Walking in Others' Shoes

Walking in Others' Shoes

Stories from the Early Years of the Partner Church Movement

by

Gretchen Thomas

with

József Kászoni, Cathy Cordes, and Leon Hopper

Roots and Wings Press

First published 2010

Roots and Wings Press, Melbourne, Australia

Copyright © Gretchen Thomas

All rights reserved

National Library of Australia Cataloguing-in-Publication entry

Author: Thomas, Gretchen.

Title: Walking in Others' Shoes: Stories from the Early Years of the Partner Church Movement.

Edition: 1st ed.

ISBN: 978-0-646-53169-4 (pbk.)

Notes: Includes bibliographical references.

Subjects: Unitarianism—History.
            Unitarians—History.
            Unitarian churches in Romania—History.
            Transylvania (Romania)—History.

Dewey Number: 289.14498

Printed by Arena Printing and Publishing on 100% post-consumer waste

Edited by Sans Serif Editing and Publishing

Book and cover design by Mal Oram

Cover embroidery by Magdalena Gaspár

To obtain copies of *Walking in Others' Shoes* and *Hands All Around*, go too:
<www.rootsandwingspress.com>

To every pair of Unitarian and Unitarian Universalist congregations joined in partnership since 1990—each has its own stories to tell.

To Leon Hopper and Mária and József Kászoni—whose faith and friendship have inspired my commitment to partnership and reset the horizons of my life.

József Kászoni and Gretchen Thomas exchanging birthday presents in the Homoródszentmárton churchyard, June 1993

Also by Gretchen Thomas, together with Judy Robbins,
Hands All Around: Making Cooperative Quilts

Contents

—∞∞∞—

Foreword

❦

The most radical thing we can do is introduce people to one another.
—a Unitarian Universalist Partner Church Council bumper sticker

In celebration of the twentieth anniversary of the Unitarian Universalist Partner Church movement, Gretchen Thomas has collected these wonderful stories about how, when we reached out to re-establish connections with Unitarians in Eastern Europe, they began walking with us in ways that have deeply affected many lives in North America and Europe. To begin such a book, you need themes worth exploring and stories worth telling. To finish it, you have to care passionately about those themes and stories, as Gretchen clearly does. For me, the best part of our partnerships are the stories we remember and tell again and again because they make being in partnership a living, vital part of both congregations' lives and histories. The stories in this book are especially valuable, first because they bring to life and preserve the first three years (1990–93) of our partnership movement before the Unitarian Universalist Partnership Council was formed, and second because congregations just starting up a partnership can learn from them what they might do, and not do, as they begin their connection.

We need to find many ways to continue telling our partnership stories, ways that enliven our relationships and weave our lives together. Isn't that how history is created? As our shared history grows and connects us with others around the globe, the world becomes friendlier and smaller. It helps us realize that we may have different stories, but we have common hopes. Hearing our stories leads others to tell their own, which in turn increases the number of threads in the tapestry of partnership. The next time Gretchen visits with the Homoródszentmárton (Mărtiniş) Unitarians, they will tell the stories again about her "first communion," about the wonderful day a church tractor was delivered during the Easter Sunday service, about her urging a bride to smile during her wedding ceremony. And they will laugh, and history will be written.

I hope reading the wonderfully touching, historic, funny, sad, and wise stories in *Walking in Others' Shoes* will inspire everyone who has ever reached for connection across cultures and borders to find their own ways to tell their own stories. In the process, perhaps we will all come to see that we are a part of the same story.

Cathy Cordes

Executive Director of the Unitarian Universalist Partner Church Council
Bedford, Massachusetts, United States, 2010

Preface

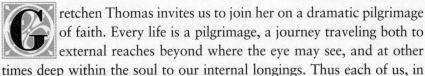

> *In our interconnected world we must learn to feel enlarged, not*
> *threatened by difference.*
>
> Jonathan Sacks, Chief Rabbi of the United Hebrew Congregations
> of the Commonwealth

Gretchen Thomas invites us to join her on a dramatic pilgrimage of faith. Every life is a pilgrimage, a journey traveling both to external reaches beyond where the eye may see, and at other times deep within the soul to our internal longings. Thus each of us, in our own way and time, are pilgrims searching—searching for meaning, wholeness, peace, and freedom. Gretchen says: "Partnerships are one of our most promising means of broadening and harmonizing a pressing world need—for people everywhere to think globally and care for one another."

My pilgrimage, related to Gretchen's, had its beginning many years ago in the little Unitarian Church where I grew up. On the wall of my minister's study hung a shadowy print. To me it was dark, mysterious and foreign in its presence. Why was it there? My minister explained that it was Ferenc Dávid declaiming at the Diet of Torda on behalf of religious tolerance and the Unitarian religion. The date of the Diet was January 1568, a time when Transylvania became an island of religious tolerance while the rest of Europe's religions were determined by the point of the most powerful sword.

I listened with fascination to the story of the founding of the Unitarian Church in Transylvania, and how Dávid would later die under the next king in the castle dungeon in Déva (Deva) because he insisted on the right to continual innovation within the Unitarian faith. Listening to his story, I longed and dreamed that one day my pilgrim feet would take me to the "land beyond the forest" (the meaning of the Latin word,

Transylvania) that had given birth to both the first proclamation of religious toleration and to Unitarianism. Surely, I thought, there in Transylvania I would find my holy land, my holy ground on which to stand.

The year 1990 marked the beginning of a unique and transforming adventure for many North American Unitarian Universalists and our congregations when we became partners with Unitarian churches in Transylvania in Romania. What moved 120 Unitarian Universalist congregations to spontaneously volunteer to become a partner church with a church in Transylvania? What provoked us to connect with Unitarians in a land we had never seen, when we knew next to nothing about them and did not speak their language?

Deep in the human soul there is a yearning for wholeness, for connections stretching across boundaries of state and ethnicity. In 1989 we had witnessed, with fascination and hope, the rise of the Solidarity movement in Poland, the opening of the Hungarian border, and the earliest cracks in the Berlin Wall. But Romania remained locked in Nicolae Ceaușescu's iron grip, with his designs for the destruction of hundreds of villages, many with Unitarian churches, in order to create massive agricultural co-operatives. His grim program was halted by the remarkable events of December 1989, sparked by the determined resistance of the Hungarian Reformed Church minister László Tőkés, in Temesvár (Timişoara), who dared to challenge Ceaușescu's grip on the people. In July 1989 Tőkés had openly protested the destruction of Transylvanian villages in a video interview made in his parsonage and shown on Hungarian television. In December members of his congregation stood bravely in front of the parsonage and church to prevent Tőkés from being arrested, and then both Hungarian and Romanian citizens of Temesvár rallied in support. This was international, prime-time television news. As a result of their courageous protest and the fighting that followed, the power and rule of Ceaușescu came tumbling down.

The borders of Romania opened. For the first time since World War I the Hungarians and Romanians living in Romania—who had each suffered in their own ways under Ceaușescu's increasingly megalomaniac leadership—had a common cause and needed one another. After such a dramatic, well-publicized event, it is not surprising that Unitarian Universalist congregations promptly responded to an invitation to be paired with and support their clearly beleaguered Unitarian colleagues in far off Transylvania.

But after we responded, and were "assigned" a Transylvanian congregation, what next? What avenues would congregations follow to become a symbol of solidarity? The reality is that in the beginning there was no plan or program for what this new relationship should be, or how to build it. Yet from the initial and undefined beginnings in 1990 there emerged an unusual, wonderful, and transforming program. Our work slowly evolved out of the wide variety of personal experiences and visits between Transylvania and North America that took place during those early years.

First there was an exchange of letters slowed by an unreliable, sometimes corrupt, mail system and struggles with translation. Our letters were followed by tentative visits and an early trickle of pilgrims in both directions that would in time become a flood. There was no question that lives were being stretched, enriched, and transformed. But how were we to make sense of what was happening? What were the pilgrims experiencing? What was going on in the lives, thoughts, and feelings of the newly connected Transylvanian Unitarians and North American Unitarian Universalists?

In those early days we did not imagine that re-establishing the connection between Transylvanians and North Americans—picking up the earlier sister church program of the 1920s—would eventually extend to include Unitarian and Universalist churches in Hungary, the Czech Republic, the Philippines, the Khasi Hills of northeast India, and Africa. Every time we reached out to new partners in new places we relearned that partner church connections hold far more possibilities than casual or one-time relationships do. We relearned to ground our connections in the vital imperative of commitment and continuity.

Gretchen deftly describes how what began as a "relief connection" focused on rescuing friends in need, evolved into a "partnership" relationship with a focus on mutuality. She calls upon us to move beyond our ethnocentric perceptions, for partnership exacts a radical patience and understanding if we are to find common ground. At the center of her book is her exploration of the ways in which North Americans find partnership connections meaningful and inspiring, and how they have deepened our understanding of our Unitarian heritage and faith.

Through the stories of her personal encounters in Transylvania, carefully woven together with stories about key figures in the history of our earlier partnerships, she seeks to answer how this deepening of faith and understanding happened.

Telling stories of our personal experiences helps us make sense of where we have been, what we have seen, and what we have been doing. Listening to others' stories, we soon recognize that the same event can be experienced differently, sometimes in contradictory and ambiguous ways. The mix of stories in this book enables deeper truths and meanings to emerge, revealing that human interactions can be messy, especially when they cross national, cultural, and linguistic boundaries.

Today's partner church program

The twenty year old Unitarian Universalist Partner Church movement began in response to a widespread impulse to reconnect with the Transylvanian Unitarian churches in Romania, which became possible only after the fall of the Iron Curtain and the opening up of Eastern Europe. The program started informally in 1990, and in 1993 it became an official organization affiliated with the Unitarian Universalist Association.

This program establishes links between interested member congregations of the North American Unitarian Universalist Partner Church Council and congregations of Unitarian or Universalist denominations (some with their own partnership councils) in Romania, Hungary, the Czech Republic, the Philippines, the Khasi Hills in northeast India, and other parts of the world. Congregations from these countries are paired in a long-term relationship with a Unitarian Universalist congregation in the United States or Canada. On first entering into partnership there is a lengthy, self-searching process designed to ensure a healthy start-up and ongoing connection. Once the congregations have met and built trust and understanding, they work together on both short- and long-term projects of mutual benefit. At the beginning of 2010 there were close to

Every one of us has a story that reaches deep down into the core of our being. Listening to the stories of others—as one does when reading these remarkable pages—enables us in small but often profound ways to crawl into others' experience and understanding of life, and in turn to see our own life anew.

Leon Hopper
Former president of the Unitarian Universalist Partner Church Council
Seattle, Washington, United States, 2010

200 pairs of partner churches supported in North America by a small hard-working staff and district networkers, and in several other partner countries by their own volunteer councils and district networkers. There are additional activities that provide for individuals' involvement.[1]

The 1920s sister church program

A previous partner church (then called sister church) program was established in the 1920s, pairing two Canadian and 116 US Unitarian Association churches with Transylvanian Unitarian congregations. Before World War I, Transylvania was the large, eastern-most part of the Austro-Hungarian (Habsburg) Empire. In the 1920 Trianon Treaty settlements that ended the war, Transylvania was ceded to Romania, and the Transylvanian Unitarians who had been Hungarians all their lives became Romanians overnight. Through the sister churches North American and British Unitarians contributed substantial aid to Transylvanian and Czech Unitarians, including for the emergency needs of the thousands who immigrated to Hungary rather than live in Transylvania as Romanian citizens. All but two of these early connections were severed as a result of the 1930s Depression or because sister church pairs were on opposing sides during World War II.[2]

Introduction

❧❧

The UU partner church movement may represent the greatest UU social activism since the civil rights movement.

John Buehrens, former President of the Unitarian Universalist Association

Sometimes life offers you an unexpected chance to become part of something new, something that promises to change your life. If you decide not to take up this opportunity, time surges ahead, leaving you standing still. Or you can step out of who you have been and ride these new experiences into a new life. As Elizabeth Gilbert urges in *Eat, Pray, Love*, "One must always be prepared for riotous and endless waves of transformation."[3] In 1990 the partner church movement, then simply a hope born of longing for wider connection, presented me with my own wave of transformation when it set me down in the middle of the intense changes taking place in Eastern Europe following the end of Soviet domination. Riding the partnership wave, I discovered new ways of being in the world, and I found myself eager to keep the stories in this book from being lost.

The impulse to write about our partnerships first struck me during a massive snowstorm that grounded thirty-three North Americans and seven Transylvanians inside a chilly, historic Beacon Hill mansion in Boston, Massachusetts. We were attending a five-day meeting of partner church networkers—church leaders in Transylvania and North America who serve as catalysts and supporters of the partnered congregations in their districts. Following our dinner of leftovers prepared without electricity and featuring Coco Pops for dessert, we held a hastily scheduled question and answer exchange. We were relaxed and tired after several days of hard work and a spirited snowball fight that afternoon on the Massachusetts State House lawn, which one of the Transylvanians had declared was "a post-modern partner church ex-

1

change." The unexpected storm gave us a golden opportunity to get to the heart of things we found hard to understand about each other's congregations, countries, and cultures.

Our discussion began with questions of fact ("Is it really true that...?") and clarity ("What is the reason for...?"), but we soon moved on to more probing questions of meaning and faith. In the candlelight, the Transylvanians kept returning to one question: "We are very clear why partnerships are vitally important to the future of Transylvanian Unitarianism, but we don't understand why you North Americans are so passionately committed to these connections. With all the time and energy partnership work takes up in your busy Western lives, how can working together with us be this important? Why do you find it so meaningful?"

Some of our answers centered on an unexpected moment of self-realization: "In that moment I saw my life (my work, my world, my faith, my self) in a completely new light." Or we told of how we set off as tourists to visit our partners hoping to find picture postcard sights, but returned as pilgrims. Cathy Cordes, who would in 2001 become the executive director of the Unitarian Universalist Partner Church Council, spoke about her realization that "human encounters are our most precious currency." Several North American networkers described their surprise that instead of functioning as change-agents, they found themselves changed—into more deeply spiritual beings. I said, "I was hungry, and this work fed my soul. My faith was given back to me."

But the Transylvanians did not buy it. While the blizzard raged outside, they kept circling back to the same question. They didn't believe that these wake-up experiences about faith, or values, or priorities could possibly have made such a difference to us, could be powerful enough to "grow our souls," as fellow Unitarian Kurt Vonnegut would have said.

Those of us in the North American part of the circle understood why our partnership work mattered so much. Quite a few of us felt we had unknowingly been living semi-conscious lives until these new connections with our partners in Eastern Europe completely unsettled our assumptions about what mattered to us, forcing us to reframe important aspects of our lives in new and provocative ways. Being in partnership had helped us confront how we had limited our faith and our understanding of global concerns through caution, complacency, arrogance, or ignorance. We North Americans returned home from visiting our partners in Transylvania awake in new ways. We had brought home with us deepened understandings of ourselves, our fears, and our commitments to Unitarian Universalism, and we had begun to question our previous assumptions about economics, history, and the place of Canada or the United States in the world. These new understandings and challenges lasted long after we finished sharing the stories and photos of our partner church visits.

On that dark, snowbound evening, we North Americans struggled hard to explain how our partnership experiences had stretched us to face squarely the injustices of economic difference, to honor the role history plays in our day-to-day decision making, to overcome our language limitations, and to stop taking many aspects of our North American lives and economy for granted. It made me wonder if any of us spends enough time seriously considering our life experiences—what they have taught us, and how they have redirected the course of our lives. "Why don't I collect these remarkable partnership experiences into a book?" I impulsively asked myself. Such a book could advocate for the value of partnership, and writing it would help me understand just how these partnership involvements were changing my life—how they were growing my soul.

Warmed by our close companionship on that chilly evening, I realized my life-changing partnership experiences were different in a significant way from those of my colleagues. I was the only networker who framed my answer by talking about something that had happened in North America. I described a "learn about Transylvania" gathering during our partner church minister's first visit with our congregation. One of our members asked József Kászoni, "What has surprised you most about Unitarian Universalists in America?" I was distracted by a too-full cup of coffee and nearly missed József's answer. He replied, "I'm beginning to wonder if your religion is important enough to American UUs. Why do you hold your faith so far from the center of your lives?" József's question haunted me until, step by step, I allowed my faith to become the bedrock center of my life.

It was several years before I took up the challenge to write down the stories that would answer the question Transylvanian networkers raised on that wintry evening: Why do we North Americans find our partner church connections meaningful and inspiring? Why have we continued year after year to work passionately for their success and deepening? What do we mean when we declare, "Working for the partnership movement has given me back my faith" or "transformed my life"? As we celebrate the twentieth anniversary of our movement, I hope people of every faith who are intrigued by the possibilities of building cross-border and inter-faith partnership connections will find these stories useful, provocative, and inspiring.

Gretchen Thomas
Melbourne, Victoria, Australia, 2010

Note to Readers

———— ⸎ ————

Speaking and writing across partnership borders and language barriers raises challenges for authors.

I often stumble into understanding Transylvanians—not only their language and history, but their feelings and needs, intentions and desires. Three Transylvanians have read this entire book, and many others have read the individual pieces in which they are mentioned. All have sent me helpful corrections and explanations of things I misunderstood. Sometimes, in fact rather often, their corrections and objections conflicted with each other. I have done my best to sort out these conflicting truths, opinions, and memories. Any mistakes that remain belong wholly to me. Information from my North American colleagues has sometimes also been contradictory, but I am more confident that I have managed to sort out the North American differences accurately and fairly. I welcome suggested corrections for a later edition.

Hungarian names start with the family name, but as this book is in English, the Hungarian names have been reversed to keep them parallel with English usage.

Because places in Transylvania have both Romanian and Hungarian names, the first time a place in Romania appears in the text, both its Hungarian and Romanian names are given. Thereafter I use only the Hungarian name. Because knowledge of Western placenames and locations should not be taken for granted, the first time they appear, North American places are given with their state or province, and cities elsewhere in the world appear with their countries noted. Thereafter only the city name is used. A complete list of placenames appears before the endnotes.

Since there is no term for "United Statesian," when I have used "American", I mean a US citizen and not "Canadian" or "American and Canadian." Though we do not yet have partner congregations in Mexico, my stubborn use of "North American" is an effort to emphasize that in North America our partnership movement is continental.

I have used double quotation marks (or indented text) for direct quotations from written sources and also for conversations either recorded at the time or recalled from memory. Where accounts of conversations are written from memory, the content has been confirmed with the speakers.

Several people who are quoted or whose stories are told or touched on have died since these events in 1990–93. They include Ed Cahill, Attila Csongvay, János Erdö, Peter Fleck, Natalie Gulbrandson, Don Harrington, Rosamond Reynolds, Alan Seaburg, Harry Scholefield, Helen Seitz, and Jules Seitz. I am noting these deaths here, rather than in the text.

My partnership experiences have been primarily with congregations partnered with Transylvanian and Hungarian Unitarians, so I have not included any stories about our many co-religionists in other parts of the world, though I believe these Transylvanian and North American experiences contain much of interest to the many Unitarians and Universalists who live, as I now do, outside of Europe and North America. I hope these stories will also be of use to those in other denominations who have their own partner church or sister parish programs.

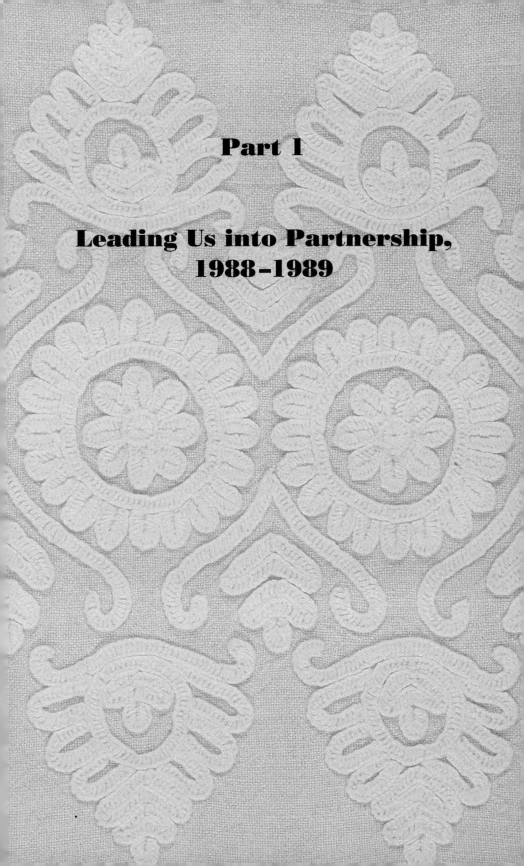

Part 1

Leading Us into Partnership, 1988–1989

I grew up in the 1940s and '50s in the Tennessee Valley Unitarian Church in Knoxville, Tennessee. The only Unitarians beyond the United States that we knew about were the Czechs. Our first minister, Richard Henry, had passed on to us his profound respect for Norbert Čapek (1870–1942)—the Czech Unitarians' founder and heroic leader. Our congregation in East Tennessee must have been among the earliest to celebrate Čapek's annual flower communion.[4]

Thirty-five years later I was in seminary, working to become a minister. Our Unitarian Universalist history class brushed lightly on the early 1500s Polish Socinian Brethren, the mid-1500s Transylvanian Unitarians, and the 1920s and '30s Czech Unitarians. In 1983 that was all I knew, and I did not care much about any of it.

Five years later in Switzerland, I happened upon a photographic exhibition about Transylvanian villages (some with Unitarian churches) about to be leveled and collectivized by Nicolae Ceaușescu's Romanian communist government. In the spring of 1990, following the December "revolution" in Romania, I read that the Unitarian Universalist Association was launching a project that would help North American congregations like ours work together with Transylvanian Unitarian congregations in some of the same villages.

These were my tentative, unpromising first steps into involvement with our fellow Unitarians and Universalists around the world.

But today, when someone says "Unitarians in Europe" I can picture members of the Unitarian and Free Christian Church congregations in Great Britain, the Unitarian Church in Dublin, Ireland, the fellowships and scattered individuals of the European Unitarian Universalists, the meet-by-computer Finnish Unitarians, the struggling Unitarian Church in Poland, and the revived Czech Unitarians. But I can see most clearly many Transylvanian and Hungarian friends and colleagues. Through our working together for the last twenty years, they have become my brothers and sisters in faith. We have struggled—and often succeeded—to stand in each other's shoes, to walk each other's paths, to appreciate and care about each other's lives.

"Revolution" in Homoródszentmárton

Many years passed before I heard an eyewitness account of the 1989–90 uprising in Romania. I had known the Transylvanian Unitarian minister József Kászoni and his wife, Mária, quite well for more than a decade when they came as guests to a summer conference of religious educators on Star Island, off the coast of New Hampshire in the Atlantic Ocean. The theme speaker for the conference asked József to "tell us about those momentous events in 1989, so we can understand better the lives of our Transylvanian brothers and sisters."

A lifetime of oppression has so deeply engrained in every Romanian caution, and the wisdom of leaving opinions unexpressed, that few Transylvanians share stories from their lives openly with anyone they do not know well. After a sleepless night of debating with old fears and discussing with Mária what he would and what he could not say to us, József told us the following about his experiences during those life-changing days in Romania:[5]

> Through the long years from 1952 to 1965, when Gheorghiu-Dej led the Romanian government, followed by the Ceauşescu dictatorship from 1965 to 1989, the only place the Transylvanians could express our Hungarian ethnicity and culture or even feel safe to be ourselves was in church. For the last ten of those Ceauşescu years and then four more after our so-called revolution, I was the Unitarian minister in Homoródszentmárton in the Harghita (Harghita) district—one of the larger villages in the Unitarian heartland of Transylvania. It is a place—unique in the world—where it is possible that everyone you will see during an entire week in the villages will be a Unitarian.

> I decided to become a minister while I was still a *gymnasium* (high school) student because I believed that a minister should be able to bring the light of hope into the darkness of those anguished years. I knew that my becoming a minister meant persecution and suffering would be inevitable for my family. It would mean always being on guard. It would mean performing the high-wire dance of conforming without becoming one of Ceauşescu's "new socialist men." That's someone who has lived so long under police censorship that even their own thoughts have become automatically self-censored.

The Romanian government believed Transylvanian Hungarians were its number one enemy. Refusing to collaborate with them was our way of holding on to our Hungarian identity. We Hungarian Transylvanians regularly refused to co-operate in small ways that were expected by the local police or even the state's secret police force, the Securitate. But anyone who openly refused to collaborate when officially pressed to do so was listed as "an enemy of the state." To be branded in this way could be a death sentence. The Securitate officer who was responsible for our area was stationed 17 kilometers (10 miles) away in Székelyudvarhely (Oderheiu-Secuiesc). He was rewarded if he reported a lot of these "enemies." He convinced the mayor and the police chief in our village to work with him to impress the Securitate chiefs in Bucharest (Bucureşti) that they were all "doing their duty." So our local village officials began spying on and recording the activities of every person who might possibly become classified as "an enemy of the state."

Hungarian-Romanians in Transylvania between World War II and 1989

In August 1940, Northern Transylvania was taken back from Romania and returned to Hungary by the Axis powers. But as a result of the 1945 treaty agreements at the end of World War II, Transylvania once again became part of Romania. By 1947 the Soviet Union was in direct military and economic control of Romania, the king was forced to abdicate, and large farms and most church-owned agricultural land and school buildings were confiscated by the government. While he was head of the Romanian Communist Party, Gheorghe Gheorghiu-Dej developed Romania's new political system, which was both Stalinist and highly nationalistic. Amazingly, Gheorghiu-Dej forced Nikita Khrushchev into withdrawing Soviet troops from Romania in April 1958. In 1964 Gheorghiu-Dej broke with the Soviet Union completely, and Soviet Proletarian Internationalism was replaced with his party's National Communism.

The people expected improved freedoms from the break with the Soviets, and many Western governments applauded by awarding the Romanian

Our village's Reformed Church pastor and I—as well as the circuit-riding Baptist pastor and Roman Catholic priest who often held Sunday afternoon services for their parishioners in Homoródszent-márton—were all on the Securitate list of "enemies" because we were leaders of our congregations of Transylvanian-Hungarians. The police kept close track of who visited us, and those we visited. Mária and I were particularly suspect because just before I came to serve as a minister in the Homoród Valley, we had spent New Year's Eve in Kolozsvár (Cluj Napoca) with László Tőkés, who was the most closely watched minister in Transylvania. No doubt the Securitate also knew that László and I were lifelong friends. From the time I was eleven, László and I lived on the same street in Kolozsvár, and we studied together at the Protestant seminary until László became a Hungarian Reformed pastor, and I became a Transylvanian Unitarian minister. Another mark against me was that ten years later we were visited in Homoródszentmárton by some of Mária's relatives from

Communist Party many significant honors. But in the 1970s and 1980s, under Gheorghiu-Dej's successor, Nicolae Ceauşescu, conditions for all Romanians, but particularly for the scapegoated minorities, including their churches, became even more oppressive, cruel, and economically crippling than they had been under Soviet domination.[6] In *Paprika Paradise* James Jeffrey describes Ceauşescu's rule as "a dictatorship that was equal parts viciousness, florid hypocrisy and elephantine narcissism...turning Romania into the virtual prison it would remain until 1989."[7]

The Securitate was Romania's equivalent of the German SS, Soviet KGB, East German Stasi, and US FBI rolled into one internal secret police and security force. In March 1990, the Securitate was reinstituted as one of the early acts of Ion Iliescu's interim government. Both Hungarian-Romanians and Romanian-Romanians believe this reinstatement was not in any sense a reformation, but only a surface change of name (to the Romanian Intelligence Service).

Kolozsvár. They brought with them an Asian woman who was a Romanian citizen and therefore not a foreign guest, which would have been illegal. But everyone who saw her, including the local policeman, assumed she was a foreigner. This moved our family higher on the police and Securitate's "enemies of the state" list.

Mária and I had a signal—if our gate was locked it meant I must not come into the yard or the house because the Securitate was looking for me. Fortunately, our country roads were awful, and there were almost no cars. The Székelyudvarhely police would not lower themselves to walk the 17 kilometers (10 miles) to Homoródszentmárton—the way we villagers did whenever the bus broke down or we couldn't afford a bus ticket. For many years Securitate officers had only come to remote areas like ours about four times a year.

In the villages we all knew each other very well, so only a few villagers were willing to inform on their neighbors, or ministers, or family members. It was much easier for the police to recruit informers in the large, anonymous cities. Of course we could never be absolutely sure of this because the Homoródszentmárton police chief and mayor relentlessly pressured everyone they could, especially their employees, to give evidence against the other villagers. And they refused to let anyone read the records we knew they were keeping.

But if you were very careful, it was possible in the countryside to speak out against Ceauşescu and his government and still escape being arrested. Without openly preaching anything against the government, ministers could use carefully selected stories from the Bible to speak out against the repression and the injustice of Ceauşescu's regime. It was inevitable that anyone who dared to preach in this "outspoken" way would be detained and questioned. Then if they refused to stop—if they continued "to be outspoken"— they would be arrested and imprisoned.[8] A former Romanian policeman—he was dismissed from the police force when he married a Hungarian-Romanian—confessed to me several years after 1989 that the police chief had forced him to spy on our Sunday services. We had been suspicious of this non-Unitarian who suddenly became a regular attender. The police chief had told him, "We just need your signature on a few sentences saying that József Kászoni spoke against the government in his sermon. Then we can arrest him." Fortunately for me, whatever I preached, week after week, he told them I had said nothing subversive.

There are many wonderful examples of church members who acted courageously and loyally to protect their ministers. The Securitate managed to stop individuals, but as hard as they tried, they never gained any control over our faith. The people trusted their church leaders, and together we all strove to faithfully follow the guidance of the way Jesus lived his life and his teachings. The people's trust and faith were the source of their minister's power, a power that was one of the few things the Securitate feared. They hated the fact that our faith remained strong, no matter what they did to us.

Remembrance Day, the 6th of October, is when all Hungarians celebrate the thirteen Hungarian generals who rebelled in 1848 against the Habsburgs. It was very significant that our part in the events of those next few months started for us on Remembrance Day. I came home from visiting our sick and elderly church members and found the parsonage gate locked. I started to leave and hide, but Mária was watching for me. She motioned through the window that I should come inside but relock the gate behind me. Two members of

The 1848 Uprising in Hungary

During the 1848–49 war for independence from Habsburg rule (a clash within the Austro-Hungarian Empire between the Austrian monarchy and Hungarian separatists) the generals who led the rebellion were captured and executed at Arad (Arad). Their decomposing bodies were left hanging as a horrific warning. In punishment for the Hungarians' rebellion, the Habsburgs demoted Transylvania to being a province ruled by martial law.

Transylvanians vowed to wait 150 years from the day the beer-drinking Austrian officers toasted the execution of the Hungarian heroes before they would again clink together their own beer glasses. Hungarians around the world celebrated the end of the century and a half mourning period with many toasts throughout 1999.

László Tőkés' congregation were hiding inside. These brave young people had traveled 400 kilometers (245 miles) from Temesvár near the border to deliver an aid package. It contained small amounts—just what they could carry without raising questions—of flour, sugar, oil, and vinegar. A large delivery of humanitarian aid had arrived at—had been smuggled into—their Hungarian Reformed church in Temesvár, and eighty members of the congregation were delivering it in this way to forty families László Tőkés knew had been doing what they could to build a protest against the Ceauşescu regime.

After our young visitors left, Mária and I repacked the food in Romanian containers and gave them to ten of our congregation's families in the most pressing need. We said they were relief packages from the government. We felt so good. It gave us great hope—not because there was extra food, but because it was our first connection with people from outside who cared about the horrors occurring inside Romania. We felt the earth was shifting beneath our feet, that finally we were not alone in our fight, that perhaps, after all, there was a way out of our isolation. That was the day I decided to risk walking the dangerous tightrope of openly speaking out against the government while doing everything I could to keep from being arrested. From that day, we lived every hour like high-wire acrobats with no safety net.

Because the government's agricultural headquarters in our area was in Homoródszentmárton, ours was one of the few Transylvanian villages not scheduled to be demolished. In our Sunday services, I began to pray aloud for all the nearby villages listed for destruction. What I said out loud was, "God, protect (this village) and (that village)." Everyone knew these coded words meant: "Do not let these precious places be destroyed by our insane government." Then I would preach a sermon that put forward an innocent message on the surface but on a different level carried for those with ears to hear it an anti-Ceauşescu message. Because I was now openly delivering these subversive messages to the people, I had to leave Homoródszentmárton immediately after the service, sometimes for several days, until after the Securitate arrived to interrogate me about my prayers and my preaching. After they gave up on finding me and had driven back to Székelyudvarhely, Mária would get an "all clear" message to me, and I could come home for the rest of the week until I went back into hiding after the next Sunday service. We could not risk my being questioned in any way by the Securitate in Székelyudvarhely because someone who acted in such an openly subversive way would immediately be put in prison.

This very tense situation was made worse when a villager, who resented the fact that his family had not received one of the aid packages, denounced me to the local police. The man believed our cover story that the relief packages had come from the Romanian government. He assumed that since the government knew there were 700 people living in Homoródszentmárton and we had given aid packages to only ten families, I must have kept most of the "government supplies" for my own family. Mária and I had given away every bit of the aid from Temesvár, but since it had been carried in backpacks by two people, there was only enough for a few families. Humanitarian aid is inevitably too little too late, and I fear the contentious question of what are fair and just ways to distribute it will be with us forever. Even in those very early days this difficult question created havoc in our lives.

We lived like this—playing cat and mouse with the police—through ten Sundays until the 16th and 17th of December when, listening eagerly to the radio, we were astonished by reports of the resistence against the soldiers in Temesvár. Courageous members of László Tőkés' congregation, even young children and grandparents, had made a human wall around their church building, which also contained the Tőkés' apartment. The church members refused to move because they were absolutely determined to prevent László's being exiled to a remote village, imprisoned, or worse. But after three long days and nights, soldiers forced their way into the church and took László and his pregnant wife, Edit, to Menyő (Mineu)—a remote hamlet with no telephone lines which could be reached only by horse cart along rutted wagon tracks. It was a perfect place to interrogate them, and condemn them to silence.

And then a great miracle happened, the miracle that changed the course of our lives. The Temesvár church members were joined by hundreds, and then thousands, of citizens who were not part of the Hungarian minority. At first soldiers with machine guns and armored cars rolled in against this growing mass of unarmed, protesting civilians. There were many heroic acts from the 16th to the 22nd of December, and a hundred people were killed in the fighting in Temesvár. But when the soldiers realized that continuing to follow Ceaușescu's explicit order—"Give one warning, and if they don't submit, they'll have to be shot"—meant they would have to kill children and Romanian Orthodox priests, they stopped firing. Some of them even joined the protestors. That was when the Romanian "revolution" truly began.[9]

The revolt swept in a powerful, unstoppable wave from Temesvár across Romania to us in Homoródszentmárton. Our first step was to form what you North American UUs call a committee—of the chief of the agricultural co-operative, the forester, the dentist, the carpenter, and me. Hour by hour we had to decide what to do. Convincing everyone to work with the committee rather than acting on their own was our hardest job. And we had to stop rumors and panic.

On the 22nd of December I went across the road to conduct a funeral service. While the mourners and I were in the church, Mária saw television coverage of what was happening at the big political rally in Bucharest which had been called by the government to counteract the Temesvár uprising. The crowds began chanting slogans against Ceaușescu, defying him! That had to be impossible, but Mária saw it with her own eyes. She watched as fighting broke out between protesters and soldiers. Shots were fired directly into the crowds killing many people, and some of the large government buildings were set on fire. Then the television news people announced that the Ceaușescus had left the country. Mária went to the houses of families with televisions and urged them to put their sets in a window so everyone in the village could see what was happening. The local policeman told her to stop agitating and go home. But she answered him defiantly, "Ceaușescu is gone. There's going to be freedom soon!"[10]

When our sexton, Rózsika Nagy, rang the bells for the funeral, the minister two villages away in Homoródszentpál (Sinpaul) heard them. Out of concern for my safety, he walked all the way to Homoródszentmárton to warn me: "József, everything about this remarkable day will be under severe investigation. You must write out the exact words you used in your funeral service so you have proof that on this day you have said nothing subversive." It had not yet occurred to him that the police could be defeated, that they would not forever be running and ruining our lives. Then we learned from the wife of a policeman who worked in Székelyudvarhely that the Securitate headquarters there was on fire, and that a government official named Coman had been caught and killed by a crowd of protestors. So we felt both horror and elation on top of a great deal of fear as we slowly let ourselves begin to believe the Ceauşescu government was truly going to be overthrown. There was no time for me to write out anything. In fact, though all this happened fourteen years ago, today is the first time I have ever written down any of this story.

Early the next morning the phone startled us awake. Villagers had captured the Homoródszentmárton mayor and police chief, and some of the crowd wanted to kill them. I have never dressed so fast! I ran all the way to the village hall where I found the two extremely frightened men tied up in the middle of an angry, agitated crowd. Standing on the steps I delivered the most important sermon of my life. Its message was, "Jesus has taught us that we must never adopt the ways of our enemies." I convinced the people to release their prisoners. I told the two officials who had for so long held all our lives in their hands that they must leave the village immediately and stay away for a long, long time. It was a complicated moment for both them and me when those two frightened men realized that the Unitarian minister, whom they had hated and considered to be their number one enemy, was now their protector and only hope.

For days after that we did not really sleep. Our committee met again and again as emergencies and unexpected issues arose. At first the government claimed that foreign terrorists had captured Ceauşescu and announced that more terrorists were on their way to attack us in Transylvania. It was a blatant maneuver—thankfully unsuccessful— to trick the Transylvanians into welcoming the protection of army soldiers who were in fact being sent to put down the rebellion. The forester was the only member of our committee who owned a gun. He needed us to declare to everyone that no one except him would be allowed to use it. We declared it and then prayed there would be no reason for the forester to have to shoot it.

There was panic in the streets and poetry in the air. The legends we had heard all our lives about the heroic but failed uprising of 1848 suddenly came to life. We felt it was our turn to make history—that we had unexpectedly become part of the great upheaval already taking place in many parts of Europe, the same Europe we had been cut off from for so long. For many weeks, all across Romania, completely autonomous, locally formed committees like ours were the only functioning government. Some used the old rules, others made up new rules as they went along. Too many local leaders modified the rules for their personal gain because corruption and acceptance of corruption had become a way of life in Ceauşescu's Romania.

December 25th, 1989—Christmas day for Protestants and Roman Catholics, but not for the Romanian Orthodox majority, who follow the Julian calendar—was the day Nicolae and Elena Ceauşescu were tried for two hours by a special military tribunal. It was certainly not a fair trial, but they were the ones who created a state in which a fair trial was impossible because Ceauşescu's legal system existed to terrorize any opposition. So it was not difficult for us to convince ourselves that they died by their own hands. When we woke up that morning and learned they had been captured and were being tried, we realized the Christmas angels had visited the village during the night—as they do every year to leave fruit and nuts and decorations on the Christmas trees—but this time they brought us the miraculous gift of an end to horror, of peace on earth, and hearts finally able to be full of good will.

As the Christmas hymn says, we were a bare-branched tree that came miraculously into bud in the midst of winter. Instead of ruling Romania for the next five-year term as head of the Romanian Communist Party, our despotic, insane dictator was sentenced to death in the same moments we were holding our first truly free worship service in twenty-five years. That service was actually the first time in my entire ministry that I could preach completely from the heart without cloaking my self-censored message in double meanings and smoke screens.

In other church services across Romania, where pastors and priests were still not convinced that lasting change would come of the uprisings, nothing about the rebellion was even mentioned. In our Unitarian service, we rose to sing the *Székely Anthem*, and then, because we were crying too hard to sing with full voices, we sang it again, and then again.[11]

That morning, for the first time, our village's Catholic and Baptist families came to worship with us. It was such a momentous day, and they did not know if their itinerant priest and pastor would be able to come to the village to hold their own Christmas services. It was the most meaningful communion any of us had ever shared. We felt a complete renewal of our commitment to live our lives according to God's will and Jesus' teachings. We all sensed a tangible force that was feeding us courage and holding us tenderly at its heart. We needed its power and its comfort because now we had to face the legacy of evil in our lives. We had to face the harm of our hating others, even more than the harm we had suffered from being scapegoated and hated, because even justifiable or inevitable hatred always does great damage to the one who hates.

When we went to bed late that Christmas night, Mária prayed for the outside world to come to us in Transylvania. Four months later, when we received a letter from the San Jose Unitarians asking if their minister, Gretchen Thomas, could visit us, I was surprised. But Mária wasn't. She always believed the world outside our closely guarded borders held huge potential for us. It took me longer to trust that the rest of the world would replace its previous indifference and lack of knowledge with caring about our tiny but steadfast congregations, nestled so far away in the heart of Transylvania.

At that time, József knew there were Unitarians in the United States and Canada, "But you North Americans might as well have been living on another planet," he later told me, "because no foreigners had ever played any role in my daily struggle to preserve and protect the Transylvanian Unitarian Church, my congregation members, and my family. I truly did not believe that anyone beyond our locked-shut borders cared if we lived or died."

Unitarians? In Romania?

I was the minister for religious education for the Unitarians in San Jose, California in late October 1988 when my husband, Robin Room, attended a meeting at the World Health Organization in Geneva, Switzerland, and I went along. One afternoon, Robin left his meetings to join me on a bone-chilling walk across the already wintry hills of that ancient Calvinist stronghold. "I want you to see the Monument Wall of the Protestant Reformation Heroes." In the deserted park, I stood in awe before the many statues of "protesting" theological leaders who wrote and politicked their way through the religious and governmental upheavals of the 1500s. It occurred to me that the tumultuous creation of the new Protestant movement in those years was similar in many ways to the emergence of the European Union, the body on which all of Europe is hanging its hopes and future.

In the formal, bare-limbed park below Geneva's ancient city wall, enormous granite statues of John Knox, William Farel, and Theodore Beza stood next to the dominant figure—a grim-faced John Calvin, who glowered down at us. (There are six smaller statues, including one of István Bocskai, a martyred Hungarian noble who won privileges for Hungarians and Transylvanians under the Habsburgs, including the election of their own rulers.)

"Why isn't there a statue of Servetus?" I complained, stamping my feet to keep warm in my Californian shoes and coat. For me, the most important of the Reformation's many passionate, unorthodox theologians was this brilliant, obstinate Spaniard who was a persuasive proponent of positions that would later be adopted by Unitarians and Universalists. Who could forget the dramatic story of Michael Servetus' three-month long heresy trial in 1553 that culminated—as Calvin intended—in Servetus' death?

Along with the Council's order to burn Servetus, there was an order to burn the 1000 copies of his last and most heretical book, *Christianismi Restitutio* (*The Restoration of Christianity*), which had been printed, but not distributed. Three copies escaped the flames,[12] one of which was used to guarantee the survival of the Transylvanian Unitarians when they were under attack during the Counter Reformation. Robin told me that there was a simple memorial stone marking the place where Servetus was put to death.

Standing beside the Monument Wall in 1988, I was a new minister,

Romania in the European Union

Romania became part of the North Atlantic Treaty Organization (NATO) in March 2004 and a member of the European Union in January 2007. Despite the European Union's requiring democratic practices and protection of human rights, many Transylvanians report the present government still uses the Romanian Communist Party's methods and its vision still rests on Ceauşescu-era perspectives. Western Europeans question if the Romanian government's widespread and deeply entrenched corruption will create insurmountable problems for Romania's EU participation. The Transylvanian Unitarians hope the government will eventually be forced to recognize and obey the European Union's strict requirements for the protection of minority rights, or even recognize the three countries of Székelyföld as an EU area with special minority rights. But they cynically point out how the government managed to side-step the minority rights reforms that were supposedly a condition of becoming an EU member in the first place.

Although the cost of living has increased, nearly all Romanians, including the Hungarian and other minorities, are proud and grateful the country is now an EU member. Unitarian farmers and entrepreneurs have made good use of EU regional development funds and the blossoming tourist industry. They say, "We are so glad that we are Europeans now, instead of Eastern Europeans."

guiltily aware that I knew far too little of the history of Unitarians and Universalists outside the United States. "Do you have time for a pilgrimage?" I asked Robin. Forty minutes later we found Servetus' neglected memorial stone. It was twenty feet up a steep hillside, overgrown by untended bushes and surrounded by litter and weeds. The stone cube was so well hidden that our official Geneva guidebook referred to it as "the lost monument." Its neglect brought home to me that despite the enormous courage it takes to die for your beliefs, the odds still favor martyrs' slipping into obscurity.

To read the inscription on the back of the stone demanded a hazardous scramble over piles of slippery leaves near rue Michel Servet. We did our best to work out the convoluted "expiatory" French message: "The dutiful and grateful followers of Calvin (the great Reformer)—who condemn an error that was of [Calvin's] time and who are strongly attached to freedom of conscience according to the true principles of Calvin's Reformation and the Gospel—have erected this expiatory memorial. October 27, 1903." On the opposite side of the monument, beneath Servetus' name, were the words, "physician" and "died at Champel by burning at the stake." Servetus' date of birth—1509 or 1511—and death—27 October 1553—were not given.

As Robin and I made our way back from our sobering pilgrimage, we happened upon a temporary photographic exhibit hung outdoors in a narrow laneway. Three vibrant young adults dressed in native costumes were urging passers-by, "Do not miss this important exhibition." They were trying to raise awareness and funds to help save several hundred

Why there is no statue of Servetus anywhere in Geneva

After months of lengthy, intense debates with the prosecutors, and eventually with John Calvin himself, Michael Servetus was declared a heretic by the Council of Geneva. There were thirty-eight charges, including a denouncement of Servetus' arguments against infant baptism and his assertion that the doctrine of the Trinity had not been established by God but rather by the Council of Nicaea. There was also a charge of insulting Calvin. But Servetus' most fatal heresy was his universalist insistence that God existed in all people and things, rather than only in the chosen, as Calvin claimed. For putting forward these heretical positions, Servetus was chained to a stake and burned to death. He was punished so severely because he had dared not only to have these ideas, but to publish a radical, brilliant defense of them using the printing presses that had become the engines of the Protestant Reformation.

When the Monument Wall of the Protestant Reformation Heroes was erected in 1909, no statue of Martin Luther, Calvin's greatest rival, was included. Luther's name is merely listed on the perimeter wall along with Huldrych Zwingli and other reformers. If Luther and the founder of Transylvanian Unitarianism, Ferenc Dávid, were not considered Protestant heroes by Geneva's 1909 Calvinists, then there would certainly be no villages "scheduled to be destroyed in Ceauşescu's latest round of grandiose agricultural development plans."

This did not ring any bells with me. I knew next to nothing about Ceauşescu's Romania, which had been hidden from me all my life by the Iron Curtain. "Romania...Bulgaria...Eastern Europe...is that on the Black Sea?" I muttered, yearning to go straight to the hotel to get warm and rest my aching feet. Thanks to years of *New York Times* reading, Robin knew enough about Romania's contentious dictator to join the articulate, multilingual young people in convincing me not to miss the exhibition.

I dragged myself reluctantly past the first section of photos. They showed lovely agricultural villages clustered around steepled churches with interesting bell towers and massive, heavily carved wooden gates.

statue or any other recognition of Servetus, who was the protester and innovator Calvin appears to have feared the most.

The Servetus entry in Wikipedia, the on-line encyclopedia, explains that between 1903 and 1908 there was a fierce battle between Calvinists and Free Thinkers over which group's proposed monument would be installed by the city to honor Servetus. The Calvinists won, and their wording was used on the stone cube they chose to install on rue Michel Servet. The Free Thinkers found a more welcoming home for the statue they had championed, in Annemasse—in France, but a suburb of Geneva. Their inscription openly condemns Calvin's role in Servetus's death. It is a larger than life statue of Servetus bound in chains and holding his book with flames burning around his feet. (A copy of this impressive statue stands in front of the 14th Arrondissement's town hall in Paris, France.)

The massive Monument Wall of the Protestant Reformation Heroes was erected at the end of this conflict over if, and how, to honor Servetus. Perhaps the decision to build the Monument Wall in the 400th anniversary year of Calvin's birth was sparked by the ongoing controversy over how much the city was willing to disapprove of Calvin's "error" in putting Servetus to death. If that is what happened, one could say Servetus does have a vital, if invisible, presence at Geneva's Monument Wall of the Protestant Reformation Heroes.[13]

Churches always grab my interest, and the hilly countryside in the photos was quite beautiful, so I began reading the captions that were provided in several languages. One word jumped out—*Unitarienne*, *Uniatier*, *Unitárius*. Could these be Unitarian churches? We hurried back out to the sidewalk to learn more from the young fund-raisers. Once she understood that I was a North American Unitarian, the young woman declared passionately:

> My grandmother was born in a *Reformát* village in the Homoród Valley [a village where almost everyone is a member of the Hungarian Reformed Church]. Eleven of the fourteen Unitarian villages along the Big and Little Homoród Rivers are scheduled for destruction. A Roman Catholic village and my grandmother's *Reformát* village—the one where I have spent every summer and school vacation— will also be completely torn down. Only the central "market" villages—

Were the Transylvanian villages destroyed?

Ceaușescu's original "systemization plan" was to demolish 8000 of the 13,000 villages in Romania, but before any action was taken the list of threatened villages was reduced to 3200. In the end, bulldozing and leveling did take place in villages near Bucharest. The number of destroyed villages varies widely from a few to more than a hundred, depending on the source of the data. More than 100 historic Orthodox churches were also demolished when urban blocks were cleared in Bucharest for Ceaușescu's grandiose palace, government buildings, and industrial projects. From 1955–65, one million individuals and their families were forced by government decree, or by the ruined economy, to move out of their villages into densely settled high-rise suburbs of block after block of bleak, poorly built concrete towers with broken elevators and erratic electricity. Many farmers were forced to become industrial workers. In 1972–73, forty more of these new towns were hastily built.

In 1981, after the harvest failed two years in a row, Ceaușescu announced that neglecting agriculture in pursuit of massive and rapid industrialization had been a mistake. To revitalize Romania's agriculture, 7000 villages (not yet those in Transylvania) would be replaced by 250 new towns called "agro-industrial centers." Demolishing villages in rural

Homoródalmás (Mereşti), Oklánd (Ocland), and Homoródszent-márton—will be left standing. The leveling of villages has already happened near Bucharest where productive village farms were bulldozed wholesale to make way for smoke-spewing factories and prefabricated, lifeless, concrete block housing. The Transylvanian villages in our photos will be next. These historic, generations-old homes and churches will be torn down by a regime that has already reduced so much of the Hungarian minorities' lives to rubble.

We have to stop it! It is devastating and unjust. At the end of World War I, our grandparents' parents made the heartbreaking choice to give up their Hungarian citizenship so our families could remain on the same land and in the same homes our ancestors had occupied for many centuries. Since 1920 our families have stayed in Romania, even though Romania has broken promise after promise to honor the

areas all over Romania would create "an agricultural revolution using proven Stalinist collectivization methods." Very little of this planned destruction was carried out.

In the late 1980s, the government announced yet another plan—the leveling of most Transylvanian villages to break up (the Agriculture Ministry said "to reform") the centuries-old pattern of family-owned farms throughout the region. The intention was to force the absorption of the minorities into homogenized communities in which Transylvanian minority children would lose their ethnic identity—usually Hungarian, German, Jewish, or Roma.

In 1949, when the first agricultural collectives were imposed under Soviet guidance, farmers who protested were arrested, imprisoned, and tortured. From then on, protests against Romania's systemization and collectivization efforts could be initiated only from outside the country. Romanians have long resented the ability of Hungarians living in Romania to inspire support and receive funds from other countries. Outsiders made far more effort to help the Hungarian ethnic minority than to help Romanians, though for the most part it was the Romanians who suffered from forced relocation of families and the leveling of villages.[14]

Hungarian Transylvanians' minority status. Now this is our thanks—our land will be stolen, our homes bulldozed, our families ripped apart. These are the places where our ancestors are buried, and where we and our children should be buried, too.

I tried to imagine a government that had the power to summarily tear down churches hundreds of years old. I tried to imagine a government that would want to do that. Robin and I could sense the complexity of this history and knew we did not understand these Romanian-versus-Hungarian battles, but we were moved by the plight of fellow Unitarians. After looking carefully at every photo, we were glad to make a contribution.

As the weak sun gave way to winter's early dusk, that market village name, "Homoródszentmárton," slipped right by me.

A year later, during the 1989–90 holiday season, while the Homoród-szentmárton Unitarians were living through the momentous changes in Romania and struggling to come to terms with the lasting damage Ceauşescu had inflicted upon them, I was extremely busy in San Jose orchestrating our congregation's many end of year celebrations—Hanukah, Winter Solstice, Christmas, Kwanza, and New Year. But I made time to watch CNN's coverage of the dramatic uprising of Romanians against their dictator and his government. All that autumn I had followed the unexpected, exhilarating changes in Poland, Hungary, Czechoslovakia, and East Germany, and especially the fall of the Berlin Wall. I thought of these as "Solidarity" and *perestroika* and "ending the Cold War" movements—exciting happenings that I assumed would in the end have little effect on my life. For us in San Jose, the most dramatic moments of the 1989–90 holidays were during the Christmas Eve service when a member's well-sprayed hair nearly went up in flames as we sang *Silent Night* and lit our world peace candles, one by one, in the darkened church.

The impact of World War I and its Trianon settlement treaty on Transylvania

From 1914 to 1920 four empires fell (the German, Russian, Ottoman, and Austro-Hungarian empires), communism first took power and Fascism began, the League of Nations and other peace-seeking institutions were formed, and the faces of the Middle East and Europe were re-mapped, creating bitter disputes, many of which remain unresolved nearly a century later. Early in World War I, Romania remained neutral, but it eventually declared against Britain and its allies. In mid-1916, with Romania's very large army in mind, the Allies bribed Romania to change sides and declare against Austria-Hungary and Germany. Recently released war documents reveal that Romania changed sides at this point in return for a promise that it would be given Banat, Bukovina, and Transylvania at the end of the war.

In the war settlements, the defeated Kingdom of Hungary lost two-thirds of its territory and its population to five surrounding nations: Romania, Czechoslovakia, Poland, the newly formed Kingdom of Yugoslavia, and Austria. At the time, President Woodrow Wilson said: "The proposal to dismember Hungary is absurd." Later Winston Churchill said: "Ancient poets and theologians could not imagine such suffering, which Trianon brought to the innocent."[15]

Under the terms of the 1920 Trianon Treaty, the two largest of the Austro-Hungarian Empire's reassigned areas—Eastern Hungary and Transylvania—were awarded to Romania. Not able to be fully faithful to either their new or their former country, the Hungarian minority became fiercely faithful to their ethnic heritage, the villages of their forebears, and their churches. The government subdivided large Hungarian estates and gave the land to Romanian farmers.

Democracy failed to develop, as a succession of governments manipulated elections to ensure a predetermined outcome. In the 1930s the Iron Guard—often seen as a forerunner of the Securitate—gained in power and persecuted ethnic minorities and Jews. Right-wing parties flourished—in part by blaming communists, Jews, liberals, and outsiders, rather than World War I or the Great Depression, for Romania's long-standing economic devastation. Economists say Romania has never recovered from the 1930s Depression. Among ethnic Hungarians, longing for their pre-Trianon lives was intensified by longing for the pre-Depression economy.[16]

The pain Transylvanian Hungarians felt over the injustices of Trianon are still keenly felt, but today most ethnic Hungarians living in Transylvania have come to terms with the likely reality—that their families' future generations are going to be Romanian citizens and that Transylvania is not going to be rejoined with Hungary. Some see the best way forward as working to be officially recognized as "Hungarian-Romanians"—ethnic Hungarians with Romanian citizenship. They hope to gain a stronger guarantee of rights for all ethnic minorities in Romania and special minority rights for areas in Transylvania that are densely settled by Hungarian minorities, based on precedents already established in other parts of the European Union (e.g. Catalonia, the Basque regions, and the South Tyrol).

Today, Transylvania contains one-third of the land and one-third of the population of Romania. In the 2002 census, of the 7,221,733 people living in Transylvania, 75 per cent were ethnically Romanian, 19.6 per cent Hungarian, 3.4 per cent Roma, 0.7 per cent German, and 0.1 per cent Serbian. Within the European Union, ethnic Hungarians living in Romania are the second largest national minority (after the Catalans in Spain). Although there are Hungarian-Romanians living in every part of Transylvania, fourteen Transylvanian counties have Romanian-Romanian majorities, while only two (Kovásna and Harghita) are mostly Hungarian.

The Transylvanian Unitarians are both a religious minority and an ethnic minority in Romania. In 1989 there were 68,500 Unitarians in Transylvania; in a 2005 census there were 58,000. Other minority religious groups are members of the Reformed (Calvinist), German Lutheran, Baptist, Roman Catholic, and several rapidly growing Evangelical and Pentecostal churches, particularly Jehovah's Witnesses. Many of the Jews who remained in Transylvania after World War II emigrated to other countries in the early 1990s.

Part 2

In Homoródzsentmárton, 1990

In March 1990 I read an editorial in The World, *our church magazine, that described Transylvanian Unitarians' efforts to hold on to their hope and faith while enduring thirty-seven years of first Gheorghe Gheorghiu-Dej's Soviet Proletarian Internationalism, and then Nicolae Ceauşescu's National Communism. It made me remember the passionate young people in Geneva with their photographs of Romanian villages scheduled for destruction. What had happened to all those villages and the Unitarian churches? I constantly stumbled across articles about Romania. The next issue of* The World *said Ceauşescu's dictatorship was widely believed to have been the most oppressive in Eastern Europe. A New York Times editorial about conditions in Romania made clear that the old guard had not actually been overthrown by the peoples' uprising and the Ceauşescus' deaths. William Schulz' editorial in* The World *ended:*

> [A concrete way to] help rebuild religious freedom in Transylvania....is by encouraging your congregation to become a "sister church" with one of the 130 Unitarian congregations in Transylvania.[17]

Though I was still not clear where Transylvania was exactly, as soon as I read this invitation to become a sister church, our congregation in San Jose signed up, and I began making plans to visit the Transylvanian Unitarians. I didn't realize it, but we were not alone. It was the same year as the Tiananmen Square protests in China and Nelson Mandela's release from prison in South Africa, a time when hope for freedom, dignity, human worth, and human rights abounded, not only in the halls of government, but in countless people's daily lives.

From 1948 to 1998 it was nearly impossible for foreigners to visit Romania or even to speak with Romanians. So in May 1990 I became one of a tiny number of North Americans who had ever visited our fellow Unitarians in Transylvania. But just two months later, ninety more North Americans arrived in Romania eager to meet their Transylvanian brothers and sisters. Within a year, several hundred more had visited Transylvanian Unitarians, motivated by the possibility of building congregation-to-congregation partnerships. Most of us knew very little of what we needed to know before we could understand Romania, Transylvania, and Transylvanian Unitarianism. I could not even find the village of our proposed partner church on the map because it had not occurred to me that of course it would appear on a Romanian map as 'Mărtiniş'—its Romanian name. No one had mentioned Hungarian

*versus Romanian placenames to me. And I was inside Romania before I
realized that "Homoródszentmárton" would also not appear in any
transport schedule, postal list, or telephone operator's directory. It was
not like me to set off for a foreign country so ill-prepared. It was a good
thing Judit Géllérd had told me to expect the unexpected!*

*Unconsciously, I think I must have assumed this visit would be
different, and easier, because I was going to meet my Unitarian brothers
and sisters—certainly a naïve notion, but one that proved to be
absolutely true.*

Wheresoever You Go, Go with All Your Heart

What do you pack when you are about to leap into the unknown of a proposed partner church relationship with a remote village congregation halfway around the world? I sought the advice of Dr. (now also Reverend) Judit Gellérd. This remarkable Transylvanian, daughter of a heroic, important Transylvanian minister, has worked tirelessly throughout her life to help the Unitarians living in Romania.[18]

Seven weeks proved too short to allow a written reply from the Homoródszentmárton Unitarians to my letter asking if I could visit them, but—as she would generously do many times in the future—Judit bailed us out. She telephoned her mother, who lives in nearby Székelyudvarhely, and then delivered the good news to us: "Your history-making letter made it through the Romanian censors, and all the Homoródszentmárton Unitarians eagerly await your visit. József will meet you on the station platform." Great! But which platform? And what station? I had long been aware I had too little trust in "things working out." This trip to Romania was clearly providing an opportunity to turn that around.

When I asked Judit how to prepare and what to pack for my five days in Transylvania, she advised, "You just need to expect the unexpected, and it's hard to pack for that." She asked if I would take along two suitcases of items for a women's church group project. When I think now of the many times Judit has personally delivered packages, suitcases, computers, and books for the Transylvanian Unitarians and their North American partners, I am very glad I trusted that if Judit said getting those suitcases to Transylvania was important, I should feel honored to make it happen. Since that time, I have found that trusting Judit's judgment has led me to many valuable insights and exciting experiences. I could not have had a better introduction to partnership with Transylvanian Unitarians than the happy circumstance of meeting with her and receiving her advice.

In my own suitcase were presents—a very basic camera, a lot of film to go with it, a colorful tee shirt with our San Jose church logo on it, and a hand-held tape recorder with batteries. (Two more years passed before we thought to supply a European-current battery charger.) In my backpack was a copy of a Unitarian history text I was sure our partner church minister would value. Judit had assured me József Kászoni was learning English. (Until I began learning Swedish, I did not appreciate how long he would need to study English before it would be possible for him to read this scholarly book on the history of the Transylvanian, British, and North American Unitarians.)

I expected to need Kleenex packets, but it did not occur to me that I would need a minister's robe. I packed a blank journal—blank except for the first page, where I had written Confucius' advice: "Wheresoever you go, go with all your heart."

The alarm rang early on Wednesday morning, 23 May 1990. Our plan was to fly from San Francisco in California, to Chicago, Illinois, to London, England, and on to Vienna, Austria, then take a direct train through Budapest in Hungary to Segesvár (Sighişoara) in Romania—a fifty-hour journey from Berkeley, California to Homoródszentmárton in Harghita County, Transylvania. We had passed on this itinerary to József Kászoni via Judit's mother, who assured us that we would be met at the train station in Segesvár on 25 May, which turned out to be the Friday morning before Pentecost—one of the four major Transylvanian Unitarian holidays. We had only been able to buy train tickets as far as Budapest, but Judit assured us we should have no trouble buying our tickets to Romania during the train's one-hour layover in Budapest. Or if there was not enough time, for an extra fee we could always buy tickets on the train from the conductor. Never having spoken with József Kászoni, and not having a train ticket for the most crucial leg of the trip, it all felt like a blind leap into the unknown.

While waiting for our first flight at San Francisco airport, Robin read with dismay a newspaper report that in the night there had been a 7.8 earthquake in Romania's Carpathian Mountains. Northern California is earthquake country. Say "7.8 Richter scale" to us and we assume collapsed bridges and twisted train tracks. Our adventure in Eastern Europe gained a whole new edge. We had come quite early for our plane and decided to try to telephone the Homoródszentmárton parsonage to learn if it was still standing. (The phone number Judit had given us was

"Homoródszentmárton 8.") But the phone company said it would take at least forty-eight hours for them to schedule an operator who spoke both Romanian and Hungarian. That didn't surprise us. We had already learned it took the US and Romanian postal systems more than seven weeks to manage to deliver one letter and return the reply. (None of us had e-mail then.) Robin and I turned to each other and agreed, "Of course we're going. This earthquake may mean the trains into Romania will be empty." With our hearts in our throats, but our eyes wide open, we leapt.

Thirty-three hours later, our train—called the Orient Express, with Istanbul as its last stop, but with none of the amenities that "Orient Express" evokes—pulled into the Keleti (Eastern) railway station in Budapest, where our tickets ran out. There was only an hour-long layover, and we were all set to jump off the train and rush to the ticket office to buy the basic seat tickets we needed for the rest of the journey into Romania. We were also hoping to obtain the sleeper car places that would keep us from having to sit up all night. But as we looked out the window of our carriage we could not believe what was happening. A heaving sea of people covered every inch of the platform and reached all the way out into the street. We could not have been more wrong about people staying home because of the earthquake. What was going on? If these thousands of people already had tickets, there could not possibly be any tickets left for this train. What a disappointment it would be to have come all this way and not make it to Transylvania after all!

We split our efforts. Robin sat guarding our two seats and four suitcases, hoping to purchase seat tickets or even tickets for standing (if such a thing existed) from a passing train conductor, while I plunged into the nearly rioting crowd to search out the ticket office and tackle the probably impossible task of getting seat and sleeper tickets for this obviously sold-out train. We had come so far. The Homoródszentmárton Unitarians were making special preparations. I simply couldn't imagine writing an apology for not being able to show up. We were determined to make this visit happen.

I pushed against the tide, clearing my way with great difficulty through the horde of people surging toward the far too few train carriages until I came to a section of the platform where only a few people were milling about. I spotted a young man I hoped might be from the United States because he was wearing Nike running shoes and a North Face backpack. "Could you please help me?" I asked. He turned out to be Hungarian and quite eager to practice speaking English.

I asked, "What has brought all these people to this particular train? And where must I go to buy a ticket to Sighișoara?"

He replied sympathetically, "Do you mean Segesvár?"

"I don't think so," I answered.

"Segesvár is the name Hungarians say for Sighișoara," he patiently explained, smiling. I gave heartfelt thanks for the kindness of strangers. "I am traveling with a group. We are twelve Catholic pilgrims going to the Black Madonna shrine beside Csikszereda [Miercurea-Cuic]."

"Is that in Romania?" I asked, wondering how long it would take me to get my tongue around these Romanian placenames. Or were they Hungarian? In any case, it didn't look like we were going to have a chance to learn anything about that because twenty minutes of the hour between our train's arrival and its departure were already gone.

"Csikszereda is close to Segesvár in Romania where you need to go," he said. "Our group has to change trains in Segesvár to get to Csikszereda, so I have a ticket to Segesvár. I will sell the ticket to you."

I stared at him in disbelief, followed by a flood of relief...until I remembered Robin. "I want so much to buy that ticket from you," I said eagerly, "but my husband is with me, so we need two tickets."

"You need two tickets to Segesvár? We have two tickets to Segesvár."

Who was this saint? Or was he a con-artist? And what had miraculously set him in my path? I asked, "Do you know what 'too good to be true' means?"

He nodded, "But it is true. Two of our group must work and cannot go with us. We have two empty tickets to Segesvár on this train. You and your husband can use the tickets and become Catholic pilgrims," he grinned. "Or," he frowned, "maybe you do not want to pay the extra for the sleeper carriage? The cost is too big?"[19]

Thinking of all the passengers who would certainly be standing up in this train all night, I assured him Robin and I would be overjoyed to pay them for the tickets and join their group in their two comfortable six-person sleeper compartments.

"But if I go back to get my husband and we give up our seats, will you still be here when we come back?" He promised me he would. To seal the deal, I told him I was a "pastor," hoping a person on a religious pilgrimage would do his best to keep a commitment he had made to a minister.

"You are a priest?" he gasped.

"I am a priest," I said emphatically, telling myself it was not a lie, just a translation.

"I have never met a womanly priest before," he said, and turned to tell his companions that he had found interesting people to buy the extra tickets.

Pushing back through the surging crowds, I managed to reach the train carriage where Robin was waiting anxiously. But no one would let me join the crush of people squeezing into the carriage. I had to stand on the platform and yell up to Robin through the window. Of course he was very reluctant to give up our seats, but once I convinced him to come with me he made two travelers who had resigned themselves to standing all the way to Romania as happy as I had been to meet my Catholic pilgrim. Robin had to pass the luggage out the window to me. While he pushed his way out of the carriage through all the people still pressing in, I stood protectively beside our two suitcases and the two larger ones for Judit Gellérd's women's group. I certainly was learning to trust in the kindness of strangers, or at least the kindness of Hungarian pilgrims. I puzzled over what the young man meant when he insisted they were "pilgrims" instead of "visitors." And I still didn't know why so many people were fighting so hard to get on this Thursday night train to Romania.

Our rescuers were still waiting on the platform for the railway porter to finish making up the sleeper berths. They were delighted to be paid in US dollars for their two "empty" tickets. Sitting with these young people who were so eager to talk with us felt exponentially better than being squashed by the aggressive crowd in our original carriage. Besides, here we had tickets. If we had stayed in our original seats we might well have been forced to leave the train at the next stop if the conductor said he could not sell us tickets. It did not occur to us or our rescuers that using someone else's ticket for an international destination might be illegal.

While our overloaded train chugged across the Great Plain of Eastern Hungary, we ten Catholics and two Unitarian Universalists found a lot of common ground. The Hungarians were in their twenties, and every one of them aspired to live for a while in an English-speaking country, working in a job that would help them gain fluent English and advanced computer skills. They declared that what I was doing—connecting a California congregation with one in Transylvania—was its own kind of pilgrimage.

We discovered all of us were secretly carrying religious texts and history books to give to Transylvanians. Books, especially foreign books, were particularly precious possessions because communist doctrine had long determined and limited what books could be imported, sold, or published in Romania. For years the Ceauşescu government had maintained its draconian position on the history of Transylvania by forbidding any books that indicated Transylvania had previously been Hungarian territory. To me this was as outrageously false and harmful as claims that the Holocaust never happened. The law that made it highly illegal to bring unapproved religious texts or history books into Romania was still in effect. My "unapproved" religious history text was *A History of Unitarianism: in Transylvania, England, and America* by Earl Morse Wilbur. We were all nervous about what might happen to the books—and to us—if our baggage was searched when we crossed the border into Romania.

There was no difficulty with the initial ticket collection, but around midnight, when we reached Arad, on the border of Hungary and Romania, the new Romanian train conductor collected our passports and the group ticket and then began arguing loudly. Oblivious to how I was making a serious problem worse, I gave into my nervousness by talking more and faster—until Robin scribbled a note, "Better if you don't speak English." In the midst of my anxiety attack, I had to smile. He had used such a kind way to tell me, "Shut up." I knew enough to fear an earthquake, but not enough to fear a border crossing. Interrupting the conductor's diatribe, the oldest, and very attractive, woman pilgrim convinced him to discuss his concerns with her in the empty corridor outside our compartment. Robin whispered to me that he had figured out that the problem was the names in his and my passports—they didn't match the names listed on the group ticket.

I never knew if the young woman successfully got us into Romania because she was so savvy, or lovely looking, or willing to try speaking Romanian. It occurred to me later that perhaps she bribed the conductor.

In any case, this mature and clever young woman had skillfully averted a dangerous moment that could have forced us off the train and ended our partner church experiment before it had even begun. It was the second time we were rescued by these generous Catholic pilgrims.

Stretched out on my comfortable bunk near my husband and ten new friends in our compartment and the one next door, I felt enormously grateful not to be standing in the crowded corridor or put off the train to search the streets of Arad after midnight for a hotel room, or (I realized with horror) locked up in detention at the train station until the next west-bound train appeared. I soon fell into guilt, asking myself, "Who am I to be sleeping so comfortably when all those other travelers are standing, packed in like sardines?" And, "Who am I to have been living comfortably through all the years while our brother and sister Unitarians in Romania were suffering unspeakable deprivations?"

It brought home the truth of Pico Iyer's assertion in *Why We Travel*: "All good trips are about being carried out of yourself and deposited in the midst of terror and wonder....We travel, initially to lose ourselves, and we travel, next to find ourselves."[20] I could see already that this was turning out to be a trip that would take me out of myself and put me down somewhere else, a journey from which I could not return to being the person I had been when I left home.

Sometime later Robin shook me awake and pointed silently through the window to a lonely mountain topped with stark ruins outlined by moonlight. It was the castle at Déva near Torda (Turda). In 1568 during the Diet of Torda, Ferenc Dávid (the founder and first bishop of Transylvanian Unitarianism) had won a ten-day debate that resulted in Europe's earliest pronouncement of religious tolerance. Eleven years later, after his teachings were declared an illegal innovation, Dávid was sentenced to life imprisonment. In November 1579, after five months in Déva castle's cold, dark, wet, and lonely prison cell, this Protestant Reformation hero died a martyr. I had dressed up as Ferenc Dávid to tell his story for our children's Sunday school classes. And now I was looking out the window at the Déva castle with Ferenc Dávid's prison cell somewhere within—a pilgrimage site for Unitarians from all over the world.[21]

Pilgrim-style, we merged our leftovers for breakfast. While the porter converted our bunk beds into seats, I stood in the corridor next to the young man who had offered me the unused tickets on the station platform in Budapest. He was watching the passing countryside with a broad smile on his face. He turned to me, "The doors to Erdély have finally been thrown open. We are entering Székelyföld. It is the heartland, the mother country. This land, this special place stirs up great longings for all Hungarians." He added with great feeling, "We have been denied it for so long."

Sixteen hours after it left Budapest, our still full-to-bursting train pulled into Segesvár. I leaned far out of the window searching every male face for József Kászoni, as if I could spot a Transylvanian Unitarian minister simply by how he looked. I saw an elderly man handing down a heavy appliance box to a smiling woman. And look at that! She was using a red Radio Flyer children's wagon, exactly like the one from my childhood, to roll home their new television. Crossing the road that ran

The Székely, Erdély, and Székelyföld

The origins of the Székely people—a Finno-Ugric tribe separate from the Magyars—are uncertain and subject to much debate between scholars, as well as among the people themselves. The answer may be settled decisively in the next decade by genographic investigations. Today, people with Hungarian ancestry living everywhere in the world consider the Székely in Transylvania—Erdély, as Hungarians call it—to be their ancestors and "the truest Hungarians." They consider Székelyföld—the "heart of Transylvania" counties of Harghita, Kovásna, and Maros—to be their spiritual homeland and the most valuable and romantic region of historical Hungary. In part, this is because present-day Székely have been locked away inside a ring of protective mountains and had little contact until recently with the modern world. Their isolation has helped them retain many of their ancient customs, though the internet, automobiles, and air travel are making rapid inroads. The Unitarians in Transylvania feel it is their sacred duty to preserve their heritage of Székely culture, language, and traditions. Preservation of the Hungarian identity of villages in Székelyföld is central to this effort, and every Unitarian church in Transylvania and Hungary plays a vital role in this preservation.[22]

alongside the station was a sturdy wooden cart drawn by two massive horses. A broken-down automobile had somehow been loaded up onto the cart. I was about to step into a world where televisions are moved on wagons when there is no car, and cars are moved on horse carts when there is no tow truck.

A balding man wearing a crisp white short-sleeved shirt was searching along the platform from carriage to carriage. Instead of a tie, he wore an International Association for Religious Freedom medallion featuring a flaming chalice. (Sometimes it is possible to know a person is a Unitarian by how they look.) Of course it was József Kászoni from Homoród-szentmárton, 60 kilometers (37 miles) up the road. Robin and I were so relieved and delighted to have made it to this important meeting. Thanks to the kindness of strangers we had not been stopped, or even delayed, by the earthquake, or the huge crowd of travelers, or our lack of tickets.

We exchanged deeply grateful goodbyes with our young pilgrim rescuers, and I stepped down onto the platform—forty-five years old, wearing comfortable travel clothes and sturdy walking shoes. I had cut my hair short to accommodate our stay in a rural area with sporadic water supply. I was the product of a childhood Unitarian congregation in the Appalachian Mountains in East Tennessee (mountains strikingly similar to the Transylvanian Carpathian foothills) that had been university-based and more humanist than "spiritual." Through years of participation in the civil rights movement, the women's movement, and education reform campaigns, I had become a committed leftist. My greatest satisfactions came from working with social action organizations and congregations to better the lives, and schools, and churches of future generations. I had always had an adventurous spirit, but it had never led me this far from home. I wondered how this Transylvanian minister would describe himself and how he might understand "adventurous spirit," "committed leftist," "social activism," "civil rights," and "the women's movement," since what needed doing in his world must be so different from mine.

Before the final leg of our journey by car to Homoródszentmárton, we dropped into the local Unitarian parsonage in Segesvár, as we would several times every day, each time we passed through a village, town, or city with a Unitarian church. A red wagon was parked next to the front door. Pointing to the new television set it held, Ferenc Nagy, the Segesvár Unitarians' minister, who had indeed been on our train from Kolozsvár, beamed at us, "Here's our new window on the West."

Ferenc spoke beautiful English, learned the year he was a visiting scholar at Manchester College (the Unitarian seminary in Manchester, England). He told us that for the last fifty years, only he (in 1973) and Elek Rezi (in 1985–86) had been allowed to leave Romania to study there on a fellowship (as a Sharpe Hungarian scholar). That morning none of us imagined that four months later József—chosen in part because of his initiative in learning English—would board the train in Segesvár and head for England as the next Hungarian scholar.

Ferenc and his wife, Piroska, invited us into the Segesvár parsonage for tea and cake. They told us the 7.8 earthquake we had read about had occurred so deep underground that it caused almost no damage. "In Homoródszentmárton, a few stones fell off the old wall around the church, but that was all," József said.

We finally found out why the train had been so crowded. Ferenc explained that Romania's first true election in many years had been held three days before Robin and I left California. Immediately before the election and for the first time since the 1970s, the border between Hungary and Romania was opened for travel by any Hungarian citizen who had a passport. Pentecost was a four-day holiday weekend, and it seemed that every Hungarian who had relatives in Romania was making a visit that was many years delayed and longed for.

Suddenly allowing this "unwatched" travel (travel without a visa) between Hungary and Romania was a blatant maneuver by Ion Iliescu, head of the interim government, to gain at least some of the Hungarian-Romanian minority's vote on 20 May. When they won the election, The Front, as the new National Rescue Front (FSN) coalition party was called, also offered a significant amount of money to any group that started a new party. Foreign journalists lauded this as evidence of "a real democracy," but this tactic was actually another election manipulation to make sure the new parties would prevent a united opposition that could win a majority vote and thus wrest government leadership from the FSN.

In times of social and political upheaval, it is usually the trains going *out* of the country that are full—of people escaping into exile. But few

Romanians possessed the passport or the funds that would let them take advantage of the newly opened border to travel outside the country. Instead, people from all over the world were about to pour across the borders *into* this forgotten, sequestered country. "If you thought *your* train was impossibly crowded, come back to see the Saturday morning train full of people who will leave when they finish their work week," Piroska told us (with Ferenc interpreting). "Grandchildren will be coming to meet their grandparents for the very first time. Landowners will be visiting their family's holdings after living in exile since 1947 or even seventy years, since Trianon." These were, I realized, the dramatic stories I had missed hearing in the crowded train corridor.

Ferenc Nagy took József, Robin, and me on a walking tour that began at the Segesvár church, known as the *Kicsi Templom* (the Little Church) because its sanctuary is quite small. Ferenc had to lead three services there each Sunday to accommodate all of the service attenders. Located near the river, the church bore the imprint halfway up the sanctuary wall of a high-water mark from a devastating flood a few years earlier.

From the church we climbed up through the picturesque, historic Saxon town of Segesvár with its impressive stonework. Ferenc's stories made its history come alive. I was struck by the dreariness of the buildings and the hopefulness of the people. As our tour ended, it seemed to me that Ferenc Nagy was reluctant for our "dropping in" to come to an end because, even more than a new television, our visit marked not just a window, but a door opening to the West.

At the last stop on our tour of the old town, Ferenc Nagy pointed to a large, interesting corner building. "The rumor is that Vlad the Impaler may have been born in this villa," he said. "Vlad was the Romanian despot from the fifteenth century who…" He interrupted himself to glance expectantly at me, but this time I knew to keep my mouth shut. "You surprise me," he said. "Americans are always so eager to ask us all about Dracula." I confessed, "Judit Gellérd told me what Transylvanians think about the myth of Dracula and the reality of Vlad, and I completely agree with you." There were smiles all around when Ferenc and József realized I shared their disgust and disappointment that their beautiful countryside, and ancient walled city with its important history as a vital European crossroad, was only famous among North Americans

The Transylvanian Saxons

The Saxons were Germanic immigrants in the Middle Ages with special building, stonework, and craft skills who were invited (from 1141–64) to settle in strategic areas in southern Transylvania which King Géza of Hungary felt needed fortifying. The Saxons call Transylvania "Siebenbürgen," the seven fortress areas. Their seven walled citadel cities were built between the twelfth and the fifteenth centuries. The Saxons eventually gained an administrative autonomy for themselves rare among feudal Europe's absolute monarchies.

Other Germans, who were crusader knights, passed through Transylvania on their way to conquer the Holy Land and Jerusalem. They built their own string of forts and castles to guard the commercial route they established between Western Europe and the Holy Land. Since a massive 1990s exodus to West Germany, there are far fewer Saxons living today in Transylvania. The founder of Transylvanian Unitarianism, Ferenc Dávid, was a Transylvanian Saxon from an artisan family in Kolozsvár.

for its connection with Dracula, a fictional monster, and Vlad the Impaler, a blood-thirsty tyrant.[23] But I was stopped cold by what Ferenc said next: "Ceauşescu is going to haunt Romania more than Dracula ever has. If North Americans are so intrigued by Dracula, how long are they going to think of Ceauşescu whenever they hear something about Romania?"

Though I knew there had been a violent uprising and change of government in Romania, I understood little of its meaning or impact. In the 1960s, when I learned the truth of Stalin's systematic murder and imprisonment of his political enemies, I became disillusioned with communism, but that did not prepare me for what I was learning about the communist Ceauşescu years in Romania. The Western media called the 1989 uprising of the people "a revolution," but Romanians soon began to sarcastically call it "our so-called revolution." Robin and I knew that much of Eastern Europe was in turmoil, including the overturned governments of Hungary and East Germany, their communism replaced by as yet undefined alternatives. Thanks to watching CNN throughout the previous fall and over Christmas, we knew that except for Romania these had been peaceful revolutions. Romania was the only country in Eastern Europe where shots had been fired into the protesting crowds, and Ceauşescu was the only head of state, together with his wife, to have been executed. ("Shot down like rabid dogs," as one Transylvanian minister characterized it.)

It is one thing to watch media reports of an uprising and quite another to move among the very people whose lives have just been changed forever, to experience alongside them a time when abandoned dreams once again feel possible. There had to be both fearful and hopeful questions in every Transylvanian's heart: Is it truly possible to overthrow such a repressive government? What will our lives be without it? How do we learn to live free of fear and subterfuge?

I journeyed to Transylvania focusing on one small aspect of these upheavals—the possibility of connecting North American Unitarian Universalists with Unitarians in Transylvania. When Robin and I stepped

Romania's "so-called" revolution

In 1995 a Transylvanian minister explained to a group of partner church pilgrims:

> It is a mockery to say there has been a true revolution in Romania. We call the uprising "the events of 1989" or the "so-called" or "stolen" (*ellopott*) revolution. How could it be a revolution when it simply returned the communist government to power? Most of the present leaders were former communist leaders under Ceauşescu. Day by day they run the government using the same oppressive totalitarian practices as before. Their "new" Romanian government claims to be democratic, but they are still acting as communists in their hearts and in their strategies. After our so-called revolution we expected all the secrets of the Ceauşescu years to come out, but in fact we still know only a small part of what really went on. The question all Romanians are now asking is: Were the events of 1989 a people's revolution or actually a coup to get rid of Ceauşescu?

off the train in Segesvár, we did not expect to be plunged into the center of the enormous changes so recently experienced by everyone we met. But we quickly shook ourselves awake, adopted "a beginner's mind,"[24] and remembered Judit's admonition to expect the unexpected.

That afternoon we would delight in the energy, joy, and hope we found waiting for us in Homoródszentmárton. Thanks to the warmth and hospitality we received from our pilgrim friends on the train, and from József, Ferenc, and Piroska on our very first day, I was intrigued rather than overwhelmed by this world where the unexpected was an hourly occurrence. I was eager to step right into the heart of this revolutionary time, so like the euphoric, liberated feeling that flooded much of Europe during the French Revolution, about which Wordsworth wrote: "Bliss was it, in that dawn to be alive."[25]

Thinking American

When we arrived in Homoródszentmárton we ate the first of many delicious meals made for us by József's mother, who had come from Kolozsvár to help with the celebration of my visit. Then we used precious gasoline to drive to a high mountain meadow where several village elementary schools were taking part in a Friday afternoon end of school year field day. A former local official—one of only four villagers who had the use of a car—had volunteered to do all our driving, which included his having to wait several times in up to five-hour queues to obtain the scarce gasoline needed over my five-day visit.

The village children, including József and Mária's eight and ten year old daughters, had hiked up the road to the meadow. In the early summer sunshine they were performing Hungarian folk dances and singing traditional songs. There were individual competitions in fire-building, plant identification, and knot-tying, as well as tests of strength in an energetic school-against-school tug-of-war.

Looking down on the village, with its ancient Unitarian bell tower rising high above the homes, barnyards, and fields, I had my first of many lessons about Unitarian life in Romania. József explained to me that in Homoródszentmárton there were 700 adults, half of whom were Unitarians and the other half Hungarian-speaking Calvinists, Baptists, Roman Catholics, and a few Roma (Gypsies). This mix is unusual, even for the three Homoród Valley market villages, and was explained by the workers who needed to live where the bus ran (when fuel was available) from Homoródszentmárton to the nearby town of Székelyudvarhely to the west, and to the city of Brassó (Braşov) to the southeast.

József said wistfully, "It would be better if everyone in Homoródszentmárton was a Unitarian." I questioned him closely, keeping my English as simple as I could, saying that our San Jose church members value religious diversity as an opportunity to practice our commitment to defending religious freedom for all people; that we believe diversity is a gift, because living within its demands makes us stronger. I asked, "Isn't that exactly what Ferenc Dávid made possible by his Reformation Unitarianism?" József replied:

Yes, I understand—but Gretchen, you are thinking American. If your government announces a plan to destroy your home, your church, and your entire valley, you must unite in order to resist. But before you can risk resistance you have to be able to trust each other completely. Without this kind of trust we would never have survived the endless years when half the telephones in the country were tapped by the Securitate, every piece of mail was opened and read, every contact with a foreigner had to be reported in detail, every leader's actions were scrutinized and reported on, and all typewriters were registered so everything written on them could be traced to the author. Informing was always a tempting source of income for our people who were starving.[26] With only four hours of heat a day, six hours of electricity, and one 40-watt light bulb in each room, people slept away the winter months. Dairy farmers and cheese makers never ate cheese themselves, because most—certainly the best—of our agricultural and manufactured products were exported. Parents regularly went hungry to give what food they had to their children, so that much of the adult population now looks ten to twenty years older than their actual age.

To survive such terrible conditions, you must be able to approach each other without suspicion. To live without fear, you must have leadership. Our church services and religious education classes were the only times we could count on being allowed to gather in a group, so in the villages, ministers were the only possible leaders. The survival of every villager rested on the shoulders of their ministers, and Homoródszentmárton, which is served by three ministers and one priest, has a dangerously divided leadership. At least here in Székelyföld we are nearly all Hungarian-Romanians.

As I struggled to take in this horrifying description of Unitarians' lives in Romania, I was still having a hard time with József's conclusion that a homogeneous, all-Hungarian minority population was an advantage, even a necessity. My immediate family includes members born on five continents, so seeing diversity as a disadvantage was an upside-down idea that was hard for me to swallow. Standing in these new partnership shoes was going to be hard, and it occurred to me that on many levels giving up "thinking American" would be difficult.

In part of my talk during the Sunday service, I described our North American Unitarian Universalist congregations as a loosely connected body—an association of congregations with an elected president and

Hungarian-Romanians and Romanian-Romanians

Hungarian-Romanians have Hungarian ethnicity and Romanian citizenship. Romanian-Romanians have Romanian ethnicity and Romanian citizenship. Hungarian-Romanians are sometimes referred to as Transylvanian-Romanians, but today the large majority of people living in Transylvania are non-Hungarians who may also call themselves Transylvanian-Romanians. Hungarian-Romanians are often referred to as ethnic-Hungarians, but that term applies to all the Hungarians who live anywhere in the world. An accurate, but much too lengthy, description is: the Hungarian minorities who are Romanian citizens and live in Romania.

moderator rather than a denomination with a Bishop at its head.[27] Later József told me: "The Transylvanian Church would never choose to be 'an association.' It would be a disaster to be a separate congregation when you are under attack. And we have been under constant attack since 1920—some would say since 1579 when Ferenc Dávid died."

Another Transylvanian Unitarian minister told me, "My life has been hard, but not impossible, because I have my family. I know the history of my people. I have church. I have my faith." I felt humbled every day of my visit by the commitments and sacrifices they had made to keep their faith strong, their families together, and their congregations vital in the face of such severe oppression. Connecting with Transylvanians could teach us in North America a great deal about faith and hope, about loyalty and patience, about sustaining inner strength in the face of injustice, evil, and attack.

As the governments that ruled Transylvania changed again and again, its ancient communities and culture survived only where neighbors and relatives fought to stay on their land and protected their churches from unwanted change. The land and the church formed the common ground on which they could stand together, where they could trust, support, and protect one another and their faith.

It occurred to me that, in a parallel way, becoming Unitarian had enabled my own family to become more trusting and honest through dragging into the light several generations of family secrets involving addiction and abuse, which certainly helped us move beyond them. But unlike the Transylvanians, my sister, my brother, and I moved on from those hard times separated from one another. Our North American Unitarianism did not hold us together. As a teenager in the 1950s and early '60s, being Unitarian forged a path for me to walk away from my parents' values and their unhappy marriage to a different life-view that grew out of the political commitments of my own 1960s generation. As a young adult I knew I would always be Unitarian, and I was sure my church was an important ground-breaker and change-bringer for our modern times. This new connection with Transylvanian Unitarians who were just as radically engaged, but in holding onto, rather than changing, their values and their culture, made me stop to consider how my life would have turned out had I chosen a different path.

In *The Sum of Our Days*, the Chilean matriarch Isabel Allende concludes from her astute observation of the Northern Californian Americans she now lives among, that "though [individualism and freedom] may help in getting ahead in this world, it brings with it alienation and loneliness."[28] What if my sister, brother, and I had knitted our lives together for safety and survival instead of each setting out alone, insisting on the right to be independent and to follow our individual paths to change?

In Transylvania I was confronted with families I admired who had made the opposite choices from my own, people who were fighting with all their being to stay together and stay at home. They preferred a close-knit family tribe to the American dream of absolute individual freedom. I was also confronted by a people who treasured their faith and constantly used it and needed it to strengthen their hope and trust. I was told that when he was elected a bishop of the Hungarian Reformed Church in 1990, László Tőkés said, "I am not a hero. The scenario and the message were written by God: 'Do not be afraid.' For forty years we have been sick with fear. Then last winter we rose up, sick with courage. Today, we are a people who must re-learn how to dream."[29] I wondered what it was like to be a people and a church who did not believe, as I always had, that they could successfully change their lives and their world for the better; who did not believe, as I always had, that they were the ones who could successfully guarantee their church's future, who could mold its destiny with their own hands.

I had another lesson in "thinking American" when I met with five journalists from several of the small newspapers that sprang up immediately after December 1989. It left me with no doubt that participating in this partnership would demand I change my attitudes, welcome surprises, and learn to stand, even to walk, in those always unfamiliar, often uncomfortable Transylvanian shoes. Clustered around the parsonage dining table with pens and paper ready, the journalists were eager to talk with me because I was the first North American they had ever been able to interview openly and report accurately. To publish their newspapers and to hold such an interview were until recent months acts of subversion and defiance because, I was shocked to learn, there had been twenty years of crushing government censorship of all written material.

At one point in the interview (conducted in simple sentences, with József interpreting) I felt uncomfortable when I heard my words through their ears as I expressed a strong criticism of some US government policy. So I added, "But if I don't like what my government is doing, of course it's up to me to work to change it." The journalists asked József to translate that sentence two more times because they could not believe I had meant to say it. That individual Americans would assume the responsibility and shoulder the moral burden for the misdeeds of our US government officials was a concept none of them could understand. These Hungarian-Romanians said they would never feel responsible for anything the Romanian government did, nor would they even refer to it as "their" government. Why not? Because they did not believe there was anything they could do to change, or even influence, the government's positions and policies. Of course I can see why members of an oppressed ethnic and religious minority with next to no real power in the Romanian parliament would feel that way. But I thought it was sad, because how could any form of democratic freedom and responsibility take root among a people who completely distrusted, and indeed seemed to hate, their government?

Perhaps learning about democracy from North Americans was not what Transylvanian Unitarians wanted. On the other hand, in *Transylvania and Beyond*, Dervla Murphy records a quite different conversation, from January 1990, with two Romanian-Romanians:

Justinian: It's bad to give [people] passports they can't use. It makes people discontented and angry.

Dervla: But in a democracy people must be free to travel....[and] it's the government's duty to provide passports.

Mihai: We have much to learn about democracy—everything! Can you send us some books when you go home? We need to study democracy. No one in Rumania can understand what is it, really."

Dervla Murphy added: "I promised to do what I could and didn't say what I thought—that the practice of democracy cannot be learned from books."[30]

I began to wonder what things we North Americans would and would not be able to talk about with our Transylvanian brothers and sisters. Were there essential differences between us that we would never be able to reach across and understand? Could the North Americans come to respect and value the Transylvanian's origin-focused Protestantism? Could the Transylvanians respect and value the North Americans' "accept all comers" position, which has produced Unitarian Universalist congregations that deliberately reach out to include people rejected by mainstream society—mixed-faith couples, gay and lesbian families, atheists and agnostics looking for a spiritual home? Would the Transylvanians be surprised to learn some of these "outcasts" are third and fourth generation Unitarians or Universalists?

Could we reach across the strikingly different roles that ethnicity, economics, and faith play in our lives and congregations? Which worship practices could we share, and not share? Which of our social action concerns might the Transylvanians join in, understand, or sympathize with? Which of the Transylvanians' causes would we eventually work for together?

How difficult would it be for the Transylvanians to trust idealists like me, inexperienced with the savage realities of Soviet imperialism and National Communism, idealists the Transylvanians dismiss, no doubt rightly, as ridiculously naïve? And how difficult was it going to be for North American Unitarian Universalists, who have placed innovation and choice at the center of our religious beliefs, to learn to respect the Transylvanians' resistance to change and celebration of tradition?

Clearly, it was going to be both demanding and complicated to build real connections between Transylvanian Unitarians and North American Unitarian Universalists, because the Transylvanians have spent their lifetimes standing *against* their enemies and *for* maintaining their faith traditions and heritage, while we North Americans have strived to live and worship in ways that *move us toward* ever-evolving beliefs and *move us away from* the historic doctrines and no longer satisfying traditions of the past. What would become our common ground?

Could we manage to stand in each other's shoes? Could we nurture a radical patience with ourselves and each other, while we reached for trust and understanding? Would it ever be possible to actually understand and respect each other enough to read each other's thinking and understand each other's hearts—the crucial prerequisites for our being able to work together in trust, as partners?

And if these things did prove possible, how long would they take? How long would it be before both Eastern and Western partners stopped shaking their heads and asking themselves, "Are these new partners of ours *real* Unitarians?" How long would it be before they could trust our deeply entrenched democratic practices, and how long would it take for us to respect their hierarchical decision making? How long would it take every partner to stop thinking "us" and "them"?

I had no answers. I only knew I wanted to remain in my new state of grace, conferred on me by this new "old world" I had entered so unexpectedly, so unprepared (despite Judit Gellérd's warning) for what I was experiencing there.

Back at home, a long-time member and pillar of the San Jose congregation took me aside one Sunday morning to ask, "Gretchen, just how different are these Unitarians in Transylvania from us?" I drew a deep breath and said, "Very different, I think; probably more different than we will ever know." His face fell with disappointment. "But isn't that the dance," I said, "the point of partnership with these very foreign Unitarians—to stretch across our differences until we find connection and common ground?" His face brightened, and he said, "Of course it is. Well then, let's jump in with both feet."

Standing on Holy Ground

When I was in seventh grade, our Sunday school curriculum was called "Church across the Street." It taught us about the beliefs and worship practices of many of the major religions and helped us consider the universals of religious experience. It certainly strengthened our respect for cultural diversity. The six of us would squeeze into our teacher's car and drive across town to a different church or synagogue (but no mosques back then) to learn about yet another way of "doing religion."

At my first worship service with Unitarians in Transylvania, I felt I had stepped back into one of those Sunday school visits to a neighboring, but very different, faith. I was acutely aware of the differences between our North American and Transylvanian worship practices—the clothes we each wear to church, the ways we enter or leave the sanctuary, where people sit, the music we play, the songs we sing, what the minister does, the telling, or not, of stories that invite us to laugh or cry, the serving, or not, of communion, how we pray, or do not pray. I have always been grateful that growing up Unitarian instilled in me a sincere respect for religious beliefs and practices different from my own. But how true is that, really? It took me much too long to accept, and be glad, that our new partner church's practices and beliefs were so different from ours in California, and so closed to change.

For example, I wonder if North American Unitarian Universalists can ever fully understand or appreciate communion's vital role in the lives of our Transylvanian partners. This question is often raised when partners participate in each other's holiday worship services. Judit Gellérd's father, Imre Gellérd, believed, "If the rituals of our practice disappeared one by one, the last to go would certainly be communion."[31] When a visitor explained to several Transylvanians why their North American partner congregation no longer shared communion, one of them asked with deep concern, "How can you live without the sustaining joy and comfort of sharing the Lord's Supper?" Another began to weep for her partner church in the United States which had lost so much.

On my first Sunday morning in Transylvania, Mária offered to iron out the wrinkles in my robe. "What robe?" I responded. József's jaw dropped and he sputtered something strong-sounding in Hungarian. It had not occurred to him that a minister might come for a visit over a weekend without bringing a robe. He frowned in disbelief when I explained that since World War II only a few Unitarian Universalist ministers in California have worn robes when conducting weekly worship. If I had thought about it when I was packing, I would have guessed, correctly, that Transylvanian ministers always do. Teaching myself to think ahead about such things has been an important part of learning to walk in others' shoes.

I had not realized that my first visit in Transylvania was over Pentecost or that this meant communion would be served at the special holiday church service. I knew I should feel honored when József invited me to serve communion with him. But I had grown up during the years when US Unitarian congregations were stridently moving beyond being Christian, and even in seminary I had never been invited to take communion. Of course I suffered a mixed reaction to József's invitation—I felt honored, but quite anxious.

Astonished to learn that I had never taken, much less served, communion, József became my teacher: "Sharing communion affirms the strong roots of our faith—roots in our religious community and in its heritage. It is essentially about communion with God, as well as communion with out forebears and each other." I could certainly feel enthusiastic about that, and I was relieved to be assured that the bread and wine carried no physical "body and blood" implications. József points out in his contribution to David Steers' collection of articles about communion practices in different parts of Europe that baptism, confirmation, marriage, and burial happen only once in a lifetime, but Transylvanians share in communion about 200 times during their lives.[32] He told me, "Communion is the most important event of the church year for us." Elek Rezi echos this in his article, "The Lord's Supper in the Transylvanian Unitarian Church":

> The Lord's Supper or Communion is the central ritual of the Unitarian Church in Transylvania....Communion is a time to remember Jesus, his teachings and devotion to what he firmly believed. It is also a time to re-examine our own lives and to re-dedicate ourselves to the sort of religious life taught by Jesus. The aim of the communion service is to improve the quality and value of our human life.[33]

Feeling completely reassured, I consciously shifted gears to a "take what you like and leave the rest" frame of mind and refocused on learning how to serve communion with understanding and grace. József tried to hide his surprise that any minister could be completely ignorant about this important ritual, but it was clear he felt embarrassed for me. "Don't worry," he reassured me, "only you, me, and Gabriela Popa understand English [Gabriela was József's English teacher, and was helping József with translating], so I can help you in English when you need it." He did not say, "*if* you need it," and I could imagine the words he was not speaking aloud: "And we must hope that no one else will realize that you are so ignorant."

Explaining the choreography, József said that the traditional practice of rural village churches is for the men to share communion and then leave the church. After the men have left, the women gather in their circle around the communion table. József registered my look of shocked dismay as I pictured that—to me—sexist practice, and he quickly added, "Of course I am eager to see reforms not only in the Romanian government and the Romanian economy, but also in some of our worship practices."

József's sermon that day was based on Exodus 3:5 "Remove the sandals from your feet, for the place where you stand is holy ground." "Communion," he told the congregation that filled every pew in the large sanctuary, "is the moment of facing God, of standing with God, of grasping something from God's very being, the moment of God's nearness. It is a revelation in faith. It means receiving God in our lives and God receiving us. In one word: communion with God." Judit Gellérd had warned me to prepare for the unexpected, but how does one prepare to leap into the unknown of such an intense communion with God, especially since I had never believed in that kind of personal God?

Ruth Gibson, who served with me on the Partner Church Council, has written about the first Transylvanian communion she attended:

Without understanding much of the verbal content of the sermon or the prayers, and only a bit of the hymns, it was clear to me that something meaningful was going on. It seemed to me to have something to do with the sense that everyone knew and accepted that they had all fallen short, that their circumstances had meant compromise and doing what had to be done to survive, that even God had not answered all their prayers, and that nevertheless, their longing for something better was enough, their willingness to gather for the Lord's Supper was enough. They were celebrating their faith that as far as God is concerned, we are all welcome at the table. I think the sense of being sustained by faith has more to do with the experience of being held by an accepting community than with theology and doctrine.[34]

I remember that the light bulbs in the elaborately carved wooden chandelier were switched on (maybe because turning on electric lights in the daytime was finally allowed?) though their light was superfluous in the bright sunlight streaming through the twelve clear, very high windows. The distinguished visitor's pew, just under the high pulpit, where I sat alone on neither the men's nor the women's side, was quite hard, and its back met mine in all the wrong places. The well-used hymnal's broken back made it easy to leave open on the slanted rail in front of me. The communion table, covered by the whitest cloth I had ever seen, with elaborate cutwork and scalloped edges, had been made that week to honor our fledgling partner church relationship. I wondered which of the black-clad women had donated her skill, imagination, and hundreds of hours to make the tablecloth. I had met the remarkable black-suited man who sat alone in the front pew. He had carved the chandelier and painted the traditional flower designs that danced across the organ loft and the fronts of the first pews.

As József lifted the chalice for me to drink from, I suddenly remembered a US Baptist seminary professor telling us the true work of ministry is to strive, by grace alone, to embody God. As I offered the bread to each of the men, our eyes locked. "You are looking deep into each other's souls," József had instructed me. At first I felt vulnerable and anxious about having these people look deep into my soul, but very soon it became a blessing.

After József said the traditional prayer that ends the men's part of the service, he whispered to me in English, "Gretchen, I have an idea. Please be ready to pray." Then he said in Hungarian to everyone else: "Our honored guest is going to say the prayer at the end of the women's communion, and I am worried she might feel we are being disrespectful if the men leave and miss hearing her prayer. So perhaps the men should remain here during the women's communion." In the memory of anyone there, it was the first time the men sat respectfully in their seats while a circle of women shared communion. Those moments were a benchmark in the many new and challenging experiences the partnership has brought to the Unitarians in Homoródszentmárton and the Unitarian Universalists in San Jose.

It was my first communion, and it marked a crucial turning point in my personal faith development. I grew up in the Bible belt of East Tennessee where, for the first nine years of my life, I was the only Unitarian in every school I attended. Being constantly alone in my faith had made me defensive—eager to convince my friends that the Unitarians were as established as the Catholics, as organized as the Presbyterians, and as fervent as the Southern Baptists.

As I prayed my unexpected prayer in that sanctuary where dedicated religious liberals have gathered faithfully for more than four and a half centuries, my defensiveness about being Unitarian dropped away completely. When I "removed my sandals" and stood on that sacred ground, I understood with my whole being that I am a living part of a very old and significant religious movement. For the first time in my life I had no reservations about being a person of faith who fully belonged within the generations of North American Unitarians and Universalists. There in Transylvania I was no longer a stranger in a strange land. I could picture our two congregations walking a path together on common, holy ground.

I helped József conduct that first Transylvanian service wearing the most somber clothes I had brought with me, but no robe or stole. My credibility was seriously undermined. I had no idea then how bizarre it was for Transylvanian men and women to be served communion by a minister dressed in a bright green skirt and blouse. I am sure both József and Mária had to explain, and re-explain, my unorthodox attire to every congregation member.

As soon as I returned to Northern California, I bought a traditional black clerical robe to wear in Transylvania. (The pink robe especially made for my ordination was no help.) On my second visit to Homoródszentmárton, after I had worn my new black robe while assisting at a wedding and two more Sunday services, a respected village elder declared that I was, after all, a real minister. He had no problem with my being the first woman to have served him communion. His problem was that I had performed this important sacrament without wearing a minister's robe.

Leon Hopper told me this story from his first visit with his congregation's partner church in Torockószentgyörgy (Colteşti): Leon had been invited to preach the sermon for the Sunday service, and he had brought a robe and the most conservative tie he owned. The tie was dark

Communion practice—East and West

Between World Wars I and II, North American Unitarians (and to a lesser extent, Universalists) incorporated humanism into their perspectives and enlarged the sources of their faith beyond the original Judeo-Christian and Protestant roots to include many major religious traditions. As a result, most North American congregations stopped using worship practices like communion, which were specifically Christian.[35] A few congregations, including those that identify as specifically Christian Unitarian Universalist, continue to serve communion, though not every Sunday, while others have returned to serving it either once or four times a year.

The Transylvanian Unitarians are Christians whose communion practice was set in the early Protestant Reformation. The high points of their church calendar have always been the four Sundays (Pentecost, Harvest, Christmas, and Easter) when communion is served. Communion is also served—though often not to everyone attending—during confirmations and ordinations.

Transylvanian Unitarians are ardent unitarian, rather than trinitarian, Protestants. Jesus is a great person and teacher—not a divine being, and not referred to as "Christ." Quite a few Transylvanian Unitarian ministers are ardent followers of the Jesus Seminar's scholarly debates about the historical Jesus. At the heart of communion is the example of Jesus' life, because his teachings form the foundation of Transylvanian Unitarian understanding of the world—what it means to be human, how to live one's life, and what one might hope for one's children.

blue, so dark it was very hard to tell if it was blue or black. When Leon joined the family for breakfast at the parsonage on Sunday morning, his partner minister took one look at his tie, said, "That won't do," and loaned Leon a black tie to wear. Beneath his robe.

The Transylvanian Unitarian Creed is:

I believe in One God, creator of life and providential Father.
I believe in Jesus, the best son of God, our true teacher.
I believe in the holy spirit.
I believe in the mission of the Unitarian Church.
I believe in forgiveness of sins and eternal life. Amen.

The Transylvanian Church Affirmation is:

I am Unitarian,
I live and work in this faith.
Jesus is my guide,
And God is my help.
We, humans, are all brothers and sisters,
Our law is one: LOVE.
The goal of our work is shared,
Happy are those of God's Kingdom.

Infants in Transylvanian Unitarian families are baptized and named. When they are around fourteen, youth are confirmed. To prepare for confirmation, they attend a year of weekly classes where they thoroughly discuss and then memorize the questions and answers of the ages-old Transylvanian Unitarian catechism. They take their first communion at the confirmation service.

Learning to Pray:
Join Me as You Will

I noticed that when we entered the Homoródszentmárton church sanctuary, József sometimes paused for a moment and seemed to withdraw inside himself. When I asked him about it, he said, "If you want to experience how Transylvanian Unitarians worship, you must pray silently within yourself as we do when we enter and leave the church." So that's what he was doing—praying! Then he taught me the prayers Transylvanian Unitarians pray when they enter a worship service:

I have entered your house of worship, oh gracious God.
My prayers are seeking you, and I hear your voice.
Loving God, be with me, show me your holy face,
Fill my heart and my spirit, let me feel your loving presence.

And when they leave the service:

I depart with joy in my heart filled with peace and stillness.
My soul has found rest here because you have been with me.
Guide me, protect me, help me always, oh loving God.[36]

When József urged me to reach out through prayer to God each time I entered a church, and when he invited me to pray the women's prayer during the communion service, he had no idea he was forcing me to face my deep-seated ambivalence about prayer and plunging me back into an ongoing, thirty-year struggle. Over time my growing respect and trust of Transylvanian worship practices made it possible for me to confront my ambivalence about prayer and move beyond struggling with it.

———————

Prayer is a tense and tender place where I work out my religious ambivalences. My first real theological discussion—with my mother, while she washed and I dried the Sunday dinner dishes—was about prayer. That morning in my religious education class at church we had debated whether or not it was a good practice to pray every day at school, as all students in the state of Tennessee were then required by law to do. My mother and I asked each other how praying actually worked in people's lives and hearts. What were the different kinds of prayers, and why were there so many? Was praying part of every culture and an inevitable part of being human?

As I stacked the clean dishes in the cupboard, I declared, "I think praying is just a special way to convince yourself that you can do, or be, or have something. You may tell yourself you are communicating with God, but it's really just a conversation with your deeper self." I went to bed convinced I had reached the heart of the matter. At twelve I was already the product of a religious tradition that lifted up skepticism as a righteous path for faithful individuals. Thereafter I dismissed praying as a well-intentioned blend of self-encouragement, self-management, and self-deception. I decided I was radically different from people who prayed, and I deliberately chose to stand outside "all that." I did not pray except when it was my turn to say grace before meals at my Southern Baptist grandmother's table.

When our minister, Richard Henry, led our annual flower communion service, I couldn't understand why Norbert Čapek, a strong religious Humanist, had created a ritual of praying over the flowers people had brought. He had called it "consecrating" the flowers, but I knew it was a prayer. The point of the flower communion was to celebrate each member as both a separate individual member and a part of the congregation and to see that everyone both gives to and receives from their congregation. That is what I thought religion should be about, not consecrations or prayers.

In junior high school it angered my home-room teacher that I kept my eyes open and my lips closed during the daily recitation of the Lord's Prayer. I declared it was my right not to pray at school, citing the early Unitarians who had established the United States' foundational separation of church and state. Whether I prayed mattered more to the teacher than it did to me, but I knew my rights. I was convinced it was hypocritical to pray if I didn't believe in it, and it was definitely against my religion to be a hypocrite.

In my early thirties I began practicing Zen Buddhist meditation and found that sitting in silence and group chanting came naturally to me. It felt right to stop digging into the past or poking into the future, and rest fully in this moment. At that time, praying with words never came naturally. I always tripped up on to whom, or to what, I was speaking, and I was never sure about what, or if, to ask.

Fast forward ten years to the demanding apprenticeship called clinical pastoral education (CPE), a requirement for ministry students of most faiths in the United States. CPE is an intense three months spent working days, nights, and weekends with mental patients, hospital patients, or prisoners. At the end of my first day on a hospital oncology ward, the supervisor helped our small group of seminarians role-play conversations we could expect to have with patients in different stages of illness or dying. Evaluating my practice turn, he said, "Gretchen, you didn't say a prayer. Patients need you to pray for them." That night I telephoned my mother to tell her I was finally going to have to learn to pray.

"You know how to pray," she said. "Just take their hand and invite them to pray in their way, while you are praying in yours."

"They don't want me to pray *with* them. They want me to pray *for* them, to ask God to help them get well. Out loud."

"Out loud!" she gasped. Then we both laughed, embarrassed by how narrow-minded we were being. Surprisingly, both of us could remember hearing very few Unitarians pray a prayer aloud. I think most of my parents' generation of Unitarians were too busy discarding the orthodoxies that had been forced on them as children to seriously consider what benefits praying might hold. Our services' closing benedictions were the closest we East Tennessee Unitarians had let ourselves get to praying. We felt fulfilled when we rose to the challenge of defending our often changing beliefs and affirmed together every Sunday that "service is our prayer." We held off on experiencing mystery or connecting to the sacred until we were on a retreat or surrounded by Nature. We held little in reverence, but were fiercely faithful to our small, hardworking church community. And Sunday after Sunday we were filled by the spirit of something important but unnamed when we sat together in silence or sang familiar, moving hymns.

All of it was religious, but none of it was really prayer. In fact, we often defended our right not to pray, like the chaplain in Maine who—when a police lieutenant asked her, "Listen, Reverend Mother, as long as you're here, couldn't you pray for it to stop raining?"—replied, "I'm a Unitarian Universalist. We don't do weather."[37]

There are a lot of Unitarian Universalist ministers of my generation who have an unsettled relationship with prayer. Zoltán Veress and his

Unitarian wife, Magdalena, are well-known Hungarian authors who were able to leave Transylvania as political refugees in 1986 to live in Sweden. They have written and published many books for their loyal readers among Hungarians in every corner of the world. Their special delight is in the pleasures of heartfelt conversations over celebratory meals. At the end of a wonderful evening in Stockholm, Zoltán told me how astonished he felt when a visiting Unitarian Universalist minister respectfully declined his invitation to end a similar evening by praying the *Our Father*. Staring pointedly at me over the top of his eyeglasses, Zoltán declared, "Sometimes it's hard for me to tell if you Unitarian Universalists are building a church or a trade union."

It was a steep learning curve, but working in hospitals taught me how to pray. There were a surprising number of patients (including a few Unitarian Universalists) who found they needed to connect with God but had no experience with praying. Emergency room and operating theater deaths came faster than I was ready for, deepening my respect for the comfort of prayer and its power to connect us to strength, acceptance, and faith.

I was forty-four when, during my ordination service, a different kind of prayer swept through me in the San Jose church sanctuary filled with people praying for me and my ministry. I accepted their faith-filled connection to me. I believed in their trust and felt through and through the power of their life-giving love. I knew that we were one, with one another and with God. But I assumed that this unexpected moment of spiritual connection, like ordination itself, was a once in a lifetime experience. Once ordained, I swam steadily up the stream of being called upon to pray. We blessed each child we dedicated and consecrated the flowers during the annual flower communion. We said grace before special meals. (I carried one I could use in my wallet so I didn't have to pause while I sorted out my ambivalences.) Church members asked me to pray comforting prayers with them, though seldom for them, at the bedsides of their seriously ill loved ones. We moved together beyond worship that was locked into a reaction against the past and instituted a time in every Sunday service for meditation and prayer, usually led aloud by the minister. My prayers were fine, but in my heart I was not at peace. I was still engaged in my decades-long battle with how to pray, if I really wanted to pray, and what it all meant.

Then I found myself in the back of beyond, in a remote village church nestled in the foothills of the Carpathian Mountains being warned during my first Transylvanian Unitarian worship service, "Please be ready to pray." To pray out loud, on my feet, with no pre-determined prayer pulled out of my wallet. Just pray, however it comes, straight from the heart. In that moment my ambivalent dance with prayer took an abrupt turn. I finally understood that in prayer my heart must not be full of the words I want to say. It must be filled to overflowing with the people I am praying with, and for. Standing on that sacred ground, my heart sang a prayer to me and I prayed it...aloud. As my Southern Baptist grandmother would have said, I was filled with the spirit.

I am always stubborn about adopting anything that moves me away from the Unitarianism I grew up with. So it was several more years before I completely set aside my battle with prayer. And once again, it was a Transylvanian minister who opened the door to where I needed to go.

One winter afternoon, while a feeble sun cast long shadows across the historic homesteads of Concord, Massachusetts, the transforming power of prayer unexpectedly moved through me in the midst of that most mundane of our religious institutions—a committee meeting. Kinga-Reka (Zsigmond) Székely—the Transylvanian minister serving in Homoródszentpéter (Petreni) who was studying in the United States — had joined us for the afternoon. When our Unitarian Universalist Partner Church Council executive committee ended an openly contentious and hard fought session of our (usually more peaceful) meeting, someone invited Kinga to say a few words to close our afternoon's work. She broke into a broad smile and said, "I will gladly pray for you. I can see you need it." Kinga prayed in Hungarian, but in the saying and the hearing, while holding hands with the colleagues with whom I had been fighting moments before, I was swept up in that same earth-shaking conviction I had felt at my ordination—that I was deeply connected to everyone in the room, that we were fully loved and worthy of trust, that we were truly one with each other and with God. Every cell in my body felt it, knew it, and was completely convinced of it. I felt powerfully called to recommit myself to our shared faith.

Ever since that afternoon I have rejoiced in being prayed for, especially by Transylvanian Unitarians. They are certain that there is a God, certain that God is watching over all people in the world, including me—not only in this moment, but always. Wherever they are in the world, each time these Transylvanian Unitarians pray, they are praying for me. I draw solid comfort from that. I am honored by it. I even look forward to leading prayers because it makes me feel wrapped in love and buoyed up by hope. I lift my hand and invite a blessing on our work, on our lives. This simple ritual makes itself sincere. And being wrapped in that love and hope has chased away my struggles with skepticism and ambivalence.

Learning Freedom behind
Closed Doors

All through my first visit I was astonished by the grim reality of how the Homoródszentmárton Unitarians had been forced to live since 1920, when Transylvania was excised from Hungary to become part of Romania, and the horrors of their lives since 1947, when Romania became a Soviet satellite. Every day—no, every hour—of my visit, another distressing detail would be revealed to me when I asked an innocent question about health care, church policies, the schools, the police, children, folk dancing, democracy, bus schedules, cheese, libraries, newspapers, or electric lights. Some of what I learned was quite wonderful, but it was very difficult to absorb the terrible things I heard and keep smiling. I found the upsetting answers to my probing questions difficult to believe while I was surrounded by the lovely June sunshine, the plentiful fresh garden produce, and the joyous spirit of "these new times." In fact, what I learned then was only the tip of a terrible iceberg.[38]

As József and I walked along a sidewalk in Székelyudvarhely, a crowd gathered further down. József tensed and fell silent. I talked and walked, not noticing the policemen getting out of their car across the street, or rather, I glanced at them and didn't think anything of it. József caught my gesticulating hand and returned it to my side, hissing, "Gretchen! Look down, be silent, make yourself small."

I realized how differently we lived in the world—my seeing the police as protectors (at least of women of my race, age, and economic status), compared to József's seeing them as his enemy. My North American trust in democratic practice compared to Hungarian-Romanians' cynical disgust with so many of the institutions and government regulations they had to deal with every day. Standing across the street from the burned-out Securitate headquarters in Székelyudvarhely, we talked and joked about the differences in the way we practice our religions and live our principles—our loose North American association of congregations compared to their closely woven denomination, our freedom to direct our individual lives and religious beliefs compared to their holding tight to traditional practices they fear losing. After only a few days in Romania, these striking differences between us were forcing me to remove the American filters from my way of seeing and demanding that I reframe my values.

In his foreword to *Looking for George: Life and Death in Romania* (Helena Drysdale's memoir of her time in Romania in 1979 and 1991) Tobias Wolff writes:

> Even after the 'so-called Revolution'...it is hard to break through evasion and paranoia long enough to get a straight story out of anyone. To Romanians, every question is suspect, every questioner; and they have good reason for circumspection. The Securitate invaded the whole of Romanian life, holding nothing sacred, neither friendship nor family nor one's own home....In a country run by secretive thugs...even if you weren't bugged, you thought you were, and the effect was the same.[39]

Dervla Murphy, a British travel writer, was in Transylvania at the same time as I was making my first trip. In *Transylvania and Beyond* she writes:

> Every day I was becoming more aware of the gravity of Rumania's long-term problems. Decades must pass before the country can be expected to recover from an educational system designed to paralyse independent thinking, an artistic and intellectual life warped by censorship, a legal system (if one can call it that) based on terrorism, an economic system based on the ambitions of a megalomaniac, a social life overshadowed by fear of informers, a domestic life dominated by the quest for food and medicines, a sex-life inhibited by bizarre restrictions.[40]

During the December 1989 uprising, citizens in Székelyudvarhely freed prisoners held in the Securitate headquarters and captured and killed its highest official. It rained charred paper as room after room of documents about individuals and wiretap tapes were burned. And then the building itself was burned. Was the fire set by the people so any files that were left could never again be used against them? Or was the fire set by the Securitate to destroy evidence of their culpability, now that the pendulum of political power was swinging against them?[41]

Under Ceauşescu there were Unitarian ministers who spoke out against the government, and there were Unitarian ministers who informed against their colleagues. When imprisoned ministers were released, they could not be trusted by their colleagues or congregations because the price of release was always the promise that they would become informers for the Securitate.[42]

While our small group stood and stared at the scorched shell of the Securitate headquarters, no one complained that we were blocking the sidewalk. Strangers wanted to tell me the evils of the Securitate, how its officers and agents had ruined lives and violated human and civil rights. And they relived the weeks five months before when the Romanian "revolution" leapt from Temesvár to the other cities, and then to towns like Székelyudvarhely.

A grandfather passing by our sidewalk group stopped to make sure I was "getting it right." He said:

> If the government we have now agreed with us that the Securitate was a despicable blight on Romania's history, they would turn this charred building into a cultural center. But, no, this place with its terrifying and horrible memories is going to remain a police headquarters. Those were remarkable moments last December— moments of great tension, deep fear, a lot of sadness, and huge joy. Those euphoric days will not come again in our lifetime, but they have left a hunger we will always remember.

If North American Unitarian Universalists had a motto, it might be something like Ferenc Dávid's favorite text, John 8:32 "You will know the truth, and the truth will make you free." In contrast, József told me the Transylvanian Unitarians' logo is a peace dove surrounded by a snake. It is based on the teaching of Jesus in Matthew 10:16 "I am sending you out like sheep among wolves. You must be clever as serpents and innocent as doves." I was surprised that a denomination would have a motto or logo focused on how to deal with enemies. It would not have occurred to me that this was what a church was for. But helping its members deal well and successfully with their enemies has long been, and still is, a central responsibility of the Transylvanian Unitarian Church.

I learned about the roles of teachers and churches in Ceauşescu's Romania from Gabriela Popa, József's English teacher who lives in Székelyudvarhely. Gabriela generously spent most of the long Pentecost weekend interpreting for me when I was speaking with anyone other than József. I was the first native English speaker Gabriela had ever spoken with face to face. She told me:

When a society collapses, as Romania's has, civilization survives only in those whose bonds of faith and language remain strong. Ceauşescu knew this, and he made war on our faith, war on our language, and war on our history. But we have proved stronger than him and his wars.

Gabriela was not being metaphorical when she said Ceauşescu made war on Transylvanians' faith, language, and history. Under Ceauşescu it was illegal to teach the history of the Hungarian minorities, and it eventually became illegal to teach about the history of Transylvania in the period of the Austro-Hungarian Empire because, as Ceauşescu became more and more mentally unbalanced, he became ever more determined to convince the world that before 1920 no Hungarians had ever lived within the present-day borders of Romania—an outrageous claim, since many generations of Hungarian families have lived on and worked the same land in Transylvania for nearly 1000 continuous years. In this effort to wipe the concept of a separate, Hungarian Transylvania out of the schools and off the maps, a long list was compiled of forbidden Hungarian books, especially religious books and Transylvanian history books. (The books carried by the pilgrims whom Robin and I had met on the train into Romania were on this forbidden list.) In addition to Hungarian language Bibles, the government confiscated many other books and religious items, communion chalices, flags, and banners with Hungarian inscriptions or symbols. Selling, reading, or daring to use any of these items invited interrogation and imprisonment. The Department of Education produced pseudo-history textbooks that falsified both the Romanian and the Hungarian past. These false texts were still widely available in local stores in the early 1990s. I wondered how Gabriela Popa's husband, a high school history teacher, dealt with all this. The women I met in Homoródszentmárton dealt with it by making tablecloths, pillowcases, and other handwork using what they called "subversive embroidery"—needlework that contained Hungarian tulips hidden within its patterns or the colors of the Hungarian flag woven into it.

Eventually I understood that by the 1980s Romanians truly had been at war with the Hungarian minorities. The rest of the Romanian people had been manipulated into hating the Hungarian minorities. The regime had many failures for which it desperately needed someone else to blame, and the Ceauşescu regime regularly scapegoated the Hungarian-

Romanians. In response, the Hungarian-Romanians grew to fear not only the government, but also the Romanian-Romanians. They were not imagining or exaggerating this politically fueled animosity. On a train leaving Romania after their first partner church visit, two San Jose church members started a conversation with a young Romanian who was sharing their carriage. When they said they had been staying with Hungarian-Romanians, his matter of fact response was, "We're going to kill all of them, you know."

A large number of Romanian-Romanians were forced to leave their homes and move to Transylvania or other areas to satisfy Ceauşescu's effort to maintain a Romanian majority in every part of the country. Several Hungarian-Romanians have told me that these displaced Romanians "would rather live in Transylvania now that they have seen how much better it is than in Bucharest or the south." I suppose it may be "thinking American," but I question whether people who have been forced to relocate, against their will, really live happily and without resentment in their new location.

Before I left home, I learned from a Berkeley Unitarian Universalist who adopted Romanian twins about another disturbing aspect of Romanian life—that in Romania the health care system could be your enemy. Romanian health care was used as a punitive arm of the government, for example, to promote Ceauşescu's hated "decree babies" program, which made contraception and abortion illegal for couples with less than five children in an effort to rapidly increase the population. As a result, many women underwent illegally performed abortions in dangerous and abusive conditions at a ruinous price. Ceauşescu's plan was to raise the population of Romania from 19 to 25 million immediately to supply workers for the completely unrealistic goal of Romania's quickly becoming a modern industrial nation. The "Hero Mothers" who bore and brought up ten or more children were lavishly praised for "breeding for Socialism." Punishing taxes were levied on couples with fewer than five children, and women who did not become pregnant were forced to submit to humiliating monthly gynecological exams, supervised by "the Baby Police." The birth rate increased from 6.1 per thousand in 1966, to 18.1 in 1967, 17.1 in 1968, and 13.2 in 1969. One result was that many couples delayed marriage or married without living together. Until a contraceptive black market developed, women frequently died from self-administered abortions, and far too many parents were forced to abandon their babies to state-run orphanages when there was no food for them.

One of the reasons many Romanian-Romanians resent Hungarian-Romanians is that the Romanians suffered far more from these intolerable conditions. To ensure the Hungarian minority would not once again become the majority population in Transylvania, pressure to have more children was not applied to them once they had two children, while ethnic Romanian families were forced to produce at least five (after which abortion became the legal form of contraception). When I asked József if this was indeed true, he was clearly shocked that I would bring up such a topic, but said that it was true, although he had never spoken with anyone about it—not even Mária.[43]

During the Ceauşescu era, almost everyone in Romania lived with few government services or benefits. Children were not the only group to be "discarded." The elderly, the mentally ill, the rebellious, and any otherwise "difficult" adults were seen as costing the state too much and as "better out of the way." Ceauşescu defended his position of preferring that people die soon after they ceased to be productive, and instructed doctors not to treat anyone with a chronic illness or patients over the age of seventy—condemning them to a form of state-initiated euthanasia. In order to survive, people were forced to humiliate themselves in many ways. These hated conditions continued to exist for so long because everyone was controlled and subdued by fear.

How does love survive in such brutal conditions? Imagine what such practices would do to an entire population's self-respect and how the relentless pressure to increase the birthrate could devastate a couple's love life. My questions about health care were very painful for Mária, a high school teacher, to answer. She told me, "We know how to teach lies. We know how to teach the truth when no one else is listening. What is so hard for us to learn, now, is how to speak above a whisper when we are saying what is in our hearts."

I have been a teacher all my life, and religious education has always occupied the center of my ministry. Late into my second night in Homoródszentmárton, safely nested in the parsonage study's comfortable bed with its beautifully embroidered pillows, surrounded by many books in many languages, I tried to imagine what it would be like to teach the truth in a whisper when no one else was listening. When everything important to one's soul is under constant attack, how does one go about filling that empty space inside—the place where hope should be?

Speaking as an ambassador from the Transylvanian Ministers' Association to the 1997 annual meeting of the Unitarian Universalist Ministers Association, József Szombatfalvi, Sr. said:

> Like Moses and his people, we, too, were wandering in hope and desperation, in fear and revolt, in doubt and faithfulness, in guilt and anger, for 40 years, and even more. Those were a nerve-racking 40 years—almost my entire lifetime....[But] we nurtured hope for our Promised Land....The reign of communist dictatorship seemed to have no end, no light at the end of a lifelong tunnel. The light came from within. Our faith in God and in our future was the only sustaining power we had to go on.

> Thank God, we were able to keep our religion for four decades. We nurtured, sometimes in secret, the language, and faith, and traditions.... The church has always been our fortress, not only in a physical and literal sense but also now, more and more, in a spiritual sense. And we give thanks today that we never lost the Promised Land from our sight, never ceased to struggle to recapture it.[44]

In the first half of the 1990s, the rest of the world was slowly waking up to what Transylvanians had suspected for years—that of all the Eastern European dictatorships, Ceauşescu's had been the most paranoid, the most cunning, and the most repressive. Eventually I understood that the children's field trip afternoon, with its celebration of Hungarian folk stories and dances, was actually a potentially dangerous, open act of defiance. Each of the teachers and parents there must have been feeling an unsettling, unspoken anxiety: What reprisals might come crashing down on participants at this outing if the future brought to power another Ceauşescu?

Slowly, I was beginning to understand the deeper meanings of "destroy," "resist," "trust," "united," and "family secrets" for Hungarian-Romanians, but I did not realize then that parents had taught their children Hungarian traditions and history in secret, at times inside closets with the door firmly closed. I did not know that when the congregation sang the *Székely Anthem* during our first church service together they were announcing that my visit was completely tied in their minds to their long hoped-for freedom from oppression; to their leaving their rough road and dark night and reaching a promised land.

The starkness of Transylvanian existence forced me to to see my own "American land of opportunity" with new eyes. I was surprised to discover that despite our vast differences, Romania and the United States are similar in some disappointing ways—both countries foster gross economic inequities and provide far better private than public health and welfare services. Both Romania and the United States have failed to address the lack of actual opportunity for the uneducated and the under classes. As my eyes opened to injustice in Romania, I saw much more keenly the injustice of rampant poverty and homelessness in the United States.

At the same time my experiences in Transylvania made me hugely grateful for the US system (with all its compromises) of representational government and its defense of personal freedoms. After spending time with Unitarians who had lost their human and civil rights, my own commitment to democratic practices deepened dramatically. Before I met these Transylvanian Unitarians, I spent the mornings at our Unitarian Universalist Association's General Assemblies catching up with old friends rather than fulfilling my responsibilities as a delegate at the business meetings. I was content to leave to others the democratic process of conducting Unitarian Universalist Association business and conscientiously voting up or down our resolutions for improving society. But after spending time with Transylvanians who care deeply about many of the same issues as I did, but had no hope of having an impact on government policies that decided these issues and controlled their lives, I now go to every General Assembly business session, as well as every congregational meeting, and vote gratefully through each step of even the most tedious governance process. In 1990 I mistakenly assumed these new partnership connections might "bring more democracy" to Transylvanian Unitarians, but I found instead that they were bringing a deeper democracy to me.

Re-learning How to Dream

Transylvanian Unitarians usually hold a church service every morning of the four-day Pentecost holiday. But on the last day of my visit, instead of holding their service inside the church, the Homoródszentmárton Unitarians gathered in a high meadow where we could look far down and see the village, crowned by the majestic Unitarian church steeple. Most of us climbed the long trail up the mountainside, though a few older members were transported luxuriously on the horse and cart that brought the food and blankets up. We cooked, and ate, and laughed. After we had eaten, they sang folk songs and a few hymns. With József translating the words, they even got me to sing two of our hymns for them. They especially liked the lines from "Spirit of Life" that say, "giving life the shape of justice" and "roots hold me close; wings set me free."

While we were singing, it began to rain. If it had been a San Jose church picnic, the Californians would have headed home as soon as the temperature dropped and the first threatening clouds gathered, but here no one was packing up, and I resigned myself to getting soaked through. What the Transylvanians did was tie up large pieces of canvas between the trees, and we crowded together under them, wrapped in drip-defying blankets. They didn't go home, József explained to me, because they hadn't yet done what they had come for. They had come to talk, to share hopes and information and ideas, to complain, to argue, to be truthful. They had come to re-learn how to dream. This vital, life-giving talk went on for two hours until the skies cleared, and we saw an eagle soaring overhead.

It was a worship service with no sermon and no informers. They told me that when times got very bad they would hold their church services in this place so that for a few hours, within the safety of their trusting community, they could be their true selves and speak their true thoughts.

It astounded me to discover that one quarter of the world's Unitarians had been living like this for half a century, and most of us in North America had no knowledge of it at all. This picnic service convinced me that it was absolutely crucial for us to learn as much as we could about each other's lives and stretch ourselves to stay connected, so that the lives of Unitarians and Unitarian Universalists everywhere could be changed by who their partners were, by what we have both lived, and by how our churches and our faith could sustain us through hard times. North Americans could help our partners raise the funds to build buildings or buy tractors, but buildings and tractors come and go. It would be the gift of a lifetime, and certainly a privilege, to stand together with these remarkable people as they re-learned how to dream.

Loaves and Fishes

When the Romanian borders were opened in 1990 after fifty years of increasing isolation, no Romanian expected that large numbers of outsiders would want to visit their country, a place accustomed to hiding itself from the outside world. But by the summer months the trains could not keep up with the number of relatives, tourists, and pilgrims who flooded into Romania. In the always too few trains, onboard food or beverages were non-existent, no water ran in the sinks, and the toilets could best be described as catastrophic. Nevertheless, again and again we foreign visitors came away from our visits with wonderful, sometimes miraculous, stories to tell about our train journeys—because of the kindness of strangers.

In 1990 when I stepped off the train onto Romanian soil for the first time on a Friday morning at the end of May, my husband, Robin, was with me, but he had to return alone the next night to chair a meeting back in Budapest. My five-day visitor's visa dictated that the last train I could take would leave Segesvár the following Tuesday night. We knew that getting me a return ticket was going to be a big problem, because that train was also the last one thousands of Hungarians who had come to Romania to visit their relatives could take and be on time for work after the four-day weekend. Like all of them, I did not want to leave Transylvania one minute before I had to. I had been told that when the train was so crowded that there were no empty seats, travelers simply stood in the corridor. But would that work on this night, the end of the Pentacost holiday, given the unprecedented number of passengers who had arrived in Transylvania over the preceding five days?

The third time József tried to buy me a train ticket to Budapest he had the inspired idea of showing my passport to the ticket-seller. "Please look carefully at this American's visitor's visa," he said. "When it expires on Wednesday morning, she will be illegally in Romania. She absolutely must leave before then." The ticket seller shifted her stance from unmoved to intrigued. Smiling at me she said (in Romanian), "You are my first American," and decided to risk issuing me a duplicate ticket for a seat that had already been sold to someone else. She warned, "You will have to stand in the corridor for the eighteen-hour trip, and if you make any complaint I could lose my job. But don't worry," she added, "the international trains now have a special car for foreigners. When you show your American passport to the conductor, he will arrange a seat for you in that carriage."

Late on Tuesday night, when József and Mária helped me squeeze onto the train, every inch of corridor space was stuffed with people, suitcases, and packages. The incredible crowding didn't bother me, because I felt totally exhilarated. I already knew that the last five days in Transylvania as a pilgrim-guest had changed my life. It had exposed my lack of global consciousness and expanded my too narrow national identity. I was returning home with a markedly different understanding of the power of being Unitarian Universalist. And the Homoród-szentmárton Unitarians and I had taken the first steps toward a connection that held the possibility of changing the lives of many members of our two congregations.

On the other hand I was exhausted. I was alone, unable to speak any Romanian or Hungarian. Crammed with me in the train corridor were many Hungarians making a last minute dash for home and work, as well as a few Romanians traveling outside their home country for the first time. My visa would expire before the train reached the Hungarian border, which was one worry. But even worse, Robin (now conducting his meeting in Budapest) had managed, with the help of persistent Hungarian and Romanian telephone operators, to phone me at the parsonage with the news that early two mornings before he had been forced to get off his train at the border. The Hungarian immigration guards insisted Robin's visa to re-enter Hungary had already been used twice and was no longer valid. He was calling to warn me that I must be prepared for the same thing to happen to me. Robin remembered reading in a Lonely Planet guide to Eastern Europe about this way of making Westerners pay their visa fee a second time. Cleverly, he took a taxi to the nearest automobile border crossing, walked across the border (where he was not asked to buy a new visa), and took another taxi to the nearest train station.[45] The new train Robin caught from inside Hungary actually reached Budapest before the international train he had been thrown off. "But," he warned me, "you'll need enough money to pay for your new visa and the two long taxi rides." The phone connection failed before I confessed that at the church service that morning I had contributed almost every dollar I had with me to the Homoródszentmárton Unitarians as a gift from the San Jose congregation. I just couldn't ask for it back.

Thirty kilometers from Segesvár my train passed through a strange landscape so eerie it looked like we were crossing the moon. Every surface was covered by a strange, grey, chalky substance; the few trees and shrubs looked stunted or dead. How could anyone keep from dying in such a place? How could any government have allowed this tragedy to happen?

Throughout that day my new friends in Homoródszentmárton and Székelyudvarhely had held five different send-off celebrations for me. At each one I was given a package of food and a bottle of water "for your overnight train trip." There were other wonderful presents, including a luxuriously soft lamb's fleece and a beautifully carved wooden tray that I strapped together onto the outside of my already bursting suitcase.

After an hour of standing in the packed train corridor with no sign of a train conductor, I realized the sandwiches were leaking tomato and meat juices onto everything in my capacious purse. After five celebratory meals I had absolutely no appetite, but this was a country where people had been starving, and no one would ever throw food away. Straddling my suitcase in the narrow, impossibly crowded corridor—clearly mine was not the only duplicate ticket—I realized the man next to me was eyeing my delicious smelling, if leaky, food. So I unstrapped the tray from the outside of my suitcase, loaded it up with the food, and offered it to my hungry neighbor. Once he had helped himself to as much as he wanted, I motioned for him to pass the tray on along the corridor. A long time later the tray came back, not empty as I expected, but loaded with food. Only...none of it was my food. People had taken the Homoródszent-márton food and replaced it with their own contributions. My neighbor on the other side passed the tray along to the people standing at the opposite end of the carriage corridor. All night long while I sat on the floor, cushioned by the sheep fleece, the tray of food traveled up and down.

When our religious education classes discuss biblical miracles, I like to read the passage where Jesus feeds thousands of people with only a few small fish and seven loaves of bread. And then I tell this story.

Suspended in liminal time, it was easy to stay awake while we hurtled west through the darkest hours of the night. Everyone who had shared their food began to talk to each other. Gradually, we shifted places so that people who spoke the same languages were together and began to share their stories. Through the night, people came to me to ask, "Do you know my friend, my uncle, my colleague who is in Chicago?...

Cleveland?...Houston?...Milwaukee?...Los Angeles?" This is how humans truly connect—we give gifts, we help one another, and we tell stories about our lives and loved ones.

One young person, delighted to be practicing her English, told me the town we had passed through that seemed to have suffered a disastrous chemical spill was named Kiskapus (Copşa Mică). It is one of Europe's most polluted industrial sites and the result of Ceauşescu's ruinous efforts to bury Romania under the cement and steel of a socialist industrial super-state. For thirty years the Kiskapus lead smelter sprayed a deadly cocktail of twenty heavy metals over the surrounding countryside. My fellow traveler repeated the now famous words of a Kiskapus resident: "Kiskapus is an *oras-fantom*, a ghost town, peopled by the living dead."

Only three of the people in our corridor asked if I could help them immigrate to the United States. In this dawn of a new era in Romania, I think they were eager to imagine themselves living in the West, not out of desperation, but out of the euphoric headiness of all the exciting possibilities suddenly opening up for Eastern Europeans. I felt that my life, like theirs, was being fundamentally shaken open by the changes swiftly unfolding in their country.

In the early morning, with my new friends on either side interpreting for me, the Hungarian border guards summarily approved my visa, and I did not have to leave the train. But I thought about the fate of Romanians who were captured while trying to cross illegally into Western Europe. Only five months before, they would have been beaten for days, forced to swallow "beloved Romanian soil," and imprisoned. At the Budapest train station, we fellow travelers said fond good-byes, absolutely convinced our shared journey signaled a remarkable time of connection between East and West.

———— ∞ ————

I use my carved Transylvanian tray to hold meeting nametags, and sometimes when I am putting it away I wonder: What if I had spent that remarkable night in the special car for foreign dignitaries?

———— ∞ ————

The Walls Come Down

I spent a week in Berlin, Germany on the way home from my first visit in Homoródszentmárton. Robin and I arrived in East Berlin around midnight. A long train journey had carried us from Budapest, through Czechoslovakia, and up the length of East Germany. East and West Berlin were still officially divided by the Berlin Wall, the major symbol of the Cold War.

The next week in Berlin completely reframed the experiences I had just had in Transylvania. In Berlin I woke up to the number and size of the enormous changes that were sweeping through all of Central and Eastern Europe, and through the life of every European. I began to understand our congregation's new partnership with the Transylvanian Unitarians as a part of these massive changes—though I still thought the change was happening to "them," rather than to "us." I became convinced that the new hope and the new opportunities I had witnessed in Transylvania were happening simultaneously in many other parts of Eastern Europe. In Berlin I finally understood that our partnership was one part of this exciting worldwide shift to more global thinking and connections.

When the train stopped in East Berlin on its way to West Berlin, the border guards ordered us to carry our luggage off the train and file in a single line through a special East–West checkpoint. The serious looking guards examined our visas thoroughly before we were allowed to take a local train into West Berlin. A few days later, Robin and I wanted to take a walk through East Berlin using Checkpoint Charlie to cross from West to East. Checkpoint Charlie's narrow, grim corridor was stark and intimidating. But that day both the East and West border guards were more Charlie than checkpoint. Waving aside our passports without even looking at them, they laughed and joked with us and each other. The Berlin Wall towered above us and extended in both directions as far as we could see, completely dominating the landscape. On the West Berlin side it had been covered with hectic but artistic political graffiti; here in the East it was bare and foreboding.

A friend who lived permanently in West Berlin was with us. Two weeks later she went back with a camera, but Checkpoint Charlie had completely disappeared. People were simply walking unhindered through the empty gap in the Wall where the guardhouse had been— those going from West to East carrying noticeably more shopping bags.

The history of the Berlin Wall

At the end of World War II, the city of Berlin was divided into four sections by the liberating (and then occupying) Allied forces. Berlin became an isolated enclave entirely surrounded by East Germany. Berliners were allowed to cross from their home sector into all the other parts of Berlin until the night, in 1961, when the Soviet-backed East German authorities suddenly and unexpectedly constructed the Berlin Wall to cut off any unwatched access into East Germany and stop the exodus of East Germans fleeing to West Germany. The Wall divided many children from their parents, and workers from their workplaces.

In August 1989 Hungary suddenly removed its travel restrictions at the Austrian border. While people from every part of Eastern Europe watched, holding their breath, a hesitant trickle of Eastern Europeans crossed without visas from Hungary into Austria and the West. When they were not arrested or returned to their home country, the trickle became a flood. Within a few weeks 13,000 East German "tourists" had crossed the Hungarian border into Austria, most hoping to establish new lives in West Germany.

Over several months that autumn, with no stones thrown and almost no shots fired (except in Romania), the Iron Curtain opened and then came crashing down. Music festivals and summer camps deliberately located on borders were the means of peaceful revolution. Brave new countries gave birth to themselves.

The twenty-eight year old Wall "fell"—was officially declared open and eventually torn down—on 9 November 1989, with the checkpoints still functioning as border control between East and West Germany. The Checkpoint Charlie guard posts, watchtower, and passageway were completely removed on 22 June 1990. The following October, East and West Germany were reunited as one country.[46]

(Though in 1989 many sections of the Berlin Wall were painted with the words, "Never again," in 2002 the Israeli government began building a wall to separate the occupied Palestinian territories from Israel. It is planned to run for over 700 kilometers [435 miles].)

There was no evidence that Checkpoint Charlie had ever existed.

While Robin was working, I wandered under a bleak sky, taking in the unremitting grey of the streets and the rotten, crumbling concrete. I ended up in conversation with many of the strangers I passed because people were eager to talk about the United States and Germany, the end of the Cold War, and the promise of the future. Like the Transylvanians I had just met in Romania, the East and West Berliners were joyously welcoming the changes sweeping through their lives and celebrating an end to the legions of East German informers.

Near the Brandenburg Gate enterprising vendors sat on folding chairs at makeshift tables selling souvenirs of this historic time, including, for one US dollar, what they claimed were pieces of the Berlin Wall. Of course I bought one. The morning before we flew back to the United States, I decided to take a lot more pieces of the Wall home as gifts. But now that I knew how much even one dollar could buy in Romania, I did not want to pay a dollar for each piece I needed. So I walked to the Wall and poked along its base looking for concrete pieces small enough to pick up and take home. But the ground had been stripped bare. Maybe those concrete souvenirs laid out on folding tables were the real thing after all.

Frustrated, I climbed awkwardly through a large jagged gap in the Wall to continue my search along the other side. This meant I was now standing in the empty "death strip," assigned to neither East nor West, between two parallel walls on either side of the river. This area used to be heavily booby-trapped (I hoped "used to" was correct) with trip wires attached to land mines. In the past East German guards had orders to shoot to kill anyone they saw there, and at least two hundred people had died trying to escape across places just like the one where I now stood. The steep slope down to the river was littered with pieces of the crumbling Wall's distinctive concrete and pebble composition "rocks." I happily piled piece after piece of rubble into my purse and, when it was full, into my skirt, which I scooped up like a hobo's swag. There would be plenty for friends at home. "What great presents these historic pieces of concrete are going to make," I thought, delighted...until I glanced back at the gap in the Wall I had sneaked through.

A soldier, starkly backlit by the summer afternoon sun, was pointing a machine gun at me. Was he going to arrest me? Shoot me? The soldier marched toward me, swinging his gun, and I dropped my skirt and the heavy purse, converting my gifts back to rubble. Fear blocked my dredging up a single word of German, and I waited helplessly, cursing my foolish trust that a new day was dawning in Eastern Europe. "You are at fault," the soldier called out, in heavily accented, but under-standable English. He continued to shout as he strode to where I stood, paralysed, "Those pieces are too big to carry. I will find you the good ones." He bent down to sort through the stones I had dropped, and my heart began beating again.

If this young man could so easily move from killing escapees to generously helping tourists, then the Berlin Wall had truly fallen and Eastern Europe was leaving behind its enclosing walls and stark repression. Not just Romania, but Hungary, Czechoslovakia, Poland, East Germany, and many regions of the Soviet Union would soon be looking for new connections with the West. Would joining the partner church movement lead North American Unitarian Universalists to those places, too?

That piece of the Berlin Wall, a relic of a finished era, helped me realize that when I had left Transylvania two weeks earlier, I had seriously misunderstood my experiences there. I had assumed that the experience of Transylvanian Unitarians from 1965–90 were uniquely Ceauşescu's legacy and peculiar to an isolated Romania. My time in Berlin expanded my thinking beyond Transylvania and the United States, so that I saw our new congregation-to-congregation connection as simply one example of how the world was taking on a more global perspective. And I saw that being in partnership was going to lead me to reframe my own life within this global perspective and take on thinking of myself as a citizen of the world. When the day came for the executive committee of the Partner Church Council to confront the sea change debate on whether our movement should expand to include partnerships in many countries, my vote was decided by the wider perspective I had gained and the falling away of walls within me that week in Berlin.

———— ∞ ————

I keep my piece of the Wall on my desk, turned so I can see its one flat face covered with white paint. When Robin and I moved to Canada, his new employer sent an official memo warning they would not pay to move boats, boards, bricks, or stones. I pictured us trying to talk our way onto an airplane carrying a grossly overweight suitcase filled with the many stones we have collected from each of the important places and moments in our life together. But Robin declared: "The moving company will take them. You are a minister, and these are not stones—they are sacred objects." The most treasured of our sacred objects is our piece of the Berlin Wall.

Changes in Central and Eastern European governments since 1989

The North American Unitarian Universalist partner church movement began in 1990. It was precipitated in the autumn and winter of 1989–90 by the domino-like fall of the Warsaw Pact governments of Poland, Hungary, East Germany, and Czechoslovakia, then of Romania, and eventually of Outer Mongolia and Albania.

- In October 1990, East Germany and West Germany merged to form a reunified Germany.
- In September 1991, Estonia, Latvia, and Lithuania declared and won their independence from the Soviet Union.
- In December 1991, what remained of the Soviet Union divided into the independent countries of Armenia, Azerbaijan, Belarus, Georgia, Kazakhstan, Kyrgyzstan, Moldova, Russia, Tajikistan, Turkmenistan, Ukraine, and Uzbekistan.
- In 1993, Czechoslovakia divided into the Czech Republic and Slovakia.
- Between 1991 and 1994, Yugoslavia became five separate countries (two with non-blended official names far more cumbersome than "Unitarian Universalist"): Croatia, Slovenia, Macedonia, Serbia and Montenegro including Kosovo, and Bosnia and Herzegovina including Republic Srpska.
- In 2006, Montenegro separated from Serbia.
- In 2008 Kosovo separated from Serbia.

Independence issues are yet to be settled in places where portions of these new countries are seeking a further breakaway.

Part 3

Practicing Partnership
at Home, 1990–1992

Home from my pilgrimage to Transylvania and after the Unitarian Universalist Association's General Assembly, I tested the waters for our congregation's commitment to the partnership. Despite an immediately positive response from our board of directors, I didn't feel sure of genuine, congregation-wide support for this geographically distant, long-term commitment. But once three other enthusiasts joined with me to form a "sister church" committee (as we called ourselves in the beginning) we gained confidence and direction.

From that point on, the committee members made decisions and did the work. We recruited a long list of "friends" of the partner church committee who did not want to come to meetings or make decisions but who were glad to pitch in for short bursts of concentrated work, one event or project at a time. Many of those friends have now visited Homoródszentmárton and hosted Transylvanian guests in San Jose.

At first we stumbled in almost everything we did—whether we were working alone, together with our Transylvanian partners, or with the other newly partnered congregations in our district. Through trial and error we learned to ground our work in Unitarian Universalist identity, principles, and history. Our early connection took us into the difficulties of accepting and bridging essential differences, the ethics of providing material aid, and realizing how hard it is to truly stand in each other's shoes. Everything we did was wrapped round with translation and visa concerns, postal delays, and radically different expectations about how long it would take to do things. But we stumbled most over our cultural, financial, political, and religious differences. The unexpected and exciting spiritual development of individuals and congregations that eventually grew out of our connections with Transylvanian Unitarian brothers and sisters came later in our work together.

Our San Jose committee members found reasons to visit each of the seven other Unitarian Universalist congregations in our district that were also working toward establishing healthy, active partnerships. They were eager to see the slides and hear stories from my five days in Homoródszentmárton. They had their own stories to tell us about their early efforts to communicate with their new partners. Perhaps we would not have stumbled as often if we had worked more closely with those neighboring partner church committees.

Who might make a good friend or member of a partner church committee?

- People with leadership skills who already command respect in the congregation, who know how to mold a project and keep it vital and successful.
- Congregation officers and leaders (including ministers) who are leaving their former roles.
- Church members who would be relieved to replace their old battles with positive work on new visions half a world away.
- Parents and religious educators eager to nurture globally concerned children and youth.
- Teenagers and young adults eager to learn about and visit (or live) in foreign cultures.
- Church history enthusiasts, Christian Unitarians and Universalists, people with European ancestors, farmers and gardeners, choir members, teachers, ecologists, economists, engineers, IT workers, historians, anthropologists, sociologists, ethnographers, linguists, medical workers, development and organizational experts.
- People who read, speak, and/or write Hungarian.
- People with surplus resources, time, or experience they want to contribute to vital social action efforts.
- People with few resources who are interested in the Transylvanians' ability to thrive with their limited resources.
- People excited about economic development, international relations, small businesses, farming, micro-finance, Eastern European revitalization, anti-oppression activism, toxic waste management, interfaith work, religious education reform, and global outreach.
- Immigrants, exiles, and refugees, and their second- and third-generation children, especially (but not only) Hungarians and other Eastern Europeans.
- People whose work takes them to Europe, frequent travelers, people who have lived abroad.
- People hungry to deepen their faith, broaden their experiences, make social action commitments, or build healthy church communities.

From Sister Church to Partnership

The first time I was invited to speak at a district-wide partner church fundraiser, I told the story of how our San Jose young people had changed what we called our connection with Homoródszentmárton from being our *sister* to being our *partner* church. Someone interrupted, "But that happened in our Sunday school." And then people from two more partnered congregations chimed in: "Our kids also protested that it shouldn't be called a *sister* church program." Around the room we were delighted to have this affirmation that our commitment to using inclusive and non-sexist language had so clearly taken hold with this new generation of Unitarian Universalists. The following is what happened in San Jose and simultaneously in other North American congregations.

In the fall of 1990 the San Jose church held several gatherings where I could share what I had learned from the Unitarians in Homoródszentmárton and promote our becoming their sister church. After hearing the stories, nearly all our members, including the entire board of directors, endorsed our formally becoming a sister church. But the ten to twelve year old boys raised a strong objection: "It shouldn't be called our sister church."

So we held a special meeting with all our ten to twelve year olds to discuss it. I described the original 1920s sister church program and urged the value of our congregation's carrying on this historical tradition. We talked about the close family connection implied by the name *sister* church. The boys didn't buy those or any other reasons to keep the name *sister*. "It's not inclusive language," they declared. The girls countered, "Well, don't even think of calling them our *brother* church." Our one young person with Canadian relatives said that in Canada we would be called *twinned* churches, but she said Homoródszentmárton should not be our *twin* church because, "*Twin* would mean we are the same, but, really, we're very different." That helped all of us see that the family and sibling implication of *sister* did not actually capture the spirit of what we hoped our connection would be.

One of their Sunday school teachers asserted that, "If Unitarian

Universalists are serious about not proselytizing and supporting human rights, this program's name should not imply that we are responsible for taking care of them, on the one hand, or exploiting them, on the other." His thinking was far ahead of my own at that point. We conducted a brainstorming session with plenty of flipchart notes and came to agreement on wanting a name that would convey that both churches would be in the relationship together as two quite different congregations, mutually respectful of each other and equally responsible for the program. We were convinced this new program should not be called *sister*, *brother*, or *twin*, but no one had thought of a better name

Then one of our most socially aware youth offered, "What about *partner* church?" There was a long pause while everyone considered *partner*, followed by smiles all around. From that day the San Jose Unitarian Universalists have called Homoródszentmárton their partner church. Soon we noticed that across North America other Unitarian Universalist congregations in the program were also replacing the term *sister* church with *partner* church.

After several more years, we spoke less about "having a partner church" than about "building our partnership."

I am embarrassed and dismayed to note that it did not occur to any of us at that point to ask our partners what name they would choose for our work together. As it has turned out, our Transylvanian partners have not been enthusiastic about the change of name from sister church to partner church. In part their reluctance is that they feel any change of name dismisses the original sister church program. In striking contrast to the North Americans, the Transylvanian Unitarians never forgot their 1920s sister church connections. They generously excused half a century of silence from 116 of the 118 North American sister churches by attributing the lack of contact to the impossibility of staying in touch across closed borders.

Politically correct language usage is not the burning issue for Transylvanian Unitarians that it is among North American Unitarian Universalists. When asked why they do not use the Hungarian word for partner as the name of their program, several Transylvanians have

The 1920s sister church connections that continued

Gabriel Csiki, working in Transylvania and Hungary, and Louis Cornish in North America were the original co-leaders of the 1920s–30s sister church program. Their initial assumption was that the pairings should last for three years. Of 118 North American congregations, only King's Chapel in Boston, Massachusetts and the Unitarian Universalist Church of Berkeley, California attempted to sustain connections with their sister churches in Kolozsvár and Homoródujfalu (Satu Nou). When the present partner church program started in 1990, King's Chapel and the Berkeley church asked to be re-paired with their former 1920s partners. In addition to these two, thirty-eight of the North American congregations that had 1920s sister churches are in the program today, but with different partners except for one that has been repartnered with its former sister church.

answered: "That *sister/partner* conflict is just a problem caused by your complicated English language, a problem we don't have in Hungarian. We can use exactly the same word for brother and for sister, and our word for God doesn't have a male or female connotation for us. So in Hungarian we are never required to change a name to honor feminist concerns." When I countered that *partner* versus *sister* is not really a feminist concern, the Transylvanians said they also wanted to avoid any implication that our congregations are like business partners, marriage partners, or same-sex partners. "But what matters most to us is that using the same title from the 1920s links us with our history. That far outweighs the unimportant difference, at least as we see it, between your word and our word."

What we and our partners share completely is our dedication to helping one another keep our two congregations, the spiritual lives they protect and nurture, and our relationship with each other healthy and thriving. So, as often happens in partnerships, each side does things in their own way. East and West, we have learned to respect that. I imagine the Transylvanian Unitarians will always say *partner* when they are speaking English and *testvér* (which means sibling, and simultaneously includes the concepts of sister and brother) when they are speaking

Hungarian, just as they comfortably sing the words, "spirit of life," as "spirit of God" (*Isten lelke*) when they are singing Carolyn McDade's hymn in Hungarian. Yet, in another way, we are closer than we think. *Testvér* means a blood sibling. It implies far more than North Americans mean when we say, "our brother and sister Unitarians." So by using *testvér* the Transylvanians are saying we North Americans mean as much to them as their closest family members. And by using *partner* North Americans are saying the Transylvanians mean as much to us as our most serious business or legal commitments.

The words are different, but the underlying message is the same.

The First Unitarians:
Ferenc Dávid (1510/20–1579) and
János Zsigmond (1540–1571)

In 1990 the weekly worship services at the San Jose church always included "a story for all ages."[47] On my return from Transylvania, I recruited an actor to read the following dramatic monologue for us, and we hung a print of Aladár Körösföi-Kriesch's famous painting of Ferenc Dávid and János Zsigmond's court in the social hall. It shows Dávid arguing for the Unitarian position during the 1568 Diet of Torda.[48]

Ferenc Dávid's religious freedom and
János Zsigmond's religious tolerance

Introduction

Announcer: This morning, we have an important visitor—a Unitarian minister who lived almost 500 years ago. He was the first leader of the very first Unitarian churches.

The actor playing Dávid comes out from the wings (or the announcer steps back and puts on a black robe to become Dávid, and returns) wearing a formal academic gown or black minister's robe.[49]

Story for All Ages

Hello, my name is Ferenc Dávid. In my language, which is Hungarian, my name is pronounced <u>Daah</u>'-veed <u>Fair</u>'-ence because in Hungarian the family part of our name comes first.

Thank you for coming to learn about my life 450 years ago in Transylvania. The most exciting part of my life was when I was part of the Protestant Reformation, the tremendous revolution that changed the history of Christian religious ideas for all time by making it possible for "protest-ers" to form their own religious groups. That is how the very first Unitarian churches were founded in the 1560s—by groups of protesters. I was their leader in Transylvania. Years later other people began to call us "Unitarians," because "uni" means "one," and we believe there is one God. We also believe that you and I are just as divine as Jesus was, which is a wonderful thing. Only ten years after I began to spread these new ideas, 500 Catholic churches in Transylvania had become Unitarian churches, and you could read the words *Egy az Isten*, God is One, written over their church doors.

At that time, the ruler of Transylvania was young János Zsigmond (Zjig-maund). He was crowned the king of Hungary when he was still a baby, which is certainly far too young to be a good and wise ruler of a kingdom. But the people of Transylvania were lucky, because young János had a wise mother as his advisor, and he was both brave and thoughtful. He needed to be. Our people had serious troubles.

Two huge empires sat on either side of Transylvania. To the west was the Catholic Habsburg Empire, and on our east side was the Muslim Ottoman Empire. They were at war with each other, and our small principality of Transylvania was always in danger of being caught in the middle and forced to fight in their wars.

But just as bad, inside Transylvania János Zsigmond's own people were fighting each other about their different religious ideas. After the changes brought by the Reformation, Transylvania had four different, competing religious groups. Sometimes the people of these different faiths fought each other with words—arguing and saying the worst things they could think of about each other, whether they were true or not. Sometimes they fought by taking people's jobs away, or taking away all their money, or putting people in prison, or even killing each other.

János Zsigmond thought carefully about these problems, and then decided what he was going to do. (What would *you* have done, if you were the king?) In 1568, he called the best, the most convincing speaker from each of the four religious groups to gather at Torda—an important city in Transylvania—for a debate. The debate lasted ten days, beginning each day at five o'clock in the morning! There was a speaker for the Catholics, one for the Lutherans, and one for the Calvinists. (Can you guess who debated for the Unitarians?) That's right! It was me. (Can you guess who won?) Yes, I won the whole debate for the Unitarians. Even János Zsigmond decided to become a Unitarian, because our debate convinced him that Unitarian ideas were the most reasoned, the most fair, and the ones that respected more of the Transylvanian people.

But—and this is the most important part of the story, the part you must be sure to remember and the part you can tell other people if they ask what it means to be a Unitarian Universalist—even though our Unitarian ideas had been judged better than all the others, János did *not* say all the people of Transylvania had to become Unitarians. He and his mother, Queen Isabella, said that the people of Transylvania could *debate* their ideas about religion, but they could never again fight, or punish, or kill each other because of their religious beliefs. They issued a law called the Edict of Torda which said, "Faith is a gift from God. No one should be able to force their religion, their faith, on others." This was a new and strange idea. It was the first law of religious tolerance to be declared in modern times.

Today, you Unitarian Universalists remember János Zsigmond because his law made it safe to be Unitarian and made all the people of Transylvania free to follow whatever religion they chose. And you learn about me in your church school lessons because for the rest of my life I preached Unitarianism, a faith that said all people and all religious groups must have the freedom to change their religious beliefs as they grow into new understandings. Eventually, I was put into prison for preaching that, and for practicing what I preached.

Just before I died I wrote a message on my prison wall. (If you were locked up in prison like that, what message would *you* write?) What I wrote was, "Nothing will hold up the truth on its way." The way you would say that today in English is, "No force can stop that which is right," or "There is no force that can stop the truth."[50]

It is because of the Unitarians of my 500 Transylvanian churches that there are signs today over many of your Unitarian Universalist church doors that say, "450 years of religious freedom." How good it is to know that you Unitarian Universalists are carrying on, in your own way, János Zsigmond's religious tolerance and Ferenc Dávid's religious freedom.

Was János Zsigmond a king or a prince?

János Zsigmond succeeded his father only a few days after he was born and reigned as King of Hungary from 1540 to 1570, though for much of this time the country was governed by his mother, Queen Isabella Jagiellon, with the support of the Turkish ruler, Suleiman the Magnificent. Isabella had asserted her infant son's right to be king of both Poland and Transylvania. The Habsburgs did not recognize this right, but the Ottomans did. At that point some in Transylvania saw themselves as separate from the Habsburg Empire, and therefore more a kingdom than a principality. After his abdication as King of Hungary (in favor of the Habsburgs) János Zsigmond was the Prince of Transylvania (1570–1571) for the last year of his life.

Transylvanians I consulted told me they always say, "*Prince* Zsigmond János." The depictions in Aladár Körösföi-Kriesch's 1896 painting, *The Diet of Torda,* give Zsigmond's title as prince of a principality, rather than a king of a kingdom, even though it depicts an event in 1568.

Forget Quick Fixes

In the five days of my first visit to Transylvania, I visited more than a dozen Unitarian churches and ministers in the Big and Little Homoród River valleys, met local artists at impressive artwork exhibitions, helped lead a Sunday communion service, attended a Pentecost fair, bought plants for the parsonage garden at a bustling farmers' market, and attended a funeral at the Reformed Church. I saw the burned-out Securitate headquarters and visited many historical sites and religious monuments. I shared dreams with our new partners about developing the former agricultural headquarters building. I met with the new mayor and with the former leader of the agricultural co-operative, trekked to a mountain spring to fill bottles with naturally sparkling water, learned (well, I attempted) to sew traditional Homoród Valley blanket-stitch embroidery, watched furniture painting by a renowned local craftsman and pottery-making in nearby Korond (Corund), met with the Saturday morning religious education class and with classes at the local elementary school, learned about the work of teachers and journalists, joined in a school field day, ate numerous special meals, and every morning and evening dodged cattle on the road.

I arrived back in San Jose with many ideas for possible joint projects. It is surprising to realize now how many of those activities during my visit eventually led to further work, connection, or joint projects. But we quickly ran into problems. We had no experience in planning and carrying out projects by two congregations so separated by culture, history, language, and distance. But our early difficulties grew just as much out of the differing perspectives and assumptions of rural versus urban and of poverty versus booming IT-based wealth. Also, members of our California congregation kept taking me aside to ask, "Are you sure these Transylvanians are really Unitarians?"—the same question I am sure was being asked about us in Homoródszentmárton.

⸎

In San Jose—as in every North American Unitarian Universalist congregation I have worked with—our active members included many teachers. The backbone of San Jose's religious education program was a dedicated group of retired teachers who "missed the children" and happily volunteered to teach religious education classes in teams with their friends. Soon after I returned home I met with our interested teachers to tell them about the Homoródszentmárton primary and middle schools. I told them how delighted I had been when József asked me, "Would you like to visit a class in the village school?"

We visited a mixed-age class with a bright young teacher that was located in what was, until 1947, a school owned and run by the Unitarian Church. Asked to tell the Homoródszentmárton students about my country, I led off (with József interpreting): "You live in Transylvania, which is a part of Romania. I live in California, which is a part of the United States of America." I needed a map or a globe. There was neither. Shifting gear, I described children's schools and life in San Jose, stressing the similarities: walking to school, homework and book reports (a mistake—there were no books in this school); soccer practice (did the school have soccer balls? I wished I had brought some with me); field trips (possible in Homoródszentmárton to places classes could walk to); language lessons (but Spanish in California, instead of Romanian); and graduation ceremonies. Then I invited them to draw pictures and tell me about their lives in Homoródszentmárton so I could take their pictures and explanations back to my Sunday school students in San Jose. Art supplies? There were none.

The children were eager to tell me what they already knew about the United States—big cars on super highways, skyscrapers, airplanes you shoot bombs from, cowboys and Indians, lots of soldiers shooting guns, a television in every home, a computer in every office, fireworks on the holidays. The class included second and fourth grade students. The first and third graders were together across the hall. There were several sets of siblings among the ten Unitarians, two Hungarian Reform brothers, and, unusually, a Roma brother and sister. There were no books that I could see, but plenty of chalk for the large blackboard.

The San Jose teachers were as distressed as I had been by my photographs of the completely bare school room. Surely, we thought, we could do something about the lack of even basic school supplies. They immediately began ransacking their attics for the school supplies and teaching materials they had packed away when they retired. We knew paper, pencils, chalk, and scissors would be welcome. We even had discarded metric rulers from an unsuccessful attempt by Californian schools to lead the nation into "going metric." Since we had no way to provide materials written in Hungarian or Romanian, we focused on math and science materials, along with items for pre-readers that were not dependent on language. Instead of bubble wrap, we used yarn and soft sewing supplies to stuff any gaps. We stopped at ten large, heavy boxes.

The religious education and partner church committees met one Saturday morning for a packing party and post office run. When the postal clerk learned about "our school" in Romania, she helped us repack most of the boxes to qualify them for a much cheaper library rate without customs charges. Several months later József wrote to thank us for the education supplies, and we assumed all was well.

Two years later I was hunting for an eraser in the Homoródszentmárton parsonage and stumbled upon a cabinet of carefully stored science, math, and pre-school materials, the materials we had sent from San Jose. "What went wrong?" I asked, carrying a children's microscope to the dining room table where József was finishing his sermon. József froze, pursed his lips, and ducked his head.

"We've never talked about that," he answered, clearly embarrassed.

"I'm sure you've done the right thing," I rushed to reassure him. "There must be a good reason why it's better for the materials to be here instead of at the school."

He sighed, "We should have talked about this, but I knew how disappointed you would be, and I did not know if you could understand."

József told me most of the rural elementary school teachers are quite young apprentice teachers. They come from the Transylvanian cities and speak both Hungarian and Romanian. It is not their choice to work in the countryside. Most adapt poorly to village life and flee every weekend by bus or hitchhiking back to their city. When József approached his daughters' teacher—the teacher he knew the best and trusted the most—offering some of our teaching materials, she was offended. She felt his offer of math and science materials meant he had decided she was not a good enough teacher for his children. He decided not to risk making her feel worse by offering the art supplies.

What about the materials we had sent for the pre-school children? It turned out the pre-school teacher was the wife of a local policeman. She and her husband were deeply resented and not trusted. "That teacher would not use any of these things for our children. She might even sell them and keep the money. When you wrote to us offering to send school supplies, we thought you meant paper, pencils, maybe some colored chalk. That's what "school supplies" mean to us. We realize our schools are sadly bare, but you can't turn our young teachers and the policeman's wife into American-style teachers, and we don't really want you to."

It was my turn to feel embarrassed. A hard lesson for North American partner church pilgrims is: Do not leap in to solve others' problems. When we Americans see problems—or what we assume are problems—we often long to fix them, and we assume that "getting things fixed" will be welcome.

In my heart, I still questioned how teachers and parents and Unitarians anywhere in the world would not set their differences aside when it came to improving their children's education. Eventually I came to understand that the assumptions I held—about children, education, and teaching being somehow outside politics and religion—were simply my own values, peculiar to my own history and my own Unitarian upbringing. I am not saying that my values were wrong, but that I was unreasonably naïve and idealistic about their being right for those in other countries or other cultures to live by. Often my partnership work has forced me to realize that my values and fundamental ways of being are not necessarily the reasonable way—certainly not the best, or right,

"Let's fix it" Americans

A colleague told me a joke Transylvanians tell about people from the United States. He heard it at the Protestant seminary in Kolozsvár:

> A little girl apologized to her family's American visitor for arriving home late after school. She explained that she had stopped to help her friend whose doll had broken when her friend dropped it. The American visitor said, approvingly, "Oh, you were helping her glue the pieces back together." "No," the Transylvanian girl replied, "I was helping her cry."

or universal way—and often not what everyone wants, or should want.

Facing that, I can then make the leap to accepting that my usual ways of being could, and sometimes should, change—not just improve, but become something quite different. This is not so much about learning from our mistakes as about the desire to become something new. I think an essential attraction of partnership work for many North Americans lies in this unexpected benefit—the freedom to wake up to who we truly are and, within that freedom, to become someone new.

For their part, my Transylvanian colleagues and friends have been incredibly tolerant and patient with me. They have never said, though they must have been tempted, "Look at what you're doing, you idiot." They simply asked me about what I was doing with a comment like, "That's very different. Are all Americans like that?" It was a wonderful way to help me take another look at myself and my actions.

During any visit, many ideas for ways partners might work together naturally come up. But before a project is selected and planned, both sides must know and trust each other. It takes time, repeated communication, and a lot of visiting in both directions before partners can actually understand what is happening and why in each other's lives and congregations. You must also learn about each other's skills and resources, and take these into account alongside the urgent needs and pressing dreams. When our partnership began I did not understand that even with scarce resources, local people can almost always solve their problems better than outsiders, with solutions that are sustainable by them over time.

I thought about how carefully San Jose's religious education committee moved when it was introducing a significant change. We always tried to involve the parents and the children or youth in the planning so that the launch of a new project or change could become a celebration of their decisions and their work. Homoródszentmárton's teachers, parents, and children had not been involved in any part of our effort to provide them with educational supplies. If we had stopped to judge this project by our usual standards for ourselves, we would have predicted that it was bound to fail. But we didn't stop to think about it, because we hadn't yet learned that partnership work must be mutually planned and far more than a rescue effort accomplished by providing funds and resources.

Thankfully, we no longer stumbled so badly, or so often, after the

Unitarian Universalist Partner Church Council was established in 1993, providing local district networkers to help us sort out our problems. Our early communication frustrations were eventually solved, thanks to the internet, Skype, much better language interpreting practices and, best of all, so many Transylvanians' generously learning English. But I believe our frequent mistakes in those early years were not caused by poor communication, but by unclear directions and goals. It took a very long time for pairs of partners to get onto the same page about what we wanted and believed we should accomplish together.

They Hold the Future in Their Hands

As soon as partnerships began to flourish, Transylvanian ministers and seminarians began to come to the Unitarian Universalist Association's General Assembly and to district, summer conference, youth, and ministers' meetings. It was a great pleasure to have this extended time to get to know one another more deeply. And sometimes it was not so easy. For either side.

When I attended an annual Unitarian Universalist summer youth conference outside Portland, Oregon for fourteen to nineteen year olds (called "Con-Con" because it was an annual continental convention), my task was to help its 200 participants make a quilted wall-hanging that would eventually hang in the youth program's Young Religious Unitarian Universalists' office at the Unitarian Universalist Association in Boston. Late each afternoon that week, all the conferees would meet in their small "home group" which provided a comfortable place to touch base, share feelings, and raise concerns. One of the older youths was our well-trained and skillful leader. While we talked together, many of us were sewing patches for the wall hanging, combining work of the heart with work of the hands.

Sitting in our home group circle beneath an ancient, majestic redwood tree, I listened to ten young Unitarian Universalists talk about their lives and breathed in the sharp redwood smell. Close to the huge, russet-colored trunk there was blessedly cool shade. We all slowed down. Several of the young people stretched out on their backs, because no one had been getting enough sleep and also because if you looked up through the 250 feet of redwood branches you felt drawn powerfully into a sacred space. During the "What's bothering you?" round, I shared my feelings about the difficult time our Transylvanian guest was having at the conference.

"Are these people really Unitarians? Unitarians wouldn't act like this," the visiting Transylvanian seminarian had complained on the second day to Ruth Gibson, then minister for religious education at the First Unitarian Society in Madison, Wisconsin. Hosting visiting partner-connected Transylvanians or North Americans is an ongoing activity, and pleasure, for everyone involved in partnership, and Ruth's congregation had brought him to Madison for the summer months.

The Transylvanian seminarian was the only participant who chose to wear a white shirt and tie, though Ruth knew he had more casual clothes with him. He spoke English well, but seldom engaged in conversations and sat through discussion groups and workshops wearing a disapproving expression, his arms folded tightly across his chest. I feared the respect he had previously developed for North American Unitarian Universalists and the partner church movement was fast disappearing. Ruth had asked me to do what I could to help this twenty-three year old ministry student become more accepting and appreciative of our North American Unitarian Universalist youth.

"Why do you feel they don't act like Unitarians?" I asked him.

"Their clothes! Their language! Same-sex couples!" he exploded.

"Well, they're not having sex or using alcohol," I countered.

"Drinking or sex would not surprise me as much," he said sadly. "No one here is serious. Why don't they act like they're attending a *church* conference?"

He told Ruth he was disappointed by the lack of theological discussion which proved to him that Unitarian Universalist youth were not serious about their faith. He also said that he was disgusted by their appearance, but when Ruth asked what he thought of their responsible and respectful behavior, he was too surprised to answer. (Transylvanians are often surprised to learn that Unitarian Universalist youth sign and keep agreements that they will completely abstain from alcohol, drugs, and sex during any church-related travel, meetings, or conferences.)[51]

I was struggling as I tried to make sense of this Transylvanian colleague's intolerant dismissal of our responsible and creative North American young people. I told my home group that Transylvanian Unitarians of all ages take their faith very seriously and know they can depend on their church to keep them safe and alive. For most Unitarians there, the congregation's daily life and their denomination's role in society are vitally central to who they are. I added that "since Unitarian Universalist identity and church membership are not as central or serious for us as they are for the Transylvanians, perhaps it is inevitable that this conference and our faith would appear to be frivolous to him."

There was a long silence, followed by a strong protest. A young man, whose trademark dress was a bright necklace and a baseball cap with a hole in the back for his ponytail, countered, "But being a Unitarian Universalist *is* central to my life; it *saved* my life." With that opening, in the safety of our confidential circle, he, and then other home group members, told stories about a time when their Unitarian Universalist faith and their friends at church had literally saved their lives by supporting them through and beyond a crisis of identity, broken health, honesty, addiction, or depression. I could see the entire group absorbing the underlying assurance that their congregation's youth group could be counted on, if they ever needed it, to help them face any life-threatening crisis and turn it into a life-saving turning point.

Their stories made me remember that twenty years before, when I was living in a relationship sharply at odds with my principles, a church women's group had supported me in turning my life around. I spoke a bit about that road not taken, acknowledging in a fundamentally new way the central and serious power of my religious community to save my life. It was an afternoon none of us will forget, because these were such remarkable stories. Once again, the presence of a Transylvanian in North America had led me to understand in a deeper and more loyal way what it meant to me to be Unitarian Universalist. Once again, my faith was being shaken, redefined, and reformed. Sitting in our redwood cathedral, I was fully reassured that our youth will hold tightly to their faith and lead our congregations well in the future. I went to dinner hoping the Transylvanian seminarian's home group was also helping him become able to learn from and affirm these remarkable young people. My group had certainly given me that, and more.

Postscript: When she read this story, Ruth Gibson wrote to me:
Like yours, my Con-Con home group that year was healing and energizing, just what I needed at the time. And there was a happy ending for our Transylvanian. He did make his peace with "the spirit of the Con." At the worship service on our next to the last day, he shared a story he had written about a seeker and a star that paralleled his changes over the course of the week.
I really regret missing that service as we raced to finish sewing together the pieces of our lovely wall hanging.

Part 4

In Northern California, 1992

*One year into our partnership, some members of the San Jose
congregation were still holding un-thought-through notions like, "It's
fine to be a partner church so long as it doesn't cost us anything."
Another problem was that József and I feared the connection between
our congregations was in too many ways limited to the connection
between him and me, instead of being a connection between our two
congregations. Other partner church pairs were also struggling with
these problems. In 1996 Sándor Kovács told the North American
ministers:*

> *The relationships that have grown between ministers and leaders
> in our pairs of churches are a blessing for Unitarians in
> Transylvania. My hope is that…we do not stop with a single North
> American minister to Transylvanian minister relationship. Instead,
> let these initial relationships serve as the seeds from which many
> new North American–Transylvanian relationships might flower
> between our lay leaders, our women's groups, our young people,
> our teachers of religious education, our musicians, and those of
> our laity who might find that the issues that most concern them at
> home are also of concern to members of their partner congregation,
> whether that concern be for the environment, poverty and
> economic development, ethnic relations, or the pastoral mission of
> the church.*[52]

*San Jose's Partner Church Committee decided a visit by József and
Mária would be the best way to expand the San Jose members'
interest and involvement, but Mária couldn't leave her school for four
weeks during the teaching year. Flying on a donated frequent flyer
ticket, József was delighted to be one of the honored guests who
helped blow out the one hundred candles on the San Jose building's
centennial birthday cake. That party concluded a full and festive two
weeks of talks and slide shows, partnership planning, sermons, and
injecting Transylvania into our adult and children's religious
education classes. He was learning all he could about our church and
its members, as well as our city and its citizens.*

*József then spent two more weeks visiting the growing number of
partnerships in other congregations in our Pacific Central District. We
gave him a crash course in Unitarian Universalism at a religious
educators' "Unitarian Universalist Identity" weekend workshop. He*

took a lot of photographs. We did a lot of book shopping. He visited Starr King School for the Ministry and delivered the sermon at the annual district meeting's Sunday service. József was intrigued by our worship practices and religious education classes. He was especially interested in the interfaith ministers' network, recovery programs for alcoholics, and the history of our congregation and story of our one hundred year old building.

Because József had just spent a year as a visiting scholar at the Unitarian seminary in England, his determined efforts to master English had taken great leaps forward. For the first time we were able to discuss complex and subtle ideas and concerns, which moved our partnership connection into a new stage. József saw with his own eyes that the United States was not a golden land of plenty where living is easy and all are blessed with equal opportunities. I had also stopped seeing Transylvanians' lives, churches, and villages through rose-colored glasses. As we drove through the thirsty Northern California hills from one partnered congregation to the next, we could finally talk about, and sometimes talk through, our underlying differences and the challenges they posed for our partnership work.

―∞∞∞―

A Transylvanian Look at Our Faith

In the first week of József's visit to San Jose, we held four evening gatherings so that he could answer questions about village life in Romania and explore with as many of our members as possible the ways our partnership with the Homoródszentmárton Unitarians might develop. At the last of these question and answer gatherings a congregation member asked, "What has surprised you most about American UUs?" József's answer was:

> I am surprised so many of you have changed your religion to become Unitarian, because it is very unusual for a Transylvanian of any faith to give up the religion we are born into. For us to do that would mean giving up who we are. In our interfaith marriages, daughters are automatically raised in their mother's church, and sons are raised in their father's.[53] We have a few of these non-Unitarian husbands and wives who are active in our congregations and who have come to share our beliefs. But they would not call themselves Unitarian, and we do not count them in our numbers.

He smiled and added, "Now I understand why the little book that gives an introduction to Unitarian Universalism is called *A Chosen Faith*.[54] The way you North Americans change your religious identity is a new and surprising idea for me."

As I listened to this exchange, it occurred to me that József had, after all, dedicated his life to ensuring the survival of many rural churches with a declining population, so his distress at anyone's giving up their birthright religion was not surprising.

Toward the end of the evening József told us:

> I have given more thought to the question of what has surprised me most, and there is something else about Unitarian Universalists that has unsettled me more than people here giving up the faith group they were born into and adopting a new one. I am beginning to wonder if Unitarian Universalists' religious beliefs and congregational life play too small a part in their lives. What I mean is: Why do you hold your faith so far from the center of your lives?

I reacted defensively to that question. Though it is often challenging, I strive to live by my Unitarian Universalist principles, and I know my

Unitarian Universalism and its values, responsibilities, and loyalties are central to who I am. But by the next day, when I had calmed down and thought more about it, I had to admit that, for me, being a Unitarian Universalist did have more to do with my ever-changing politics, my deeply rooted social values, and my profession of ministry than with my soul. If I had a serious health decision to make, I would go for help to a doctor, a friend, or a therapist, rather than to a minister. If I had a financial crisis or windfall, I would not discuss it with my colleagues. And it would never occur to me to pray over any of it. József's question made me realize that there were too many important areas of my life where I might look more for comfort than for principled guidance from my faith and my church. And where was God in my life? Certainly not at the centre.

That conversation was definitely a wake-up call for me. József and I have continued to talk about what he means by "faith" and "holding faith at the center of one's life." József says:

The most important thing is that my Transylvanian Unitarian faith inspires me to be my best self. When my life holds little hope, my faith is what draws me again into living optimistically. My optimism rests on trusting the teachings of Jesus as a guide for my life. As a Unitarian, I do not act in expectation of reward or of making the wheel of history turn. Living faithfully gives me the satisfaction of knowing I have been true to my principles and strong in my commitments—that I have lived with integrity—have chosen day after day to do what is right, always supported by a just and loving God.

József replied to our San Jose member's question, "What surprises you most about North American Unitarian Universalists?" with a question of his own. That question—"Why do you hold your faith so far from the center of your lives?"—has reverberated through the heart of the North American partnership movement.

The Meaning of Priceless

After spending two weeks with our San Jose congregation, József began a busy round of meetings with the other partnered churches in our district. We also visited my seminary on "Holy Hill" in Berkeley (so called because a dozen seminaries and religious centers are clustered there). József knew Starr King School for the Ministry as the place where one of his heroes, Ferenc Balázs, had been a visiting scholar from 1926–28. He also knew that Ferenc Balázs' champion, Earl Morse Wilbur, was the seminary's founding president and the author of the first modern historical account in English of the liberal religious left of the Protestant Reformation—the book I had given József two years earlier when I first visited Homoródszentmárton. József was eager to meet Alicia McNary Forsey, then Starr King School's professor of church history, who was successfully preserving the integrity of the Wilbur Rare Book Collection and opening it for use by scholars from all over the world.

When József began asking questions about Ferenc Balázs and Earl Morse Wilbur, Alicia told us that all of Wilbur's books and papers were there. "Oh, yes," I remembered, "those books in the basement."

Eight years earlier in a seminary class on Unitarian Universalist history, I had learned that Earl Morse Wilbur collected an astounding number of books and papers as he researched and wrote his two volume history, *A History of Unitarianism: Socinianism and its Antecedents* and *A History of Unitarianism in Transylvania, England, and America*, which included the first account in English of the early history of József's Transylvanian Unitarian Church and how its principles of "freedom in thought, reason in conduct, and tolerance in judgment" had developed.

My professor had led our seminary class down into an unused part of the back of the Starr King School basement to see Wilbur's 17,000 books and 13,000 papers. Searching the crowded, floor-to-ceiling bookshelves of the densely packed, concrete bunker-like room, I recognized some of the authors: Calvin, Knox, Channing, deBeneville, Emerson, Priestley, Starr King, and Tillich. But there were far more—like Balázs, Farel, and Beza—that I had never heard of, and plenty of books whose languages I could not even identify. I especially liked a book the professor showed us that had superb woodcut prints of what he said were "traditional Transylvanian Unitarian churches." In college, I had been an aspiring printmaker, and these were striking prints. It was my first contact with the remarkable quality of Transylvanian artists' work.

Our Unitarian Universalist history class brushed lightly on the Transylvanian Unitarians during the 1500s, but there was nothing about the effect on them of the Counter Reformation or the Habsburg years; nothing about their present-day denomination or what had happened to the connection the school had made through Wilbur with the Protestant seminary in Kolozsvár. I realized there were still Unitarians in a place called Transylvania, but I did not even wonder what their churches might be like today, or how they had survived the many changes of governments in Eastern Europe. It certainly never occurred to me that I might one day meet some of these Transylvanians and grow over time to care deeply about them. The professor also pointed out several books by Ferenc Balázs, who had been a visiting scholar at Starr King School in the 1920s. And there was a valuable, rare book in Latin by an early Reformation figure named Servetus.

I graduated from seminary, answered a call to serve the San Jose church 47 miles (75 kilometers) away, and forgot all about the rare books locked away in the Starr King School basement.

———— ⊰⊱ ————

József's visit to the Wilbur Collection was a high point among many eye-opening experiences he had that month in Northern California. Following Alicia into the hidden basement room, he could not believe what was there. Crowded on the many floor-to-ceiling bookshelves were unique books, papers, and letters—many of them hundreds of years old and written by Unitarian scholars József had studied ever since his seminary years in Kolozsvár. József moved slowly along each narrow aisle. He opened a book, read a bit, smiled, sighed, returned it to its place, and then reached for another. I sensed that he would have been happy to stay there for days.

Alicia showed him the school's copy of *De Trinitatis Erroribus* (*On the Errors of the Trinity*), written in 1531 by Servetus, the book my Unitarian Universalist history professor had shown us eight years before. József's hands were shaking as he reverently opened this most Unitarian of Servetus' writings. He said, "We studied Servetus in my seminary classes. This is a priceless book. But you know that."

Earl Morse Wilbur's Rare Book Collection

Wilbur went on extended leave from being president of "his" seminary—then named Pacific Unitarian School for the Ministry—to spend 1931–34 in Europe researching the rise and development of Unitarianism. His search for documents took him mostly to remote places because the facts of the history he was writing had been suppressed, and many of the documents and books he most needed had been destroyed during the Counter Reformation or subsequent wars. Wilbur was able to unearth copies in out of the way places, including the Transylvanian Protestant seminary's library in Kolozsvár.

Wilbur built the collection of books and papers now housed at Starr King School in Berkeley either by buying the books with his own and donated funds or by receiving gifts of duplicate copies from universities, seminaries, libraries, and scholars he consulted and befriended in Romania, Hungary, Poland, France, England, Spain, Germany, Italy, and the Netherlands. Eventually, the board of directors of Starr King School decided Wilbur must either resign or come home from Europe to help the seminary meet the crises of the 1930s Depression. Wilbur resigned and worked full time writing his history.

His remarkable collection of rare books and documents—many of them unobtainable or unknown to scholars in the West—would at any time have been a notable contribution to historical research. But the collection's importance increased exponentially when many of the libraries Wilbur had used in Poland, Hungary, and Romania were destroyed or their contents scattered during World War II and its aftermath. Had it not been for Wilbur's determination and passion for his subject, many of the books and copies of documents he gathered would have been lost forever. When he died in 1956 (four years after the second volume was published), Wilbur willed the priceless collection of all the books and manuscripts to Starr King School so the seminary now houses, owns, and protects for posterity the world's most important Unitarian reference library.

Alicia certainly knew that, but I did not. All I knew about Servetus was what I had learned four years before on a cold afternoon's hike to the memorial stone in Geneva that marked the place where Servetus was burned to death. I had no idea that Servetus' books were revered by theologians, physicians, book collectors, and libraries. But it was clear to me that József trembled when he held Servetus' book not only because it was 461 years old and impossible to replace, but also because he was so moved to be holding in his hands the first published book to put forward ideas that would become the foundation of his Transylvanian Unitarian Church.

When a stranger visits, it gives us the opportunity to see our own lives in new ways. As I leaned against the door jamb, listening to József and Alicia proposing exciting possibilities for connection between the Berkeley and Kolozsvár seminaries and their libraries, I was embarrassed. I was more than embarrassed. I was ashamed, because it took someone's coming from halfway around the world to make me realize the importance of Wilbur's collection to me and to every Unitarian and Universalist anywhere in the world.

Keeping Moving in the Right Direction

Another highlight of József's time in Northern California was the long afternoon lunch he spent with Rosamond (Roz) Reynolds. We rode the Larkspur Ferry across the glistening waters of San Francisco Bay on a day so sparkling it set József's usually landlocked spirit soaring. Roz was a lifelong Unitarian who had abandoned her New England roots to retire to a hillside home in Northern California. Lunch was local crabs and sourdough bread. (On the ferry home, József, who had not previously made the acquaintance of this many-legged seafood, joked, "The lunch today called for courage.") Basking in the California sunshine, Roz and József compared New England and Transylvanian village churches, headquarters politics in Kolozsvár and Boston, their differing theologies, and their dreams for the future of Eastern Unitarianism and Western Unitarian Universalism.

Her careful, participatory listening made Roz a gifted advocate and natural networker. She immediately began forging connections for József and me with people she hoped could help us reframe our partnership work in more meaningful and faith-filled ways. She kept thinking of internationally minded people from the years when she had driven into Boston from Leominster, Massachusetts to work at the 25 Beacon Street headquarters. József learned from Roz that Don Harrington had been in Transylvania in 1938, and that between 1959 and 1982, before the ban on foreign visitors, he and his Transylvanian wife, Vilma, had organized seven visits by North American groups to meet with Transylvanian Unitarians. (Don was a retired North American minister József already knew well because Don was then living near Homoródszentmárton in Jánosfalva [Ionești].) Roz urged me to interview Ed Cahill to learn about the Association's connection with Hungarian Unitarians in the 1960s and '70s, and she insisted that someone needed to read Louis Cornish's papers at the Harvard Divinity School Library to learn about the original sister church connections of the 1920s and '30s.

For much of the afternoon, József and Roz talked about the role of ministers in partnership work. Roz cautioned, "Ministers come and go, but the congregation stays." Her words came back to us later when first I, and then József, moved away from serving the churches in San Jose and in Homoródszentmárton and suffered from afar as their partnership stumbled for a while. Roz clearly felt such stumbles could be prevented. She said:

> Our congregations have learned to be quite good at going through changing ministers, and there's no reason they can't be good at keeping their partnerships lively through a change of minister. In North America, you have to get the interim minister, the search committee for the incoming minister, and the ongoing partner church committee well on board. If the new minister that the congregation eventually calls is not committed to actively supporting and building this congregation-to-congregation and minister-to-minister connection, the partner church committee must step up and get them involved. In Transylvania, you must also be sure the incoming minister is enthusiastic and positive about continuing the work the two congregations have built to that point. When ministers change, it should always be a time for more, not less, partnership activity.

Roz wanted József to describe how Unitarian communities in Transylvania and Hungary had survived their years under communism. József spoke, reluctantly at first, about the forty years of silent desperation when the Transylvanian Unitarians had little to hope for, and how what saved them was their conviction that God and their churches would never desert them. Roz, an avid supporter of Starr King School for the Ministry, was shocked to learn that for years the Kolozsvár seminary was allowed to take in only one new Unitarian student per year, and that the Protestant and Roman Catholic denominations in Transylvania had been forced to place many of their most promising and energetic young leaders in remote villages where they would have less opportunity to organize resistance. All through the 1970s and '80s, the Securitate interrogated and sometimes tortured Unitarians who spoke out against the government. Some were imprisoned for many years, one for twenty-one years. So it was very difficult, József explained, to protect the leaders who were desperately needed to keep the people's hope alive.

Roz did not get lost in the drama. She responded with thoughtful questions about ministers' roles, about their working conditions, pay, and benefits, about their support systems, and about the Transylvanian ministers' partnership expectations and dreams. And then she talked me into going halves with her to buy József a laptop computer because József had told her:

Most Transylvanian ministers want to be a catalyst for economic and educational improvements. The development of what is put forward as capitalism in Romania is bringing with it unprecedented levels of poverty, discouragement, and envy. Growing right alongside the improved economy are violence and corruption. As we go through these years of tremendous change, survival of the village and the city churches is going to depend on how well the ministers can make the sudden leap from our repressed, stagnant lives under Ceauşescu to our new lives in an IT-driven world.

Following her afternoon with József, Roz loved to ask her many visitors if they were aware of "the stunning success of the partner church program," and would make a special point of quoting the district networker who said, "This is the best church group I've been involved in for treating and respecting ministers and lay-people as equals." Roz continued to advise us from the sidelines for many years.

The truth is, much as she admired József, Roz did not share my passionate interest in Transylvanian Unitarians. The passion that connected her to our partnership work was her lifelong commitment to maintaining the health and prospects of North American Unitarian Universalist programs and congregations. She once told me, "The important thing is to keep moving in the right direction. For that, you need a congregation. Without a congregation to stand with us, most of us would just stand still." She believed emphatically that keeping congregations healthy and moving forward must always come first, because, she said, "Healthy congregations can build a healthy world."

Roz certainly understood the stages that congregational social action programs typically move through and pushed me to consider how our congregations' previous experiences with short-term international efforts would need to be adapted for the long term. Roz's message to every partner church pair would be her favorite quote from Martin Luther King, Jr.: "If you cannot fly, drive; if you cannot drive, run; if you cannot run, walk; if you cannot walk, crawl. But keep moving. Keep moving forward. And fight with all your might those who seek to move us backwards."[55]

When Roz died, I used money she left me to help bring József and Mária to Star Island, the historic New England summer conference center off the coast of New Hampshire. It felt like a fitting memorial—to share a remarkable place Roz had loved deeply all her life with this remarkable Unitarian couple she cared so much about. Describing Star Island to József, Roz had said, "It has been many years since I have attended a summer conference on Star, but the island still nourishes my soul." That prompted József to tell Roz about Budapest First Church's dream of building a family, conference, and youth center on land the church owned at Magyarkút in a curve of the Danube River. Roz replied that she hoped the Kászonis would one day go to Star Island so they would have its memorable setting and programs clearly in their minds if they built their own conference center. The members of First Unitarian Church in Budapest, and those of its current partner, First Unitarian Church in Portland, may one day build a conference center, or they may find other, better ways to work together and forge their connection. In any case, both of these congregations are solidly committed to fulfilling Roz's dream of partnerships that are built to last.

Which of Us Is Poor?

Before you drive your car into a parking space in Berkeley, it is wise to check for sleeping bodies. Berkeley's generous social services, tolerance of eccentricity, and widespread liberal guilt have made it an inviting place for poor and homeless people to settle. Every errand—to the grocery store, the library, the town hall, a café, or the bank—is punctuated by appeals from people who struggle to eke out a marginal existence by begging.

A professor once challenged our seminary class to panhandle[56] on a street corner until we had been given enough coins to pay for a night's food and shelter. "Unless you put yourself in their shoes," our teacher asked, "how can you understand the lives of the homeless who are going to show up on your church doorstep?" Part of me seriously considered it, but a bigger part was stopped by echoes of my father's scornful warnings about the shame of being reduced to begging: "Save your allowance! Do you want to end up begging on the street?" he would roar when I walked into the house carrying a comic book or ice cream cone.

Instead of trying panhandling, I volunteered to dish out breakfast at a homeless shelter in the familiar territory of the Oakland, California Unitarians' fellowship hall. And I never did take up my professor's challenge to stand on a sidewalk and beg—to walk in a homeless person's shoes. I hid behind my defensive, routine response to appeals for spare change—a sympathetic but negative head shake, a silent thanksgiving that my church sponsored several programs for people who were homeless, followed by a quick dismissal of the encounter from my conscious thought.

Then in 1992 József made his first visit to Northern California. As we walked from the photo shop to the Theological Union bookstore, József gave coins to every panhandler we passed. He found their plight confronting and upsetting. He asked me exactly where they were going to sleep that night, something I hadn't seriously asked myself. As he engaged in conversations with homeless people, he was curious, sincere, and compassionate.

I was surprised, and intrigued, because at that time in 1992, five US dollars spent in Romania would have paid for labor or supplies costing $100 in the United States. As a result of Ceaușescu's rape of the country's resources and failed efforts at industrial modernization, Romania was caught in a severe economic depression. Unitarian ministers' families survived in Transylvania on a combination of barter and whatever small contributions their often impoverished congregation members could manage to pledge, season by season.[57] So it amazed me that József parted with any of his precious coins, but he took for granted that he would give them away. "When you are desperate, even a little can make a big difference, and I am better off than they are," József said. "We can grow a lot of our food, and the members of our congregation would not let a minister's family starve or become homeless. I need to understand everything I can about homelessness and poverty in the United States, so my villagers might not have to walk those same roads as Romania plunges into capitalism."

"Who do the homeless people blame for their poverty?" he asked, explaining that Transylvanians were finding it very hard to stop blaming the Romanian government for everything that was wrong in their lives. As we talked more, we agreed that it was easier to be hopeful if you believed you could play a role in bringing about change. But I was at a loss to explain the steps of moving from blaming a dictator's oppression for one's ruined life to shouldering responsibility for changing it, much less changing the government's policies, services, and suppression of minority rights. Nonetheless, József felt ministers and priests in Romania must shoulder the task of helping their congregations, and members should take up responsibility for making such changes happen in "this new day."

József's patterns of thinking had developed during a lifetime under Romanian communism, with its ideal of shared wealth, and from Transylvanian village life, with its assumption of the need to save limited resources. On Berkeley's sidewalks, József's worldviews rubbed uncomfortably against my own ideals, which were rooted in American individualism, with its goal of increasing your family's separate status and security.

This difference between us was a deep one. Our Transylvanian partners major in community, while American Unitarian Universalists major in individuality.[58] The Transylvanian Unitarians are focused on group justice for all Unitarians, and by extension for other religious and ethnic minorities. Many Unitarian Universalists work tirelessly to bring justice to our society, but it is a justice built on individual abilities, privileges, and rights. Our church is a loose association of quite separate congregations, while the Transylvanian church is definitely one united church body. I viewed the San Jose congregation as a maverick collection of unique and special individuals loosely bound together by their love of protesting, singing, questioning, learning, and committing to our children. That is a world away from József's seeing his Homoródszent-márton congregation as one important link in a solidly united church body. He told me, "It is in the over-arching shelter of each other that Transylvanian Unitarians live."

Though József sincerely respects our social action efforts and community involvements, he still experiences Unitarian Universalists in the United States as weak in community responsibility. "You have too little sense of obligation to your church and your country, and too strong a sense of individual entitlement." It is true that it had never occurred to my congregation to question the lack of justice or lack of compassion in leaving our neighboring Unitarian Universalist congregations to sink or swim on their own. We only stepped up to help them if they suffered an unexpected, catastrophic disaster. Contrast that attitude with Transylvanian congregations who often share what they have with other congregations whose need is greater than their own. Perhaps we have been more affected by living under capitalism and they have been more affected by communism than either of us would like to admit.

Every Transylvanian who visits North America is shocked by the excess—the overwhelming choice of food in supermarkets, the overflowing trash bins, the number of cars, televisions, and computers per household. Transylvanian visitors say, "No wonder you Americans have lost touch with the essentials of life, since you have to live in this materialistically driven and environmentally unconscious society."

Another difference between József and me is that I have an embedded trust that, in the end, a government serves its citizens. But József holds a deep-seated conviction that the government is often his personal enemy, and the enemy of every minority group. We acknowledged the ironies that, while Romania may be the land of Ceauşescu's Securitate and a ruined economy, its communities have far less homelessness because of the local people's sympathetic generosity to the poor. While the United States may be a land of opportunity with a far better economy than Romania's, it offers band-aid solutions to its homeless citizens and has hollow compassion and few opportunities for its poor. We began talking about all these things during József's visit with our congregation, and we have continued to talk about them for more than a decade, on some points changing our positions, but on others agreeing to disagree.

József left for home, and my Northern Californian life went on. For years I had automatically adopted a numbed, routine response each time I passed the tired-looking woman with grey hair and missing teeth who panhandled most days in front of my bank. Sitting on a green plastic milk crate, she would look meaningfully from the bills I had taken from the bank machine to the dilapidated tote bags around her feet. I would nod, cast a half-sympathetic, half-sad smile at her, and walk past swiftly, focused on silencing my conscience.

But after I spent a month watching József move through my Northern Californian life, I no longer liked this wall I had built around myself. József's presence had dug up a lot of things I had ceased to question, or never even seen. The next time I went to the bank, I stopped to talk and listen to the woman who panhandled there. In our conversation she bragged about her grandchildren, and I told her about my family's new babies. We stumbled onto her Tibetan Buddhist connections and my Zen Buddhist meditation practice. I sympathized with her need for a car, and she understood my longing to untie my life from commuting. When we realized we were nearly the same age, she said, "We're not old yet, but our youth has been over for a long time."

She thought of herself and me as "we." Could I?

My impulse was to give her twenty dollars, but I wasn't at all sure if it was the right thing to do. I asked her if I should. She answered, "It would be stupid for you to hook your do-gooder notions on anything that passes between you and me. You couldn't transform an uneducated woman like me into a rich person, not even if you gave me all your money *and* your pension fund. Besides, your main concern must always be the same as mine—for your children. The real truth of you and me is this: you have too much money, I have too little. But if you give me some of your money, you are doing what you can to right the balance in the world. And you and I will both sleep better tonight—that has to be a good thing."

Our financial exchange was a dignified and realistic acknowledge-
ment of our different life conditions—she with her clear, rich spirit,
though very poor in resources, and me with an ever-searching, too often
ambivalent spirit, but so rich in material goods. As I turned to leave, she
pulled from one of her grubby bags a beautiful strip of rainbow-colored
Tibetan prayer flags, each printed with a blessing for the earth. Giving it
to me, she said, "Hang these in the wind. They'll keep your soul spinning
in the right direction."

Part 5

Finding Our Roots in the 1920s, 1930s, and 1940s

Learning how the Ceauşescu government had blatantly rewritten Romanian history to suit its own ends gave me a new respect for the importance of unearthing and exposing the historical truths of the past. Along the way, I learned how meaningful the past became whenever my own experiences paralleled in some way a story "from history." But valuing and enjoying history came hard to me, as I describe in the first piece in this history section.

Following my first visit to Transylvania, I felt I absolutely had to learn some Romanian history to be able to understand what I was seeing and what was happening with our partners in Romania,[59] but it took me several years to understand that this was just a first step, a baby step, really. I was far from understanding that "there is a past as well as a present, that the past has very much to do with the present, and that the past belongs to those who belong to the present."[60] After many years, a much wider and deeper acceptance of history and a hard-won appreciation of the importance of history for all of us have shown me new, exhilarating ways of embracing time and space.

Each of the biographical pieces in this section has a close personal connection for me. Whenever my intention to finish this book wavered, remembering how much Earl Morse Wilbur sacrificed to write and complete his books kept me moving forward. Louis Cornish's story matters to me because I was astonished to learn that there had been a previous sister church movement in the 1920s and that these no longer functioning connections were still vitally alive in the memories and feelings of the Homoródszentmárton Unitarians. The remarkable 1930s marriage of Ferenc Balázs and Christine Frederiksen (later Morgan) fascinates me because, like Christine, I lived in Northern California, was a university student in Ohio and then in Berkeley, married a foreigner, and followed his work commitments to a new life in Europe. Gábor Kereki's life work, including his emigration from Hungary to England, speaks powerfully to me because I share with him a passion for holding religious education at the center of our work and because I too have had to puzzle out how to shape a career as an immigrant minister. I had not had many heroes before, but the partnership movement has brought a lot of heroes to me.

Exploring the historically grounded roots of my faith makes me feel all of life is an interconnected puzzle. It is very satisfying to identify the pieces and understand how they fit together. I set out to explore the life of Louis Cornish and discovered he had helped Ferenc Balázs obtain the visa he needed to study at my own seminary. Although I was interested in Cornish because he was a founder of the 1920s partnerships, I also learned that during the 1930s Depression he saved Star Island—one of my sacred places—for the Unitarians. Soon after I realized Cornish had burned his papers to protect Gábor Kereki, I found József had a picture of Kereki hanging above his desk in Budapest.

Harry C. Meserve said it well: "It is a curious error to suppose you can carry on effectively a great liberal tradition while remaining at the same time ignorant, or almost ignorant, of the beliefs and achievements of the people who have handed that tradition over to you."[61]

I hope all partnership enthusiasts find their own vital connections to the histories that underlie and support our partnerships. I hope each of us gets to experience the thrill of tracking down a document that "makes it all clear" by filling in a crucial piece in our understanding. The particular stories that matter to each of us will be completely different. What matters is that we discover them and tell them to each other.

Warming up to History:
Earl Morse Wilbur (1886–1956)

My understanding of history has been transformed by my growing to understand, and appreciate, how the day-to-day lives of Transylvanian Unitarians are embedded in their history—a rich, sweeping, centuries-long heritage full of memorable milestones and stories. I have begun to view my own life as interwoven with history, especially the stories of the founders, teachers, pilgrims, and martyrs who cleared the paths we are walking together towards more permanent partnership relationships. I have a new awareness that we are continuing what so many before us have done, and what others will continue after us. Perhaps through understanding history we can see into the future. Certainly, history is interpreted and manipulated to meet the political objectives of governments and social groups. We will always be faced with the question of what is "the true" history.

In Transylvania I was forced to consider how it would be to hold my history and traditions so dear that I would choose to be imprisoned, or even to die, rather than be separated from them. Back at home, I gained enormous respect for Earl Morse Wilbur, who sacrificed every other pursuit during the last thirty years of his life to uncover and record the lost history of early liberal Protestantism, including Transylvanian Unitarianism.

Now I watch the world with new eyes, asking "history questions" that seldom occurred to me before, questions that grow out of the overlapping realms of history and identity. How can history help me define what is essential to my being American? How is being an American different from being a Transylvanian?...a Hungarian? ...a Canadian?...a Swede?...an Australian? What does it mean to me, after traveling as a pilgrim in Transylvania, to be a faith-filled Unitarian Universalist? In what ways have I been changed by becoming an amateur historian and a sometime pilgrim...an itinerant minister...a serial immigrant? How have others answered these questions? How will my answers be different a year, and ten years, from now?

During the month of January, students at Starr King seminary work to gain experiences in ministry-like positions. Usually we worked at a social service agency, on the streets, or in a church. Or we spent the month making an intensive study of a special topic. It was a major cheat for me to spend my January break in 1987 completing the twenty-five books that were required reading for all of us who were about to be examined by the Ministerial Fellowship Committee. In its role of opening or closing the gate to ordination, the Fellowship Committee asked students about these books and everything else they believed a new minister needed to know. My oral exam was a month away, and I was in a panic because I had not opened, much less digested, over two thousand pages of the books that were hardest for me—the densely written history texts.

A martyr to this cause, I traded in the sun-blessed, blossoming fruit trees of Berkeley for ten days of dark, freezing Scandinavian winter. I packed layers of winter clothes, my first ever pair of snow boots, and the five history texts I had yet to open. Robin's work had determined our destination—a small Archipelago island outside Stockholm, on the same latitude as Anchorage, Alaska. In January the island was dark almost around the clock, except for reflected moonlight lighting up the snow-covered rocks that marked the shoreline. Each day between breakfast and dinner I was alone with two choices—to read the history texts or to tromp round the densely forested, snow-shrouded road in my new boots. That week Robin discussed Scandinavian alcohol policy, and I finally got serious about learning Unitarian and Universalist history. My feelings about history up to that point had been close to Voltaire's: "History is after all only a pack of tricks we play on the dead."[62]

After skimming the standard work on Universalist history, *The Larger Hope*, by Russell E. Miller, I began to doubt I would ever make it through the two volumes by Earl Morse Wilbur. Instead, I read Conrad Wright's *Beginnings of Unitarianism*, which explores the indigenous New England origins of Unitarianism in the United States. Wright's appreciative son, also a historian, asserted at his father's memorial service that this book's central objective was "to protect misguided enthusiasts from drawing the mistaken inference from Wilbur that to find our [Unitarian] roots we had to look somewhere in Eastern Europe."[63] Perhaps investigating the academic duel between Conrad

Wright and Earl Morse Wilbur over the sources of our faith would prove interesting enough to get me all the way through Wilbur's two volumes— but not quite yet. I opened the third of the five books, *The Epic of Unitarianism* by David Parke, and found it was dedicated to the memory of Earl Morse Wilbur. Parke wrote, "Wilbur...has flung wide the gates of history that we may pass through."[64]

Finally, Wilbur's two volumes—*A History of Unitarianism: Socinianism and Its Antecedents* (1945), and *A History of Unitarianism in Transylvania, England, and America to 1900* (1952)—were the only books I had left to read, and remember. These volumes were always referred to as "Wilbur"—as if the man could not be distinguished from his writing. I have great feeling and respect for my seminary, the same school Wilbur served for twenty-seven years as its founding organizer, president, and professor. Maybe our mutual love for this unique institution was a strong enough connection to sustain me through the dreaded pages and inspire me to retain what I read. But maybe not. After all, I had owned "Wilbur" for several years without ever opening either volume.

It was during the earliest years of the new seminary in Berkeley—then called Pacific Unitarian School for the Ministry—that Wilbur decided to write these books. While preparing a series of lectures on the rise and evolution of Unitarian beliefs and congregations, he uncovered a lack of historical research on the parts of the early Reformation movement in which modern Unitarianism locates its roots. There was also little evidence of how Unitarian beliefs had originally developed within Christianity. Striving to fill this void led Wilbur into the studies and writing that, according to Henry Wilder Foote, made Wilbur "the foremost authority on the development of liberal religion."[65]

Out on the Swedish island I finally began reading Wilbur's volumes and soon realized that he had accomplished a daunting task—bringing to light the long suppressed and then forgotten history of the radical wing of the Protestant Reformation. It was marvelous, and truly landmark, scholarship. I concluded that Wilbur did see the rise of Unitarianism in England and the United States as later aspects of a movement 200 years earlier in Europe. But Wilbur did not address whether American Unitarianism's roots lay in Transylvania or in an indigenous American psyche or experiences. His focus was showing how each of the four primary Unitarian movements—in Poland, and successively in Transylvania, England, and North America—was firmly grounded in the principles of freedom, reason, and tolerance, and how each was a radical break from and criticism of its surrounding religious culture.

Reading Wilbur made me wonder how history is constructed and what had caused too many North Americans like me to have a short-term, impatient approach to it. What should be remembered, and what should be replaced? How does memory—and which memory—become history? When I worked at church to overturn "outdated" traditions, was I throwing out a rich heritage? Was my innate delight with innovation preventing me from connecting more deeply with the sacred because, as József raised four years later, it was stopping me from holding my faith at the center of my life?

Compiling study notes at the breakfast table of our little hut close to the Arctic Circle, I suspected Wilbur would have prescribed for me less American impetuosity and more Transylvanian persistence. I soon found Wilbur hard going, so hard that I understood why every minister who learned I had set aside this month to finish the Fellowship Committee reading list immediately asked, "How's it going with Wilbur?" In the end I decided seminarians were required to read Wilbur's two dry volumes as a warning that in ministry there will be many jobs that call out to be reframed into something that holds a redeeming reason for your pain.

The one bright spot in those lonely days of slogging through Wilbur was my reward each evening at five o'clock—an adventurous wintry walk in the dark along the snow-narrowed road and out onto the conference center's dock. Standing in the unnaturally silent, moonlit landscape surrounded by the icy black water of the waveless Baltic, I would wait expectantly for the huge passenger ferries to Finland to loom into sight around the far end of the island. At exactly the same time each evening first one and then another spectacularly lit, twelve-story floating city would squeeze between the dock and the shore of the opposite island. My heart beat in time with the throbbing engines of these monster ships, thrillingly close, amazingly huge, and glowing with an unearthly light as they threaded their careful path through the treacherously rocky Baltic islands, carrying between them 6000 passengers and their cars overnight to Helsinki, in Finland, and Leningrad, in the the Soviet Union.

Watching these magical floating palaces, I imagined Wilbur in 1931 traveling by ship from Boston to Europe. I pictured him working (for five years in Europe and in the United States for eighteen more) on his books about the past, volumes that say nothing of the people of his own time and do not mention the magnificent libraries and destinations he visited in Eastern, Central, and Western Europe. I could not imagine an author's finding pleasure in writing that sort of history. Though we were both Americans, clearly Wilbur and I were essentially different. Maybe all those ancient kings and ministers, the Ottomans and Habsburgs, and this Treaty and that Diet were not as disconnected from his life as they had always been from mine. Maybe those Transylvania, Torda, and Trianon facts and figures stirred him in a way I was not wise enough to understand. I had to wonder: Where had I gotten my narrow-minded assumption that the present was more interesting and counted for more than the past?

I picked my way back along the icy shore to dinner, and finally finished the last pages of Wilbur on the long flights home, but I didn't warm to it.

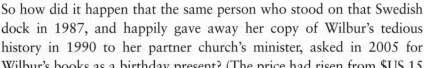

So how did it happen that the same person who stood on that Swedish dock in 1987, and happily gave away her copy of Wilbur's tedious history in 1990 to her partner church's minister, asked in 2005 for Wilbur's books as a birthday present? (The price had risen from $US 15 new in 1985 to over $US 200 for a used set. Perhaps I was not the only one who had had a change of heart about reading Wilbur.) How did these books on a subject I dreaded learning twenty-five years ago become the valued resource I now refer to frequently and sometimes recommend to North Americans who want to study Transylvanian Unitarianism?

The answer is obvious. During pivotal years in the history of the Transylvanian Unitarians, I visited the places Wilbur wrote about. I was welcomed by fellow Unitarians who were living products of this history. I rang the bells of their ancient churches and found myself held in the nurturing arms of their time-proven rituals. I grew to care deeply about these people and the future of their church. I began to burn with curiosity about the many things I saw but did not understand.

The first time I bought Wilbur's books, I really did not know if Transylvania was in Europe, Africa, or Australia. On my first trip to Transylvania, it seemed to me that our partners were as much burdened as enriched by their long and complex history. This was, without doubt, the ethnocentric view of an American who knows hardly anything about her family's history beyond the living relatives she has met. But after a second visit, I became impatient with being one of those ignorant Americans who fail—as I believe the US representatives at Trianon failed—to understand and respect the history of Eastern Europe, with its complex layers of ethnicities and religions and wars. Eventually I decided that the Transylvanians' history is vitally important to them in a way I will never fully appreciate.

I watched my husband and his research colleagues conducting their social science investigations and concluded that scholars like Robin and Wilbur could only unearth historical and scientific truths if they conducted their work from a perspective informed by but held strictly apart from their personal experiences. But after I met many Transylvanian Unitarians who seemed to "live their history," I decided that to "do history" and appreciate it I didn't need to hold it aloof from my personal stories and passions.

When I first served communion in Transylvania, I had an epiphany of understanding how ancient Unitarianism was and how important being Unitarian was to me. I had a second epiphany reading Wilbur's acceptance speech to the American Unitarian Association when he was awarded its highest honor, the Distinguished Service to the Cause of Liberal Religion Award. As he put it:

> [My vision has been] to help my brethren to appreciate our true significance, by realizing that, instead of being merely one of the minor sects of a divided Christendom, we are ennobled as a living part of a great and broadening stream of spiritual freedom.[66]

"Yes!" I thought. "That's it, exactly. The Transylvanian Unitarians and Wilbur have taught me that."

Once I finally pried open the lid of this history box, I found more and more ways to enjoy its treasures. When I returned to the United States after my first visit to Transylvania, I embarked on several historical research efforts of my own, glad to find myself sitting at the same tables in the Harvard Divinity School Library and the same chairs in the Boston Athenaeum where Wilbur must have worked. I began to wish Wilbur was alive to talk with us about all this.

I was intrigued by Transylvanian Unitarian Sándor Bölöni Farkas' accounts in *Journey in North America, 1831* of his de Tocqueville-like travels in the United States and Canada. When Farkas discovered, to his complete surprise, that there were Unitarians in North America, he wrote jubilantly to his Unitarian bishop in Transylvania, "We are not alone!"

After a frustratingly fruitless search through many other parts of the archives of the Unitarians in Toronto, Canada, the congregation's historian finally found accounts of their 1920s sister church connection to Alsórákos (Racoş) in the women's auxiliary records. It turns out that in the first half of the 1900s it was the women who managed the congregation's social action, fundraising, and international involvements.

My next historical explorations were to learn all I could about the 1920s sister church program, to learn more about Christine Frederiksen (later Morgan), including what happened when she returned to the United States after Ferenc Balázs' death, and a long, unsuccessful search for the original deed of ownership of the Unitarian Mission House in Budapest.

In the course of these investigations, I learned of a near disaster in the 1980s when the Starr King board of directors almost sold off Wilbur's collection of books and papers on advice from a rare book dealer who was close to the school. As a person who bought and sold books, he was not concerned so much with history or building libraries as with how to turn a valuable commodity into funds the school could use for good causes like repairing the roof and providing better salaries. Alicia McNary Forsey, then professor of church history at Starr King School, championed a major rescue effort for the Wilbur Rare Book Collection that included keeping it at the school.[67] One afternoon when we were both trapped by a huge rainstorm, Alicia told me a lot about Wilbur's work in Europe, including the minor miracles that made it possible for him to build his unique, invaluable collection of original source books and papers. Her efforts through the years to keep Wilbur's collection intact and make it accessible have been a great gift not only to Starr King School but to Unitarians and Universalists across the world. In his article, "Earl Morse Wilbur: Historian of Unitarianism 1886–1956," Henry Wilder Foote writes:

> The long-forgotten and fragmentary records were buried in remote and seldom visited libraries and called for a working knowledge of nine different languages, ancient and modern. Fortunately, after his resignation as President of the Pacific Unitarian School for the Ministry...[Wilbur spent another] three years (1931–34) in Europe, searching every locality where evidence could be found and gathering a great collection of books and copies of manuscript documents, most of them hitherto quite unknown to, or unobtainable by scholars in the Western world.[68]

As noted in the box "Earl Morse Wilbur's Rare Book Collection" on page 112, at any time this would have been a notable contribution to historical research, but its importance was greatly enhanced when, during and after World War II, many of the libraries he had explored in Poland and Hungary were destroyed or their contents scattered. The information gathered would, but for him, have been forever lost. These records, many of them unique, are now at Starr King School, which has the world's richest collection of Unitariana.[69]

———∞∞∞———

In 1988 Robin's mother died, and we found ourselves in Sydney, Australia. There we spent two weeks unearthing fifty years of history in the home his parents had built among the eucalyptus trees and kookaburras. We learned that Robin's mathematician father had saved every paper and journal he had ever owned, and that his mother spent the last three years of her life sorting them. It was not until I developed a profound respect for Earl Morse Wilbur and his carefully gathered collection of papers, journals, and rare books, that I could appreciate how important, and difficult, that task—both his father's original assembling and his mother's sorting and giving away—must have been. And I am far more tolerant now of the tottering piles of papers Robin continually gathers around him.

Doing the work of partnership has taught me a lot about the intersections of Transylvanian and North American Unitarian histories, but it has also taught me more about myself. No matter where one's history leads, whatever turns it takes, the greatest distances we cross are within ourselves. And, yes, there are nights when I take my replacement copy of Wilbur to bed with me to read, just for fun.

Lighting the Dark:
Louis C. Cornish (1870–1950)

Louis Cornish would have agreed with József when he said, "I can't understand why you American Unitarians hold your faith so far from the center of your lives." Cornish always searched for ways to help people deepen their faith. He would have been delighted to learn that every summer thousands of North Americans now find our way to two of the places he cherished—Transylvania and Star Island—where many of us find that whether it makes us glad or not, we are all people of faith—that every person has a basic spiritual nature which unites and balances our intellectual, physical and emotional selves, and that everyone needs tangible practices and places to which we can attach our faith in order to make it real. I know that Cornish would also have agreed with my belief that connecting through our shared history can be a cornerstone of both early and ongoing partnerships.

One dark, wintry week while I was in Boston I stole away from my religious educator's meeting to search for information about the original 1920s sister church program. Established by Louis Cornish, president of the Unitarian Association, and Gabriel Csiki, a Transylvanian minister, it paired two Canadian and 116 US congregations with 118 Transylvanian churches. I wanted to learn everything I could about this earlier sister church program, because I hoped there were old connections we might revive, as well as lessons we could learn. When I explained what I was looking for, Alan Seaburg—then the dedicated Unitarian Universalist Association archivist and curator of manuscripts at the Harvard Divinity School library—said my first step would be to read Louis Cornish's Unitarian Universalist Association papers.

Alan settled me at a large table in a glass-walled section at the back of the library. On the table he placed nine large acid-free boxes from the archives. They contained letters, minutes of meetings, and the Association's annual reports from the 1920s and '30s. There was also a biography, *Louis Craig Cornish: Interpreter of Life*, by Cornish's wife, Frances. Alan gave me a card for the copier and a door key, because the door automatically locked each time you entered or left. I realized the bookshelves behind my table must have held books too rare to be on the open shelves.

All that week I crept carefully over slippery sidewalks to my sealed-in, cozy corner of the library. I learned that Louis Cornish was an avid internationalist who had a powerful impact on the global consciousness of North American Unitarians between the wars. Cornish served as the parish minister at First Parish (known as Old Ship Church) in Hingham, Massachusetts from 1900–1915 before he became the American Unitarian Association's secretary at large and then its vice-president, responsible, among many other things, for international concerns.[70] He was president from 1927–37, through the worst of the 1930s Depression—a time when many Unitarian congregations woke one morning to discover that in the wake of a failing bank their total endowment, savings, and current pledge income had disappeared. Under Cornish's skillful leadership, the American Unitarian Association defied bankruptcy, and, remarkably, new congregations continued to start up and survive. I was surprised and delighted to discover Cornish felt the same way I did about Star Island.

Cornish inspired Unitarian congregations in the United States and Canada to look beyond their shores and engage actively with Unitarians in Hungary, Transylvania (then newly part of Romania), and in the recently created Czechoslovakia, where Norbert Čapek provided charismatic Unitarian leadership in the 1920s and '30s until his incarceration and death during World War II. There is little in the archives about Gabriel Csiki. Somewhere there should also be evidence of the role Earl Morse Wilbur played in establishing the earlier 1900s connections between Unitarian groups all over the world, connections that must have fed Cornish's involvement.

Frances Cornish's biography gives her account of the beginning of the sister church program:

> In 1921 Rev. Gabriel Csiki, a Transylvanian Unitarian minister exiled to Budapest, pleaded for help for the churches in Transylvania. Cornish [and Csiki] evolved the plan of "Adoption" of Transylvanian churches by Unitarian churches in America. In 1929 Csiki said [while attending] the annual meeting of the American Unitarian Association: "You have saved not less than one hundred and twelve churches. The Unitarians' Mission House in Budapest, founded through your

generous help....is a symbol of the friendship that binds American, British, and Hungarian Unitarians into a happy household of faith."[71]

Frances Cornish also refers to the sister church program in relation to the sacrificed (some would say stolen) bells Cornish urged many North American congregations to replace for their Transylvanian sister churches.

The sister church "adoption plan," a direct outcome of the first commission (explained below), was initiated in Boston on 9 February 1921 at a follow-up meeting between the three commission travelers, Cornish, and Csiki.[72]

The stated purpose of these first sister church connections was "to plead the Transylvanian's cause and need for aid with American Unitarians."[73] Louis Cornish's correspondence indicates that, originally, the North American congregations signed up for a three-year commitment. The congregation-to-congregation sister church connections were expected to provide moral support for the Transylvanians and education for the North Americans, while the American Unitarian Association and Transylvanian Church headquarters dealt with material aid.

Often, the funds sent to Transylvania were raised by the women's auxiliaries of the North American churches. It is unclear if the funds raised by a congregation were directed to its actual sister congregation. From Cornish's papers it is also not clear if it was separately raised funds that were used to buy and refurbish the Mission House in Budapest and the Prague Unitarian headquarters. Funds from the United States paid two-thirds of the Budapest Mission House building purchase costs. (British Unitarians paid the other third.) Mortgage payments were provided for the Hungarian Unitarians, as well as a salary for Gabriel Csiki to work with the many Transylvanian Unitarians who moved to Hungary after 1920. This ongoing support stopped as the financial crises of the Great Depression dried up nearly all charitable giving.

Cornish would have applauded the official delegation of North American lay leaders and ministers who were allowed into Romania in 1968 to celebrate the 400th anniversary of the Edict of Torda. And he probably would have jumped for joy over the official Unitarian Universalist Association and Canadian Unitarian Council delegation that met with Romanian officials in January 1990 to argue for the rights of religious minorities.

It was more than his valuing international understanding (or as we might say today, his global consciousness) that drove Cornish's commitment. Although he is known to have held prejudices about groups of people and races he considered inferior, Cornish cared deeply about, and argued forcefully for, the rights of minority groups in many parts of the world.

In the early 1920s, Cornish was vitally involved with three official delegations to Transylvania. These were called "commissions" because the men conducting them had been commissioned to carry out certain tasks by the delegating, and funding, body that sent them. All three of the commissions were sent in response to the urgent need for protection and aid for the Transylvanian minority churches and schools after it became clear that the Romanian government had no intention of honoring the stipulations for the rights of the people living in the areas ceded to Romania by the 1920 Trianon Treaty. The three commissions confronted the Romanian government with the fact that North American Unitarians were closely affiliated with the Transylvanian Unitarians and were not afraid to protest the treaty-breaking changes being forced upon the Hungarian minority in Romania.

Cornish did not accompany the first commission in the spring of 1920, but he had primary responsibility for its sponsorship by the American Unitarian Association and for raising the US$50,000 that the three North American representatives (Naval chaplain Edward B. Witte and ministers Sydney B. Snow and Joel Metcalf) delivered to the Transylvanian Church headquarters for redistribution. A newsletter from Snow's church, in Montreal, Canada, reported:

> It was a rough experience as they traveled on horseback in this remote, terrorized and anxious region. They administered such temporary aid as they could and returned to urge the Unitarians of the West not to forsake these brethren who were trying to cling to their menaced traditions.[74]

This 1920 commission—which departed Boston in March and returned home from Transylvania and Hungary in June—was called a "relief unit." The commission's report ended with, "God save the free churches of Transylvania." Witte, Snow, and Metcalf came home determined to stir up US government attention, raise funds, and address "the Western betrayal" of Transylvania.

"Western betrayal"

In 1920, Transylvanian Hungarians experienced a double betrayal—the Trianon Treaty settlement, which ceded Transylvania to Romania, followed by a lack of sanctions from other governments when Romania flagrantly broke its legal commitments under the treaty to honor the rights of the Hungarian minorities. "Western betrayal" is frequently used in Hungary, Romania, Poland, the Czech Republic, Slovakia, and the Baltic States to refer to the foreign policies of the Western Allies from the Treaty of Trianon (1920) through World War II and the Cold War. The Allies' position in 1920 settlement decisions is seen as rooted in hypocrisy because, in spite of claiming to promote democracy and self-determination, the Allies signed pacts and formed military alliances that actually abandoned Easten Europe's minorities at the end of World War I, and the whole of Easten Europe to the control of the Soviet Union at the end of World War II. In *Looking for George*, British author Helena Drysdale reports that in 1991 a Romanian friend told her: "Churchill betrayed us to Stalin at Yalta and threw us into the arms of the USSR, [so] it is your duty now to help us out of this mess."[75]

This reading of the war settlement histories is disputed by those historians who argue that Woodrow Wilson's delegation at the end of World I, Winston Churchill in Paris, and Franklin Roosevelt at Tehran and Yalta, had no other option but to accept Romania's, and then Joseph Stalin's, demands. However, recently released British war documents from mid-1916 confirm that Romania, with its huge army, was bribed by the Allies to change sides with the promise of being given Transylvania and Eastern Hungary (the Banat and Bukovina). British historians now counter that at that time a secret agreement was made among the Allies that at the end of hostilities they would not honor their promise to Romania. If this is true, then ignoring Romania's breaches of the Trianon agreements was an even greater "Western betrayal" than previously believed.

Whatever reading one chooses, it is clear that war sticks to our lives like shattered glass. Not just years later, but generations later, long "settled" wars are still playing havoc with the lives, hopes, commitments, and futures of those who won and those who lost, while minority groups suffer as ongoing victims of the enmities created by the "let's play chess with the nations" mentality of the winners.

Cornish first visited Transylvania himself in 1922. This second commission was a delegation of three Unitarian ministers—Cornish, Palfrey Perkins of Weston, Massachusetts, and Harold E. B. Speight of Boston. They were joined in Europe by Lawrence Redfern of Liverpool, England. Chaired by Cornish, the commission was sent by the American and British Unitarian churches to hearten and investigate the conditions of fifty Unitarian congregations in Transylvania and their Unitarian schools and colleges. The commission's report, *Transylvania in 1922* (which Cornish wrote) carefully describes the life and institutions of the Hungarian religious and ethnic minorities in Romania. Cornish writes movingly of the beauty of the region and the pathos of life under the radically changed conditions of minority families and churches, especially in agricultural villages operating by then under an openly hostile Romanian government. The report argued that:

> Stability of life and freedom for all peoples in Transylvania depend upon the establishment of a just *modus vivendi* under the provisions of the Trianon Treaty that safeguards minority rights, and the enlightened opinion of the world demands that Roumania keep both the letter and the spirit of the Treaty.[76]

This report laid out for the first time, for Unitarians and governments around the world, the Romanian government's severe repression of the Hungarian religious minorities.

Cornish's last important work in Transylvania was as leader of the five-person joint delegation (British and American, Reformed and Unitarian) commissioned by the distinguished American Committee on the Rights of Religious Minorities to visit Romania in the summer of 1924. The forty-one members of this committee of notables included three former or future US presidents, US Supreme Court and other high-ranking judges, senior members of the State Department, and a wide spread of US church leaders. Cornish was an initiator of this committee and, after his 1922 trip, had stirred them to take action on behalf of the Hungarian minorities in Romania. In 1924 the Committee cited "the abuse of the rights of the minorities" as its reason for sending the official commission.

After their inquiry in Transylvania covering some 2200 miles (3500 kilometers), the 1924 commission compiled a detailed report (Cornish was again the main author) of their investigation of the abuse of rights of ethnic groups in not only the Unitarian churches and villages, but also in the Lutheran, Reformed, and Roman Catholic churches and their schools. The report, *The Religious Minorities in Transylvania*, documented interferences with the guaranteed right of assembly and interferences with and closing of minority schools. It gave evidence of many instances of violence and corruption by government officials, instances of discrimination in the appropriation of land, and instances of unwarranted interference with the rights of minority individuals. In the report, each allegation reported by the minority church or individual is followed by the official response from the Romanian Minister of Foreign Affairs. He wrote hundreds of dismissive denials, admitting only two minor instances of culpability. The evasive and disdainful tone of his official replies makes clear the Romanian government did not care what the rest of the world might feel about its abuse of its new citizens' minority rights. After long delays by both the Romanian government and the minority denominations in Transylvania (whose Bishops received threats of reprisals) the report was printed, in London in 1926. Cornish concludes:

> The impression gained through contact with the Roumanian, the Magyar, and the Saxon life throughout this fertile land is that unless a solution can be found for the present problems, racial and linguistic, religious and economic, it will continue to be one of the saddest lands in Europe, and a menacing danger-spot for the peace of the world....In the grave issues pending between the Roumanian Government and the Minority peoples, it must be understood that the affiliated churches in Great Britain and the United States have a duty to perform just as long as the present conditions obtain. The Commission therefore urges upon churches and societies the continuance for the present of their financial aid to the Minority churches. The Commission believes that the American Committee on the Rights of Religious Minorities and other similar agencies, while not presuming to interfere in any respect with the rights that pertain to the civil government of Roumania, should so far as possible continue both to inform and to focus public opinion, to the end that equity for all shall be the policy of the Roumanian Government in

dealing with these problems....The entire civilized world is deeply concerned in the settlement of the issues involved.[77]

The distinguished and interfaith nature of this last commission originally raised high expectations of successfully influencing the Romanian government to change its policies toward the minorities. Other minority groups across Europe, and also the US State Department, must have been watching. It may be that the call to action of *The Religious Minorities in Transylvania* was eclipsed in the end by the crises of the 1930s Depression, which caused many US institutions to pull back from global concerns. I still hope to find an interview with Cornish or a government document that reviews the effects of the 1924 commission's work. Did the US government or the American Committee on the Rights of the Religious Minorities take any further action after they received the commission's damning report? One day we will uncover the answer.

There is a surprising reason for how hard it is to find answers to the question of the commission's influence on US government policies toward Romania. Alan Seaburg told me that when Cornish retired he destroyed almost all of his voluminous correspondence, including the papers originally kept in his office at 25 Beacon Street. In the Foreword to his 1937 book, *Work and Dreams and the Wide Horizon*, Cornish states, "Many of the problems with which I have dealt are as strictly confidential as are those brought to a physician. They cannot be told."[78] Among the most confidential were stories he could not include in Chapter XXII: International Relations. Shortly before he died in 1950, Cornish also destroyed the papers he kept at home. It must have been a heartbreaking decision for a person with such a keen reverence for history, but Cornish had been vitally connected to Norbert Čapek who was arrested in 1941 and imprisoned by the Nazis. Čapek died in 1942 in Dachau concentration camp. Cornish witnessed Sándor Szent-Ivanyi (in 1946) and Gábor Kereki (in 1947) being forced to emigrate from Hungary to the United States and England, respectively, to escape imprisonment and possible death by the communists who had taken over Hungary. Cornish's papers contained correspondence with them and many other liberal religious leaders across Europe who were still at risk of arrest, imprisonment, and worse. It is likely that Cornish feared his correspondence with the Unitarians in occupied areas could bring harm to them or to the American Unitarian Association.

At the Harvard Divinity School library, Alan Seaburg knew I needed to learn about Louis Cornish because Cornish had helped found the 1920s sister church program. But leading the commissions to Transylvania and working with Gabriel Csiki to establish the sister church connections was only one of Cornish's efforts to protect and defend the rights of oppressed religious minorities. Throughout the fear-filled Depression years when it must have been tempting to focus entirely on home concerns, Cornish did not lose his conviction that, in hard times, reaching out beyond our own walls and shores is the best way to overcome economic and psychological depression. He continued to urge Unitarians to heed the call of global connections, which he believed could revitalize any institution. At the very end of his life, Cornish fostered connections with Universalists in the Philippines and visited there. He then began writing a book about them, *Philippines Calling*, which Frances Cornish completed after his death.

Though nearly a century has passed, Transylvanian Unitarians deeply appreciate the efforts of North American and British Unitarians, and particularly of Cornish, to stir the Western Allies to enforce the Trianon Treaty provisions and force sanctions on the Romanian government, even though they were not successful. Cornish continued to plead the Transylvanians' cause by including their plight in his 1937 book, *Work and Dreams and the Wide Horizon*, which outlines his presidency of the American Unitarian Association, and more extensively in his re-examination of their situation in his 1947 book, *Transylvania: The Land beyond the Forest*.

I think it is significant that, following the unsuccessful efforts by the commission reports to stop Romanian abuse of minority rights, contact between Transylvania and North America rapidly declined. Although many of the initial sister church connections did last longer than their original commitment of three years, in the end all but two of the US congregations failed to heed Cornish's energetic assertion that the Association had a duty to provide continued support to the Transylvanians until the day their conditions improved and the Romanians adopted "equality for all" as its minority policy. In her letters written from Transylvania between 1929 and 1936, Christine Frederiksen (later Morgan) makes no mention at all of the sister church program or Mészkő's (Cheia's) relationship with the Unitarians in Lynn,

Massachusetts. Our current partnership movement can learn from this warning not to let our connections and commitments die in the backlash of any major disappointment, setback, or failure.

Star Island is named for its supposed star-like shape, though it is not very star-shaped at all. An Isles of Shoals historian told me, "Sailors named the Island. They may actually have thought it was star-shaped, but then, we have ample evidence that they drank a *lot*." For Cornish, the name meant not a shape, but a heavenly body. Cornish was fascinated by lights shining in the dark. He was a serious astronomer who spent many nights on the Island studying the stars. He was determined to ground his work and his values in a cosmic perspective, "without", as he said, "making the mistake of supposing my life had cosmic importance."[79]

Cornish and his wife, Frances, were in the Swiss Alps on Switzerland's 642nd national liberty day. He wrote this description of the celebration:

The cold darkness had fully come. Across the deep valley we spotted the distant twinkling light of the first bonfire. Soon flames appeared on the projecting shoulder of an adjoining mountainside. Then a third, and fourth, and fifth fire was kindled, here, and there, and far away yonder. The scene was a strange blending of the might of nature, with the power of human faith. Against the dark night, the stars themselves seemed to miraculously descend and linger on the Alpine mountainsides. Some celestial impulse had touched all the people in the tiny towns far below us, and led them to climb the mountains to celebrate their emancipation from the fear of tyranny, by pulling the stars down to earth. These fires were lit to celebrate the casting out of spiritual fear. These were the lights of liberty.[80]

Lights shining in the dark provided a vivid symbol for Cornish's faith. And so did the sound of tolling bells. While serving as minister in Hingham, Cornish convinced the congregation and the town to create a memorial to the town's first settlers who had come to New England as immigrants from the town of Hingham in Norfolk, England. The memorial in Hingham is a unique peal of bells in a special tower on the Old Ship Church lawn. Each of its eleven bells is an exact replica of a bell in a church in Norfolk. Those unusual bells have tolled for Hingham's important civic occasions and church services for close to 100 years.

Louis Cornish understood the power of bells calling us to gather, whether to celebrate or to grieve. And he understood the power of light shining in the darkness, to ignite hope and strengthen faith. Cornish ended many worship services on Star Island by reminding everyone of how the sparkling light of the stars "can seal within us a unity of purpose and a sense of peace," and how well "the old melodies that leap forth from bells, sound undying faith over the Island, and strengthen the souls of the listeners."[81]

In 1999, when the Unitarian Universalist Partner Church Council decided to initiate an annual award for individuals who had made outstanding contributions to global church partnership, the Council's executive committee chose to name it the Louis C. Cornish Living the Mission Award. The first of these awards honored Dr. Judit Gellérd's commitment and her work for Transylvanian Unitarianism and our partnerships.[82]

An Early East–West Partnership:
Christine Frederiksen (1903–1996)
and Ferenc Balázs (1901–1937)

Before József visited my seminary in Berkeley in 1993 he already knew
of it as the graduate school where Ferenc Balázs had studied from 1926
to 1928. Ferenc was the first of many Transylvanians to study at Starr
King and Meadville-Lombard, the two Unitarian Universalist seminaries
in North America. Today, Transylvanian ministers studying at Starr
King are "Balázs Scholars."[83] *When Ferenc Balázs completed two*
years of graduate work as a scholarship student at Oxford University's
Manchester College in England, he was invited by Starr King's
president, Earl Morse Wilbur, to study in Berkeley for two more years.
Although he then received a third offer of further academic work, at
Harvard University, he followed his Bishop's urging to return home to
Transylvania, stopping along the way to study first-hand the structure
and economics of village life in Japan, China, and India. Ferenc worked
in remarkable ways as a Transylvanian minister and scholar alongside
his American wife, Christine Frederiksen, until he died in 1937.[84]

József had read all of Ferenc Balázs' published books and poems.
But he knew little about his American wife. When I learned József was
going to give a talk about Ferenc, I sent him a copy of Christine's
book, Alabaster Village, *and filled him in on what I had learned about*
her life before she moved to Transylvania. He said, "Think of what
they went through together! Their marriage must have been a true
East–West partnership."

I wish I had learned from Christine before she died how well her
family's interest in the Danish co-operative experience translated into
Transylvania village life because my father also worked in a co-
operative study program. And I would have loved to hear more about
her life after her Transylvanian husband died—how she was, or was
not, able to continue on her own their commitments and dreams in the
United States. Soon I hope to meet in person her daughter, Enikö, and
perhaps learn some of the answers. My American–Australian marriage
feels more North–South than East–West, but it has made me especially
interested in the marriages between Transylvanians and North Americans.
Perhaps the people in these American–Transylvanian marriages are

especially able to understand and explain the differences and similarities between the lives and faith of Transylvanian Unitarians and North American Unitarian Universalists. What does it take for these East–West marriages to last—to not only survive, but thrive?

The flyer on the teachers' college bulletin board read, "You are welcome at our consciousness raising group for women seeking to live in their own way, by their own values." It was 1969 in New York City's Greenwich Village. I became a member of that group, and everything changed.

Ever since I entered that braver new world of living in my own way, by my own values, I have had some kind of women's group to aid my learning and my resolve—self-help and 12-Step groups, "Cakes for the Queen of Heaven" classes at church, quilters' sewing bees, and women ministers' and writers' support groups. I am following in my paternal grandmother's footsteps. For more than eighty years she met monthly with the same study group. In that New York City women's group, we saw that it was possible to learn from each other's successes and painful mistakes, and we learned to stand alongside each other in ways that mattered and lasted. My experiences in such groups have made me an ardent advocate of sharing our hard-won wisdom—a sure means of harm-reduction.

At one of our meetings, the women in my Stockholm writers' group stumbled onto something important that we shared—most of our mothers had lived lives built on unfulfilled dreams. Out of their thwarted hopes and aborted dreams, our mothers developed fierce expectations that they projected strongly onto us, their daughters. Every one of us at the meeting said that in essential ways we were now living out our mother's dreams. None of us regretted or resented it, not for an instant.

Our writers' group gathered every Friday for lunch at a café in the heart of Stockholm, and during one lunch we took time to salute our mothers, the women who sent us out into the world well-armed with courage and faith and hope. Our mothers' lives were interrupted and transformed by lack of education or limited career opportunities, by war or prejudice, by lack of travel and adventure, by poverty or financial insecurity, by chronic illness or depression, by addiction or abuse, or sometimes, by lack of love. They devoted their lives to making sure their daughters had the things they had longed for but been denied. They especially planted in us a hunger for learning and a readiness to risk living as a stranger in strange lands.

Many in our writers' group had moved across the world for love. The same is true of Christine Frederiksen, a young, idealistic Danish-American who dared to live an adventurous life rooted in her dreams, commitments, and passions. In 1929 Christine spent seven months journeying alone halfway around the world to join her life together with that of Ferenc Balázs, a young Transylvanian minister. She went to Transylvania—then recently split off from Hungary—because she was a young woman deeply in love and deeply committed to reform movements. Eight years later she returned to California a widow, chronically ill, fearful for her fatherless daughter, and struggling not to be bitter. But Christine recovered her health and her spirit, and dived again into living her principles, following her passions, and carrying out her dreams and commitments. She raised two daughters. She had productive, exciting careers. She helped found two Unitarian congregations. She loved again. I went to North Carolina with the hope of meeting with Christine but I had waited too long to make this visit. She was in a rehabilitation center learning to cope with the stroke that eventually ended her active life. We never did meet, and I have always wondered what kind of remarkable mother she must have had.

There is a description of Christine's family in *Poems by Christine: Spring 1994*, which was kindly given to me by her widower, Ernest Morgan. I have expanded it with information gleaned from Christine's book, *Alabaster Village*. Ernest's father, Arthur, was a Unitarian and for many years the president of Antioch College, where Christine had been a student for two years. Arthur Morgan, and his wife, Lucy, were loyal and enthusiastic supporters of Christine and Ferenc during their eight years together in Transylvania.

Christine was born in Chicago in 1903 and grew up an only child and member of the Unitarian Church in Minneapolis, Minnesota. Her father, Ditlev Frederiksen, was a grandson of Bishop Monrad who, as Prime Minister of Denmark, was largely responsible for making that country a constitutional monarchy. Christine's New England mother, Helen Brown Frederiksen, was a talented painter who had studied with Whistler and others in Paris and Italy. She painted French villages and folk peasant pottery. Because of a twenty-year struggle with cancer, Helen was an invalid much of her adult life and died in 1927. Christine had a major hand in caring for her. Christine felt her mother's youngest sister, Isabel, was her second mother.

Helen Frederiksen read an article by Arthur Morgan in *The Atlantic* magazine, 'What is Education For?' and on the strength of its wisdom sent Christine to Antioch College in Ohio. In *Alabaster Village* Christine explains that Antioch's work-study program sounded to her mother like both Jane Addams' settlement houses and the Danish folk schools that her parents greatly admired. After two happy years at Antioch, Christine ran out of money and went to live with her Aunt Isobel in California, where she finished her degree in social science at the University of California at Berkeley.

At a gathering of campus Unitarians, Christine met and eventually became engaged to Francis (Ferenc) Balázs, a young Hungarian Unitarian minister who planned to return to his native Transylvania and revitalize village life there. He left for home via Japan where he visited the Kagawa area, and India where he spent some time with Tagore and Gandhi. It was two years before Christine and Ferenc were reunited. First she had to recover from tuberculosis, which she had contracted from Ferenc (who had suffered from tuberculosis since childhood), and make the difficult decision to leave her American life behind—all while grieving her mother's death. With the blessing of her family and Arthur and Lucy Morgan in Yellow Springs, Ohio, Christine followed Ferenc, taking her own seven-month journey across the Pacific, and then Asia, Russia, and Europe.[85]

It was a visionary love that flowered between Christine and Ferenc in Berkeley in 1926. In a 1927 poem, Ferenc wrote to Christine, "Have you ever thought, daughter of a rich, advanced country, of going as a pioneer among people that are intelligent, good-willed and art-loving, yet devoid of the advantages of civilization and of a higher culture?" To cast their lot with a village, he wrote, would be like "sowing themselves under the clod" and waiting to see if they could "come up, flower, and bear fruit."[86]

Christine described the early years of their relationship: "Our world began to come together. His Old World was becoming my New World. As for my undivided heart, it just wanted to sing and dance."[87] Ferenc believed that love could seize hold of a life and move it along a remarkable, unexpected way, that it could make the impossible possible.

Great loves have a way of turning out well, even against impossible odds. Never mind that Ferenc Balázs' home and commitments were in Romania on the opposite side of the world from Christine's home and family. Never mind that their being together meant Christine had to leave behind her family and friends, career and country to live as an outsider in a strange land. Never mind that since 1920 Transylvanian Hungarians had been struggling to survive as abused ethnic and religious minorities under an increasingly oppressive and scapegoating Romanian government.

In order to join Ferenc in Transylvania, Christine spent seven months, from January to July 1929, traveling alone to the other side of the world—by train from Berkeley to Vancouver, by tramp steamer across the Pacific to Japan, by ferry-boat to China, where she participated in a course in the historical Jesus. She crossed China, Mongolia, and Russia on the Trans-Siberian railway. She continued by train from Moscow to her father's family in Denmark, took another train into Romania, and finally arrived in Kolozsvár by horse-drawn carriage, where she found her cherished Feri in a hospital with another bout of tuberculosis. She broke into a smile as she reminded him that when he left the United States she too had been in bed recuperating from tuberculosis.

The village of Mészkő (Cheia) in the Aranyos (Golden) River valley where Christine and Ferenc lived for the next eight years was short on water, wood, and eggs, and long on gluey mud. In Mészkő there were 350 Protestant Hungarians and 500 Orthodox Romanians living in 300 brown-shingled houses huddled together on a steep alabaster outcrop, their lives punctuated by the beauty of the pinkish-blue alabaster and the ugliness of the sooty alabaster dust.

Never mind that the ideals Ferenc and Christine shared—uniting belief, knowledge, and action to better humankind—meant quite different things to a twenty-three year old Danish-American social scientist who treasured democracy and a twenty-five year old Transylvanian Hungarian minister and reformer living under a hostile government. Never mind that Christine's American Unitarianism and Ferenc's Transylvanian Unitarianism had developed in worlds and centuries apart. Never mind that both Ferenc and Christine were ill with tuberculosis, about which they knew too little, or that they disagreed sharply about how to protect their daughter from contagion. Never mind that the Great Depression crashed in on their lives and the lives of everyone they knew, so that neither of them, nor either of their families, ever had sufficient money to live on. Christine felt their day-to-day life was "in so many ways idyllic and thrilling," even if it was also "far too close to a nip-and-tuck for peace of mind."[88]

Ferenc was a stubborn and eccentric radical far ahead of his time. When he gave a talk about the idea of God as a spiritual being, he was accused of atheism and questioned by the Consistory of the Unitarian Church about the soundness of his faith. He had few friends and no real supporters among the Transylvanian Unitarian Church hierarchy. But all idealists believe love can fill loneliness with light. Ferenc and Christine were burning to help bring long-lasting economic renewal to 120 Transylvanian villages. They were eager to bring spiritual renewal to 120 Unitarian congregations. And remarkably, they expected to work for the renewal of their Orthodox Romanian villagers, right alongside their Protestant Hungarian congregation members.

At the beginning of their work in Mészkő, Ferenc wrote:

I stop here. Here I shall remain.
I shall put down my roots here
and not depart till my ideas have come
to blossom and the bearing of fruit;
the winged seed may indeed fly further.
Or, if my effort should fail, should decompose
and remain sterile, without life,
then over me shall pass history's plough,
turning up and later revealing
what is required.[89]

Their love gave them courage to overcome loneliness and poverty; to create a beautiful Arts and Crafts-style church in Mészkő and build a modern parsonage surrounded by a productive orchard; and courage to turn their home into a place of lively, honest, and unconventional discussions. Together they developed the finest elementary school in the district, as well as a regional folk school for older students. They created poultry and dairy co-operatives selling eggs, milk, cheese, and butter, which eventually brought a good profit to its many village members. (The co-operatives still operate in the Torda region today.) They dreamed up and brought into being a community garden, an acting troupe, a village lending library, a lecture and play series, a youth magazine, and a Transylvania-wide series of conferences for young people. Through it all Ferenc wrote highly acclaimed books about their work and lives, commitments and faith. They had the courage to move through and beyond a devastating miscarriage and give birth to their daughter Enikö, to raise her there, in the lovely parsonage, in the orchard, in the church.

All this work blossomed until Enikö was three and Christine took her to live with relatives in Denmark and, when there was an opportunity, sent her to her Aunt Isobel in Berkeley, while Ferenc journeyed to Torda and then to Debrecen in Hungary, hoping to be healed there. But he died instead, with Christine by his side.

One hundred of the villagers from Mészkő led twelve white oxen the 12 kilometers (5 miles) to Torda to bring Ferenc Balázs' body home. All the people of the region: Hungarians, Romanians—everyone—gathered along the roads, on the bridge, beside the churchyard, in the orchard, next to the graveyard perched on an alabaster outcrop high above the Golden River. They gathered to salute the remarkable accomplishments and commitments of this man with only a few friends, with steadfast colleagues across the ocean but not at home, with support from far outside his church but too little within it. His only family was an American wife he had loved so well for eleven years and a tiny daughter. To them he gave his heart. And to the thousands of people who lined the roads he gave his life.

The love that united Christine and Ferenc expanded and strengthened their shared beliefs and values into an outward-reaching, passionate faith, an unshakeable, visionary faith—faith that tuberculosis could be healed; faith that when the Great Depression ended they would receive life-sustaining support from North American Unitarians; faith that although they were acting ahead of their times, the times would eventually catch up and their solutions for the needs of Transylvanian villages and Transylvanian Unitarianism would eventually be judged wise, useful, and just. They had faith that their vision of helping their villagers with answers from the wider world would create new hope, new prosperity, and new partnerships for Transylvania. Through extremely hard times they never lost their faith that their work in the village and the example of their lives would live on in their writings, as well as in the work and faith of others who would reach out to form life-changing, life-affirming partnerships between Transylvanians and Unitarians in North America.

Near the end of his life Ferenc Balázs wrote "Vilagitas," which means "lighting up" for 1 November, All Souls' Day, when the dead are remembered by the lighting of candles whose flames shine out in the darkness from the tops of gravestones all over Europe:

> I want everyone to know
> that I did not die here.
> My village's moods and problems
> did not drown me.
> I sowed myself only into
> this new place.
> I hid myself all over here
> under the clod.
> Let me be seen thus:
> I will sprout in these fields
> in the spring.
> There will be blossoms here
> which will bear good fruit.[90]

Ferenc and Christine's work has borne healthy fruit; their faith in the future was well-founded. József told me, "Many Transylvanian ministers dream that their partner church connections will result in the kind of work Ferenc and Christine Balázs carried out in the 1930s in Mészkő." For North Americans, Christine Frederiksen's life story opens the exciting possibility of making an adventurous trip to Transylvania and makes clear the sacrifices demanded by a lifelong commitment to our partnership connections. For Transylvanians, Ferenc Balázs' life inspires courage to take brave steps into the future—to study abroad, to act on their learning, to write, to be forward thinking, to trust that history will vindicate their work and commitments. For Christine, life was always a dance. For Ferenc, it was always a planting.

May our partnership work always be both a dance and a planting.

My own credo/My testimony—Ferenc Balázs

I believe that this world is not a chain of casual things.

I believe that everything has its own purpose.

I believe that the world's nature—predestination, fate, decision, unchangeable will—is to form persons who, with great trust, can feel and know themselves to be integrated parts of the whole world, and act as such.

I believe that the world's purpose keeps working through many small purposes, through the fulfillment of human will, and that each generation and each individual has the task of forging one of the links in the chain.

I believe in this task, in my separate small purpose. First of all, I want to clean and bring to perfection my own personality, this one dewdrop that mirrors the world. I do not repress any expression of my multifaceted personality. I live for my body as much as I live for my soul, but I keep trying to harmonize each of my wishes, instincts, and convictions with the highest and most valuable of the characteristics I have developed to this point. And I aim to build the connections of love with others among my brothers and sisters in our community. I have a strong wish to keep peace among us and to build an association for achieving our mutual interests with those with whom I am in close, loving connection.

I believe that if I can fulfill my small purpose in this short life of mine, I will achieve something valuable in itself, and not even death can diminish its meaning.

I believe in human dignity—and when it identifies itself with the world purpose, I believe in the freedom of will.

I believe that the will of my true self is the will that achieves expression in the world purpose, and if I follow the world purpose, I only follow my own will.

And I believe in God: this world is beautiful, great, and wonderful with a happy fate. It is amazing and mysterious, and when I am filled with it, overwhelmed with its infinity, its intimacy raises me, its joy makes me rejoice—then what springs forth from me is: *God*.

Do not ask what this word really means for me.

It means what *swearing* means for those in pain, what *oh* means for those in surprise, what *laughter* means for the happy. It expresses everything because it says nothing. I do not argue, I do not state, I do not prove. I am not consistent, I give no reasons. I only sigh and cry and rejoice, and I am ecstatic: *God*.

Religion gives purpose to my life, science helps me reach it, art gives me the opportunity to take pleasure in it. And it is in this life of mine— becoming perfect through all these—where I expect God to reveal Himself.[91]

My Life Has Been a Field of Stars:
Gábor Kereki (1914–1995)

In Come as You Are *Peter Fleck wrote:*

> *Today few of us live and die where we were born. We do not grow old with those we grew up with, so there is no one to share memories with, no one to verify our stories, and our history becomes vague and unreal. The reality of the past depends upon witnesses, and those who must live having nobody left with whom they shared their early years, must feel they have become, in the Psalmist's words, "strangers in the earth."[92]*

I met Joan Kereki in May 1996 while I was living as an American immigrant in Canada. It was the first anniversary of the death of her remarkable husband, Gábor Kereki. The more I learned about Gábor, the more he became my inspiration for how to become an immigrant minister in a way that turns being a "stranger in the earth" into a help instead of a hindrance, a way that celebrates the best of your past alongside your new cultures and traditions. Learning about Kereki's life also sparked my interest in all the Hungarian Unitarian congregations and their partnerships. My interest came full-circle when I walked into József's study in Budapest and found a photograph of Gábor Kereki hanging above his desk.

No immigrants or refugees will thrive—in fact they may not survive—without sympathetic help from citizens of their adopted country, the people who take them in."[93] This was the conviction of Gábor Kereki—who served from 1938–96 as first a Transylvanian Hungarian, and then a British Unitarian minister, and who, despite the dangers, enabled many to escape first from the Nazis and then the communist regimes. Another of Kereki's lifelong commitments was the welfare of children, which he expressed in this fragment of his writings:

I have seen the longest of winters.
I have seen compassion conquer despair.
I have seen that hope is a flame that cannot be extinguished.
Now we must look to our children.[94]

Gábor Kereki was eight years old before he met his father. When Gábor's father was called up to fight in the Hungarian army in 1914, his pregnant mother returned to Transylvania to live with her parents in the town of Volkán (Vulcan). Shortly before Gábor was born, his father was captured and imprisoned in a Russian prisoner of war camp. His father escaped rather miraculously, but to Asia, rather than to Western Europe. In some parts of Siberia people did not know that Russia was at war, and he learned to encourage people's assumption that he was simply a hungry traveler. After many months and many adventures he reached Japan. It took six more years and the help of numerous compassionate strangers for him to make his way back to Hungary and meet for the first time his eight year old son, Gábor.

Gábor said the many people who helped his father escape and make it safely home motivated his own lifelong efforts to help escaping asylum seekers and refugees. Perhaps it was inevitable that Gábor would develop great sympathy for the needs and hopes of Transylvanian immigrants who had fled Romania to build a new life in Hungary, as his own parents had chosen to do.

From 1937–39 Gábor, a recent Kolozsvár seminary graduate, served the two hundred families of an unusual Unitarian congregation in northeast Hungary. In 1936 the Kocsord congregation left the Calvinist Hungarian Reformed church and declared themselves to be a Unitarian congregation because they wanted to choose their own minister, which the Unitarians would give them the freedom (and responsibility) to do. Gábor was delighted to take up this opportunity to serve this unusual and unexpected spread of Unitarianism in northeast Hungary. For two years he oversaw the building—by the members themselves—of a lovely church and parsonage designed for them by Szente László, a Unitarian from Sepsiszentgyörgy (Sfântu Gheorghe), in the architectural style of the traditional Protestant churches of Transylvania. Today, the church is a Hungarian National Heritage listed building, and thousands come every year to view its painted ceiling. The first funds the congregation raised were used to buy the bell that hangs on a unique carved wooden frame in the front garden of the church. The Kocsord church buildings have changed very little from that day to this and, following Gábor Kereki's example, it has become a tradition for every minister to make their own handcrafted contribution to the interior of the sanctuary.

Gábor told his wife, Joan, about decorating the ceiling:

> Once our new church had walls and a roof, I built a scaffold and, just like Michelangelo, I lay high up there on my back, hour after hour, painting the entire ceiling with 106 of the traditional folk-style flower designs that you find in some of the older Transylvanian Unitarian village churches. It was not until the ceiling was nearly finished that it occurred to me I could first paint the square meter panels down on the ground, and then hang them up in the heavenly space above the scaffolding. We called our ceiling *the kingdom of God* or *our field of stars*.

In the fall of 1931 Ferenc Balázs was doing the same thing in Romania. In *Alabaster Village*, his wife, Christine, describes their rescue and refurbishment of the Mészkő church:

> Feri spent almost all his waking hours for three months directing the project and doing much of the labor. It gave me shivers to see him painting the many-colored designs on the ceiling with only a narrow, shaking plank between himself and destruction.[95]

The Nazis occupied Austria in 1938 and were Hungary's allies in World War II. After the Nazis were defeated, the communists consolidated their power until, by 1949, Hungary was a de facto part of the Soviet Bloc. Early in World War II, Gábor left Kocsord to serve the Unitarians in Budapest as a religious education minister for the entire area. Throughout the war and after, he worked with the Hungarian Resistance, helping people of all faiths, including Unitarians and many Jews, escape the Nazi occupation. A number of these escapees made their way to England, where some became members of Unitarian congregations. During these same years officials of every denomination, including the Hungarian Unitarians, were forced to co-operate with the Nazis and later with the occupying communists. Gábor's secret work with the Resistance, conducted at times from an office one floor above the Bishop's, was extremely risky, and his freedom and his life hung in the balance.

Meanwhile Gábor established a religious education program for

Unitarian children and youth that all Hungarian ministers could use, laying the foundation for Unitarian religious education work in Hungary today. He held special confirmation classes for the many uprooted Unitarian families who spent the war years in Budapest. Gábor established significant outreach to Hungarian cultural leaders of all faiths by serving as president of the influential cultural association named for Gábor Bethlen (a 1600s Protestant leader and intellectual).

Then, in the summer of 1947, Gábor became a political refugee himself when he was unexpectedly forced to live the second half of his life in a foreign country, England. As the Soviet communist regime began taking over the Hungarian government, Soviet soldiers moved to root out and eliminate any resisting Hungarians.[96] The Russians established their first police headquarters in Debrecen, close to Kocsord. They searched the minister's office in Kocsord and found papers they claimed implicated Gábor in working with the Resistance. The Kocsord Unitarians managed to send a warning to Gábor in Budapest.

With the combined help of several groups, including the Hungarian Resistance, the Unitarian Service Committee, and the British Unitarians, Gábor escaped from Hungary, flying via Prague and Amsterdam to England. A number of British Unitarian ministers supported Gábor while he made the difficult transition from being a Hungarian Unitarian minister to becoming a British one. He was especially helped by George James Grieve, minister of the Highgate congregation in Hampstead, England, who had met Gábor in Budapest while working for the Unitarian Service Committee.[97]

Gábor's first steps in England included two years of further theological study, improving his command of English and understanding of British Unitarianism at Oxford University's Manchester College. From then on he was recognized as a precise thinker with a fine command of English. His first ministry in England was for twelve years in Kent at Tenterden, where he established a large church school and coached many of its members to play competition level table tennis, and Northiam, where he was particularly pleased to conduct many christenings. As it had been in Hungary, religious education was the foundation of Gábor's work in England. He organized church school teachers' summer conferences and helped produce two hymnals. From 1961–84 Gábor served the Unitarians in Croydon, where, fueled by his belief in a united

Europe, his ministry extended beyond his congregation to founding and chairing the local Amnesty International branch and to working with the United Nations Association.

Gábor's fellow Unitarians provided the connections that made it possible for him to thrive in England. And he, in turn, made a home for his ward, the ten year old granddaughter of Elek Kiss (Bishop of the Transylvanian Unitarians from 1946–71). Gábor helped many refugees who sought asylum in Britain, including Asian boat people resettling from Hong Kong. Since he was certain that the Hungarian communists were still eager to imprison him, Gábor visited his home country again only after 1989. He returned to deliver the sermon at the Budapest congregation's May 1990 centenary celebrations. It was attended by overwhelming numbers of people, including the president of Hungary, Árpád Gánz, and representatives of many faiths. Following that visit, it was with great joy that Gábor was able to live in Budapest for several months each year. He delighted in leading a worship service in Kocsord during each of his visits.

Speaking at his memorial services, a close colleague said:

> Gábor Kereki stood out among British Unitarians as a courageous liberal, a democratic thinker, a faithful trustee, and a gentle, kind activist. He was a wonderful chairperson; people softened and relaxed when he spoke, and consensus became possible. He was a garden maker and a flower arranger who brought out beauty in every-thing he touched, just as he had done in the church he helped build in Kocsord. He did everything as perfectly as he could—whether it was building a church, arranging flowers, cooking a meal, or being there for someone. He never let anyone down. People were his absorbing interest, and they knew instinctively that they could trust him—animals and children knew it, strangers and enemies knew it.[98]

North American Unitarian Universalists are more aware of the work of Lotta Hitchmanova and the Unitarian Service Committee in Europe than they are of Gábor's courageous work with refugees and asylum seekers. But among the Kocsord, Budapest, and British Unitarians, Gábor Kereki is well remembered as a hero, an intellectual leader, and a skillful and beloved minister with great moral integrity.

The Transylvanian and Unitarian diasporas in Hungary

In 1989, there were 68,500 Unitarians in Transylvania. In the 2005 census there were 58,000. The number of Unitarians in Hungary is less clear. In the most recent Hungarian census, 6400 respondents indicated, "I am Unitarian," but many Unitarians have said that they answered "None" to protest having to officially report their religious affiliation in a census. A Hungarian Unitarian minister told me:

In the last 160 years, 200,000 Hungarian Transylvanians have left the Transylvania area—most in waves following the political upheavals of 1848, 1920, 1948, and 1989–90. Sharing language, history, ethnicity, and culture, many Hungarian Transylvanians have moved to Hungary, so that today almost every Hungarian-Romanian living in Transylvania has family members who now live in Hungary. To their surprise, these Székelys find they are not welcomed as a special Hungarian, but are treated like any other immigrant by the government and people of Hungary. On the other hand, most Hungarians are proud to claim relatives still living in Transylvania.

We know 10,000 Unitarians left Transylvania for Hungary in 1989, and about 1000 of these immediately went on to other countries. But we do not know how many were already here from the earlier waves. We usually say there are 15,000 to 17,000 Unitarians who were originally born Hungarian-Transylvanians now living in Hungary, where they are known as "Transylvanian-Hungarians."

Many of them left Transylvania more through force than choice, fleeing the oppression and economic ruin of Ceauşescu's Romania.

In Romania, Transylvanians do not think of themselves as foreigners but as the original settlers. The irony is that the Romanians who live in Transylvania see the Hungarians as foreigners and therefore immigrants, while the Hungarians see the Romanians as the immigrants who are occupying their ancient land.

Like other emigrants, Transylvanians who have left their homeland to live in new countries have complicated and ambivalent feelings about it. One legacy of the Romanian citizenship forced upon Transylvanians by the Trianon Treaty (including the forced learning of a new language and the pressure to adopt a new culture) has been a fierce loyalty to preserving the lands of their ancestors. If Transylvanians sometimes hate living in Romania, they love living in Transylvania, while Transylvanians who have moved to Hungary make frequent visits back to their original towns or villages and typically send their children and grandchildren back to spend any long vacation as a "Székelyföld holiday" in their family's ancestral land.[99]

Part 6

In Homoródszentmárton, 1993

Like so many other Unitarian pilgrims, I had no sooner left Homoród-
szentmárton in 1990 than I began making plans to return. I was away
from the village for only a few hours when many questions occurred
to me, and back home everyone raised other questions I could not
answer. But a further trip was not possible during the first year of our
partnership when József was studying at the Unitarian seminary in
England, and the next year our energy went into raising funds to help
the Homoródszentmárton church buy a tractor and hosting József's
first visit to Northern California.

It was not until the 1993 Easter week that I returned. It rained and
rained, the sun never appeared, and it was shockingly cold. But none
of that mattered. We were too busy with the complicated logistics of
paying for the tractor we were buying and organizing to have it
delivered as the final part of the Easter service.[100] We also celebrated
József's leaping the final hurdles for wresting his first driver's licence
out of the county bureaucracy. And all week, as one always does in
the back of beyond, we personally delivered messages and packages I
was carrying for the other North American partners of neighboring
Homoród River valley churches.[101] This time I brought my black robe.

A Transylvanian Village Wedding

On the Saturday before Easter the grandson of a Homoródszentmárton Unitarian and his bride were married in the church. The
young couple, Sándor Molnár and Enikö Lidia Balázsi, lived in a distant
city. Enikö's family was not Unitarian, but the couple wanted to have a
traditional village wedding with the customary all-night party and
breakfast afterwards. József asked me to help conduct the ceremony, and
Rózsika Nagy, the church sexton, invited me to join her in ringing the
church bells to signal the start of the wedding service.

Rózsika and I started ringing the bells as soon as one of the younger
children dashed up to the door of the bell tower to tell us the wedding
procession had started out from the grandmother's house on the other
side of the village. My bell rope was as wide as my arm and stretched far
up, higher than three stories. You grabbed the upper knot and pulled
strongly down, then let the rope slide back up through your hands to a
lower knot. If you made the mistake of holding onto the wrong knot, the
upswing would lift you right up off the ground. When there are two bells
and two ringers, it is fairly easy to keep a steady rhythm, but if there is
only one ringer for the two different sized bells (Rózsika's usual
circumstance), it takes much more skill. My arm muscles protested as we
worked up a steady rhythm, but it was cold inside the thick-walled
tower, and I was glad for the heat created by our hard work.

Earlier, guests and friends had gathered outside the bride's house for
the *busulni* (the grieving). Ruth Gibson told me about a village wedding
she attended in Nagyajta (Alta Mare) whose partner church is First
Unitarian Society in Madison:

> Supposedly, the bride is inside, weeping because she has to leave her
> childhood home. The groomsmen stand outside the door making
> jokes, laughing, and handing out pint bottles of *pálinka* (plum
> brandy) to all the men. If you are a female minister in the crowd, they
> aren't at all sure what to do with you at this point—being a woman,
> you don't get a bottle, but since you are a minister, it would be an
> insult not to give you one. Eventually, the best man ceremonially
> produces his big carved stick with a knob on one end and decorated
> with flowers and ribbons. He knocks on the door with his stick and
> makes a speech or recites a traditional poem (loud enough for the

women inside to hear) about how fine a guy the groom is and how the bride should come out now, because the groom has been waiting long enough.

Meanwhile, each of the village children has been busy decorating a bucket of beautiful flowers with ribbons and cards wishing the bride and groom happiness. They spread their buckets out in the middle of the road along the way between the bride's house and the church. At last the bride does come out, and the wedding procession begins. She is led by the best man with his big stick and surrounded by her attendants and family. Next comes the groom with his attendants and family. And then the other guests and well wishers follow, all on foot—though sometimes the groom and his groomsmen are on horseback, adding both drama and additional obstacles.

As the colorful procession passes each child's flower bucket, they drop coins into it. Then the child quickly snatches up his or her bucket and runs ahead to set it out again at the head of the procession. The money is not a gift for the bride and groom, but for the children who use it to buy candy and snacks which they enjoy during the all-night party that follows the ceremony. The storekeeper is busy that night!

Through the open door of the bell tower, Rózsika and I spotted about a dozen children running up to place their flower buckets ahead of the procession for the last time. Surrounded by her family and the two couples who were the witnesses, the bride appeared, carefully holding the long skirt of her beautiful white dress above the muddy road. She let it down again as she mounted the dry stairs and well-swept path that led through the carved wooden gate in the ancient wall, over the grass cut just for her, past the bell-tower, and on up into the church.

They didn't use the painted hand-carved wedding chairs you find in Hungarian ethnographic museums and some Transylvanian churches. Ruth explained:

The upright backs of these special chairs are carved with an exaggerated curve. When you set the two chairs side-by-side so their backs fit snugly together, it indicates that the two families are in agreement about this union. But if the chairs are set so their backs curve away from each other, it means the families disapprove of the marriage. Some couples are given a pair of these chairs as a wedding present, and in that case, when you come home and see the chairs snugly curving together, then all is well between you and your spouse. But if the chairs have been moved so their backs curve away from each other, you can see that you have a problem.

Though the sun was streaming in brightly, the church was very cold. I was grateful for the extra layer my robe provided. I found it strange that only ten people—the couple's parents, the four close friends who were serving as witnesses, and the bride and groom—came into the church for the wedding service. The children who had been moving their flower buckets along Homoródszentmárton's main road and the other people walking in the procession all went home. Even the groom's Unitarian grandmother stayed home, saying, "I'm in charge of cooking the wedding feast." Wearing my formal black robe, I contributed my part—the passage about love from Corinthians I 13, with József translating my English words into Hungarian. The service consisted of an invocation, a psalm, a reading from the Bible (my part), József's homily based on one of the verses from Corinthians, the exchange of vows, the exchange of rings, the Lord's Prayer, a blessing, and congratulations.

Since the couple had no connection to our partner church efforts, I did not volunteer to lead the Lord's Prayer in Hungarian, although I had been practicing it. Mária told me later that during the congratulations, the minister has the right—which József did not exercise—to kiss the bride on first one cheek and then the other at the end of the service. But it is not proper for the couple to kiss each other until they are outside the church. For the entire service we all stood in a close circle around the beautifully carved central table that is used for serving communion four times a year.

It was clear the couple felt it was rather special to have a North American minister helping with their wedding service. The bride said to me in halting English that she was glad to meet a woman minister, and József told me they believed my presence at their service meant theirs would be a marriage "of the new time."

It *was* all quite special, except for one thing. All through the service the bride looked very solemn, and I began to fear she was going to burst into tears. It seemed a shame that she wasn't enjoying her own wedding service. So every time she looked up, I would catch her eye and smile encouragingly. But she just frowned stiffly and looked back down at the floor. She never did smile back, not even once.

After the service we moved to the well-heated religious education room to record the marriage in the official parish register and toast the couple and their marriage with warming *pálinka*, followed, unusually, with the sparkling California wine I had brought from home. When they said they had seen Formula One racing drivers on television spraying Champagne over everyone, I thought I had better declare this bottle was exclusively for drinking. Everyone was smiling radiantly, laughing, and clearly feeling wonderful. I mentioned to József that the bride had certainly cheered up, so I guessed I could stop worrying that she was unhappy about getting married. "Whatever do you mean?" he asked, and I reminded him that the bride had not smiled at all during the church service.

"But, Gretchen!" József exclaimed, amazed that I did not already know, "We do not smile in church." As my grandmother would have said, you could have knocked me over with a feather. I had participated in quite a few Transylvanian Unitarian church services without understanding that. "What happens in church must be important, nothing you would take lightly," József explained, "so we don't laugh about it. It's all right to cry during a church service, but not to smile, and never to laugh."

That lovely young bride must have been in agony! Like me, she was "from away" and had never attended a village church service. But she had been thoroughly warned that in village churches it was the height of rudeness to laugh, and best not to smile. She succeeded in her respectful seriousness, even though I was doing my ignorant best to make it impossible for her. I asked József to explain my misunderstanding of her solemn face and my misguided attempts to get her to smile, and everyone agreed the joke was on me.

That wedding made me realize that Transylvanians who attend our North American worship services and find us making jokes and laughing together—or even bursting into spontaneous applause if we are especially delighted—cannot help but feel that we are not serious about our religion. So now, when I am asked to speak or preach in Transylvania or Hungary, I no longer include amusing stories or remarks.

The twentieth-century Protestant theologian Reinhold Niebuhr would agree with the Transylvanians. As Nancy Crumbine points out in *Humility, Anger, and Grace*, Niebuhr believed laughter occupies the space between faith and despair:

> We preserve our sanity by laughing at life's surface absurdities, but the laughter turns to bitterness and derision if directed toward the deeper irrationalities of evil and death. That is why there is laughter in the vestibule of the temple, the echo of laughter in the temple itself, but only faith and prayer, and no laughter, in the holy of holies.[102]

At first I thought it was out of balance to be free to cry but forbidden to laugh in church—but perhaps not. Perhaps the Transylvanians are on to something that is quite important when they treat everything that happens in a church service as taking place "in the holy of holies." Several times I have entered a Transylvanian church on a weekday and experienced a remarkably deep sense of sanctuary, rest, and peace. When I mused about this with a Transylvanian friend, she said, "Well, a church should be the best place to find God." Perhaps it should be, but I don't usually go into church expecting to find God—and that is one difference between me and Transylvanain Unitarians. Another is that I will always be touched, and glad, when people smile and laugh during our North American church services—for surely God is with us in our laughter.

Sounding Our Faith

As the members of the Homoródszentmárton congregation filed past József and me outside the church at the end of my first worship service in Transylvania in 1990, several members of the Homoródszentmárton church asked if I had news of their Unitarian friends in Montclair, New Jersey. I assumed that a Homoródszentmárton family must have emigrated to New Jersey, but they said, "No, we're talking about our sister church." "What do you mean?" I objected. "Isn't our church in San Jose paired with you?" They quickly replied, "Of course, you are. You're our *new* sister church. But our *first* sister church is Montclair." Could they really mean that at some time in the past they had had another sister church? How could that be?

József dug out of the church papers an elegantly typeset order of service for a 1928 worship service in New Jersey that was held to celebrate Montclair's eighth year of being Homoródszentmárton's sister church and its having replaced the bell that was confiscated by the military during World War I. I wondered if visitors from Montclair had ever actually come to Homoródszentmárton, and if they had been invited to ring "the Montclair bell" during their visit. Or was their entire sister church connection conducted with no face-to-face meetings? Perhaps the Transylvanians had held a simultaneous service on that same day in 1928 to celebrate their new bell.

Three weeks later at the 1990 General Assembly, I found the Montclair delegates and learned they were no longer aware of their 1920s sister church connection with Homoródszentmárton. But the Transylvanian Unitarians had not forgotten. In Homoródszentmárton, "the Montclair bell" rings every morning, noon, and evening to announce the time, especially for those working in the fields and for children playing in the schoolyard. With these powerful, booming, daily reminders, of course the Transylvanians still remember and treasure their Montclair sister church.

A highlight of my 1993 visit to Homoródszentmárton was being invited by Rózsika Nagy to help her ring the church bells for the wedding service on Saturday. As those bone-shaking vibrations shook through me, it came to me that I was committing myself to join in lifelong solidarity with these remarkable Transylvanian Unitarians. And I thought how thrilling it would be to make the dangerous climb to the top of Homoródszentmárton's bell tower, which is several stories high.

Transylvanian villages depend upon their church bells for much more than tolling the hours and announcing church services. In *Prisoner of Liberté* Judit Gellérd writes:

> Transylvanians would not accept a church without bells....Their role was "to call the living, to bury the dead, and to toll the alarm in times of storm, flood, fire, and invasion of enemies." When the regular bells rang, men took off their hats and rested for a moment in prayer. During thunderstorms and hail, bells "broke the storm clouds." Bells announced the sad news of a death in the village, and alarm bells called for community action. Transylvania's bells tolled the alarm during Mongol and Tartar invasions in the thirteenth century, Ottoman attacks in the fifteenth century, and Austrian tyranny in the seventeenth century. In those times the bells warned people to find refuge within the walls of the church, to store their food in the bastille. Tolling a bell was an art. It had its own language which everyone understood.[103]

Judit told me about a partner church ritual she initiated that involves ringing bells. On a pre-arranged Sunday, both of the paired congregations hold a special service. (Often this will be on the third Sunday in March, which has been designated Partner Church Sunday in Transylvania and North America, or near 15 November, which commemorates Ferenc Dávid's death.) The two services are scheduled so that, despite the time zone difference, they can begin at the same moment with both congregations simultaneously ringing their bells. A problem may arise because, while every Transylvanian church has at least one bell, many North American congregations do not. One North American congregation overcame this problem by bringing a phone into the sanctuary and dialing their partner church minister in Transylvania at the start of the service. As they had prearranged, he answered the parsonage phone and held the receiver out the window, allowing the church bells ringing in the Transylvanian village to toll through the speaker-phone inside the North American church.

When I told the Homoródszentmárton Unitarians that the San Jose church bell tower has never had a bell hanging in it, they felt quite sorry for us. They said perhaps one day they would be able to help us—as their sister church in Montclair had helped them in 1923—by giving us a bell. Then, in 1995, the San Jose church suffered a disastrous fire when melted fiberglass was applied to the hundred year old roof to stop a major leak. The Homoródszentmárton Unitarians sent their partner church a substantial contribution for the rebuilding fund. Their accompanying message said, "When you give us funds, you trust us to decide how it can best be used, and we know that now, in your hard times, you must decide how to use this aid we are sending. But we want to say to you, very seriously: *Every* church needs a bell."

During World War I, when church bells and organ pipes were confiscated by the foundries and the Romanian military to make cannon, the smallest bell was often left with the church because it was impossible to function as a church or have a village identity without a bell. It is still inconceivable to Transylvanians to gather for worship without being called together by a ringing bell. So when a church is being built, often the first step is installing a bell. Like Homoródszentmárton, many Transylvanian Unitarian churches have two bells. With two bells, it is possible to signal more complex messages: "This is a wedding" or, "This is the final call for the worship service."

On Sunday mornings, Rózsika rings both bells to call the Unitarians to worship. The bells ring for the entire time it takes the family that lives farthest away to walk to the church. Most parishioners leave home as soon as the bells begin to sound to gather in the sanctuary to sing hymns while the bells continue to ring—a choir practice of the whole. Experienced ministers, carrying their sermon notes and announcements, time their entrance through the central church door to the last of these "practice" hymns so they can warm up their voices. And then, with the minister standing in the center of the gathered congregation, the bells stop, leaving a deep, profound silence.

Six days a week Rózsika rings the larger of the two church bells at eight, noon, and four to mark the beginning and end of work in the fields. This is less often than the every half-hour of the church bells that rang in the Swedish Lutheran church tower next to our inner city flat when we lived in Stockholm. Church bells that have marked the hours of European life for centuries are under threat today, condemned as noise pollution. Italian Bishops, who have hired lawyers to defend their "right to ring," argue that the sound of the bells is an essential percussion to the rhythm of Italian life. Transylvanian villagers would agree. And after seven years of living my life punctuated by ringing bells, so do I.

A Chicago bells story

Rob Eller-Isaacs—now co-minister at Unity Church in St. Paul, Minnesota, partnered with Homoródszentpéter in Transylvania—knows the power of tolling bells. The day Martin Luther King, Jr. was assassinated, Rob wandered the streets of Chicago where he was a seminarian. He told me:

> I felt astonished, and then angry, as I passed many people who seemed to be blithely going about their daily routines. It appeared that, for them, nothing momentous had happened. Eventually, I came to my church, First Unitarian, and went inside the empty sanctuary to pray, or rant, or grieve. I passed through the empty, silent church to the bell room and began to toll the bell. Soon, another church member came, and we alternated pulling the rope down, and down, and down, for over an hour. Exhausted, we agreed the rhythmic booming of the tolling bell had given us comfort and went back out through the sanctuary. But now, every seat, and every step, and every aisle was filled with grieving people who spent the rest of the day singing, praying, testifying, and comforting one another.

They had answered the call of the tolling bell.

Why Would We Want to Be
a Partner Church?

During József's 1992 visit in San Jose we had focused on exploring our differences; during my second visit to Transylvania, in 1993, we found common ground. József had been invited by a congregation not far from Homoródszentmárton to spend an evening sharing photos and his impressions from his visit to Northern California, but they had delayed the gathering "until she comes again" so I could help answer their questions about Unitarian Universalism. Though the minister and congregation were not interested in having a North American partner, József and I decided there was no harm in our adding the possibility of partnership to the agenda. Perhaps what we said that evening might open the door for them to reconsider.

Darkness comes early to the Homoród Valley before the "spring forward" time change. József was driving, and my job was to warn him about any potholes I could see in the thick darkness. His daughters had convinced Mária to stay home and help them finish their beautifully dyed Easter eggs. József had been granted his driver's licence the day before, and this was the first time he had driven without a Romanian licence holder in the car, but I wasn't worried. He had been put through a long set of classes, rigorous testing, and then an additional six months of practice driving—a wise policy when an entire adult population of first-time car owners begins driving at the same time in a suddenly improving economy.

We were not invited into the parsonage. The Sunday school room where twenty church members and their minister were standing was dimly lit and unheated. No one removed their coats, and there were no refreshments. I felt daunted by so many tired, unsmiling faces. I wished I had brought something special from my country that we could all share. It was clear to me how much this congregation might benefit from partnership projects.

When József took his photographs in California, he had not had an evening like this in mind. His picture album was full of ocean waves, beaches, skyscrapers, and tropical plants. There were only two pictures of our church, and none of any congregation members. Why hadn't I brought the carefully prepared slide show about partnership that József and I had shown during his visit the year before to several neighboring California congregations? The Harghita District dean had a slide projector that we could have borrowed.

I didn't understand anything József said while the photo album was being passed around, but I suspected he was describing Californian freeways and the Pacific Ocean instead of the nine churches he had visited. Well, fair enough. At similar gatherings in California, I tended to say more about Transylvanian village life than about Transylvanian Unitarians' church governance or theology.

Then József asked if anyone had any questions for me. The minister and the mostly elderly men and women—all wearing many layers of black clothing topped by thick black coats with black neck scarves, hats, and gloves—stared curiously at me in a lengthening silence. I couldn't tell if they had dressed for the cold, dressed for guests, dressed to honor the dead, or all three at once. (Later, Mária told me that most were wearing black because when a family member dies, their relatives wear black for a year. I tried it myself after my mother's death and found it wonderfully comforting and helpful.)

I smiled encouragingly and bit my tongue to keep from leaping in with nervous talk to fill the awkward silence that followed József's question. After so many decades in which their safety often depended upon keeping silent, everyone in Transylvania was still stuttering haltingly into exercising their new freedom of speech. I knew it would be better for them to build a bridge to me if they were ever going to risk walking across it. And there was a chance, not a strong one, but still a chance, that reaching out to a visiting North American might be an early step toward their becoming a partnered congregation.

The minister eventually cleared his throat, and I realized everyone was waiting for their minister to ask the first question. I was delighted when he addressed me in unsure, but clear English. "Two questions," he said. "Why should any Transylvanian take the risk of becoming connected to foreigners and bringing them into our village? And why would Transylvanians like us matter to Americans?"

"Well..." I hesitated. Transylvanians were used to speakers able to impress, inspire, and win over their listeners by the force of their personality and the wisdom of their words. Clearly, József and I needed to answer the minister's concerns and relieve his anxiety. I took a deep breath, hoped for wisdom, and did my best to answer his second question—to explain how the partner church movement was becoming vitally important to Unitarian Universalists in North America through telling two stories of how being partners had changed our lives. Then I said a Transylvanian would know more about why a Transylvanian church would find it worth the risks to become connected to North Americans, and turned the uphill battle over to József.

At the end of the meeting, the minister's resistant body language made it clear he remained unconvinced. I doubted if anyone in the bare, cold room had been inspired to engage in global connection, and I doubted we had convinced them there would be any benefit in their becoming a partner church. As József drove back to the Homoródszentmárton parsonage, I was sure that we had blown this opportunity, and that we would eventually have to chalk it up as a sad example of the way we often stumbled in those early partner church years.

But I was wrong. The small, skeptical congregation József and I visited that evening has become an active partner church. The partnership came about because the neighboring minister was slowly convinced of its value by Donald Harrington—the North American minister who had married a Transylvanian and retired in nearby Jánosfalva. Once the Transylvanian Unitarian church organized its own Partner Church Council made up of elected district networkers, the networker for the Harghita district also worked to make the benefits and responsibilities of partnership attractive and unthreatening to the minister and congregation members.

The connection and projects of this small congregation's partnership may not be as visible or as lauded as those of partnerships that are older or larger, but if partnership success is measured in depth of changed attitudes and width of effort made to stretch across differences, that small Transylvanian congregation, its minister, and their North American partner have certainly done wonderful work.

Keeping Watch

At the end of my first visit, the elders in Homoródszentmárton pressed me to come back soon. "Now that you've spent Pentecost with us, you must come back for our other holidays: Harvest, Christmas, and Easter." I shuddered. Easter was my least favorite day of the church year.

I had long been in favor of Unitarian Universalists ignoring Easter altogether and had begun to ask my colleagues, "What's the point of twisting ourselves into knots to place a Unitarian frame around this celebration of a miraculous resurrection of Jesus?" More important than my theological objections was the problem that every Easter we San Jose ministers had to mediate a battle—as was also the case in my childhood congregation—between the religious Humanists and the secular Humanists, or between our Christian Unitarian Universalists and our (thankfully few) members who were stridently anti-Christian. (I worked hard, if impatiently, all year long to help this latter group make final peace with their negative childhood religious experiences.)

In my 1950s Sunday school in Knoxville, we had learned that most, though definitely not all, modern Unitarians believed Jesus was one of the world's great teachers and that he was human. It was the same "good news" the Transylvanian Unitarians have proclaimed since the 1560s— that Jesus was just as divine as you and me. Jesus' resurrection is not something I have ever believed in or related to. I can relate to and even be inspired by the Easter Passion story, as can anyone who feels strongly about social justice, but I will not let such a cruel and violent happening as the crucifixion occupy a central place in my theology or in our Sunday school program. Year after year, participating in Unitarian Universalist Easter celebrations left me feeling I was a hypocrite.

In 1993, to escape my annual Easter angst, I gratefully accepted the Homoródszentmárton elders' invitation to spend Easter with them in the Carpathian foothills. Our two congregations had raised enough funds to buy a church tractor, and the plan was for me to deliver our part of the money in person.[104] Almost three years had passed since my first visit. This time, I was looking forward to serving communion. I packed my black robe and ran away from Easter in North America to Easter in Transylvania.

It was already pitch dark outside, but our evening meal (delicious steaming polenta with wild mushrooms, a traditional Transylvanian meal that would eventually be introduced as gourmet fare in Californian restaurants) was being delayed for an hour and a half. On this Saturday night before Easter there was going to be a special music service. The whole spring lamb that Mária was marinating—slaughtered in the church barn earlier that day—was a gift from the congregation's president, a sheep farmer. Mária helped József find a pair of gloves with the fingertips cut off for Árpád László, the cantor, to wear while he played the icy organ keys. Rózsika Nagy left to ring the church bells, "in case anyone wants to join us," she said. "Not likely in this bitter cold," József remarked, and then apologized to me: "We wanted to give you the wonder of a Transylvanian spring, but you're getting our return to freezing winter. This afternoon's wedding was the first time we've held a service inside the church since last autumn. It's really still too cold to hold a service in the unheated sanctuary, but it is the only place large enough for the holiday crowds who will come tomorrow to take Easter communion. And we must be in the church tonight because that's where the organ is."

In Hungarian, Good Friday is called "Long Friday" or "Sorrow Friday." People think of this "long day" as extending from sunset on Friday through sunrise on Sunday morning. At the morning service on Good Friday, members of the congregation had gathered to hear the first half of the remarkable *Unitárius Passió* by Gyula Péterffy.[105] Now, with Rózsika pumping the organ, József and Árpád were going to sing, and I was going to hear the second half.

As József had warned me, the ten unusually large windows that I remembered lighting the new-style, one hundred year old church so beautifully during sunny summer mornings provided no protection against the cold and dark of an early spring night. Bundled in long underwear, lined boots, gloves, knitted wool hat, thick scarf, and my heaviest winter coat and József's mother's warm socks, I sat alone and shivering on the main floor of this dark, dark village church. Each time I breathed out, a cloud of warm fog disappeared into the huge empty space. József, Rózsika, and Árpád climbed the rickety stairs to the balcony and lit a few flickering candles on either side of the organ.

Earlier, József had told me that winter frost often heaved apart the rotten wooden caskets of the ancient graves directly underneath the church, and bone fragments sometimes worked all the way up into the dirt floor beneath the pews. I wasn't sure if this was true, or if I was being teased, but I sat in the dark church, shifting uneasily on the pew's hard seat, imagining those ancient bones creeping their way up beneath my feet. As József had predicted, the four of us were the only people in the village who were not inside their warm kitchens preparing the following day's Easter feasts.

The tracker-action organ wheezed into life, its aging bellows brought to life with remarkable strength by Rózsika, who steadily alternated pumping with one leg and then the other for over ninety minutes. Árpád is a fine musician. He and József launched into the second half of Péterffy's *Unitárius Passió*. I didn't understand any of the words, could not even guess its language. Their two strong voices soared. Rózsika bobbed up and down, the candles burned, the pages turned—the four of us were swept along. I felt embarrassed that no one else had joined us. If I wasn't there, would they be holding it at all? It was an uncomfortable thought, that the three of them might be creating this evening service just for me.

Slowly, I was drawn deeper into the moving music, the uniqueness of the place, and the solemnity of the moment. Waves of music washed over me. I could hear the crowd, anticipate Jesus' pain and doubt, imagine Mary's grief and Peter's regrets. My embarrassment dropped away, and the service became a blessing. My shivers changed to the tremors of mystery. From being an alienated outside observer of Easter, I was fundamentally moved to being an insider, and comfortably wrapped up in the story and the mystery of Easter.

How is it that the act of listening—of being vitally present and alert for what may come—can be so transforming? How is it that hearing this music in this place cut through my resenting and dreading Easter to convince me that people who are *unit*arians rather than *trini*tarians can claim Easter as our own, on our own terms?

The remarkable music of the *Unitárius Passió* drew to a close, and we stumbled back down the steps in the dark because there were no stars and no moon. My stomach growled noisily, reminding me how much I love the often sacred act of preparing meals. I treasure gathering to eat with others for any kind of celebratory meal—definitely my favorite form of holiday worship. It was a small miracle to emerge from the dark and cold into the bright light of the warm parsonage kitchen where Mária and the girls were hard at work on the Kászoni family's Easter dinner. Their preparations were repeatedly interrupted by boys from the village, including a sweet three year old who chose the parsonage for his first ever recital venue. Each boy would gallop through a memorized poem and then enact the ritual of sprinkling the girls with perfume (*viragozas*) to earn one of their carefully dyed Easter eggs.[106]

Mária saluted Rózsika's steadfast pumping with fiery *pálinka* and then toasted the two loyal singers. Her last toast was for me, the honored guest. "You were keeping watch for all of us," she said.

Keeping watch—that mysterious Easter ritual I had read about as a teenager in James Agee's *The Morning Watch*.[107] Agee described his struggle to overcome his doubts and to stay awake while he prayed through the long night that ended with Easter sunrise. Keeping watch is much more than staying awake. It means to be deeply aware, ready for whatever might come, without losing your intention or your connection. For me, keeping watch means rolling the stones away from the dead ends of our lives that separate us from the sacred.

Much later in that long night, I lay in the comfortable bed beside the many books in the parsonage study and considered the ways I might keep watch in my life—how all of us are called to keep watch for the oppressed and the impoverished, how we can guard against the injustices of our governments and corporate officials, how we must roll away the stones from addiction and carelessness. We need to keep watch over our health and our souls and our loved ones. That night I fully understood that I was called by our partnership connections to solve my doubts, to come out from behind my ambivalence, and become more fully faithful—faithful to the sacred, to others, and to myself. And I was surprised to realize that from now on I could look forward to Easter as simply a time when I could count on renewing my faith and my commitments. The next morning, József's Easter homily—about solving your doubts in order to renew your commitments and strengthen your faith—grew out of our conversations during the late supper about keeping watch.

Easter morning, the sun was fully shining, and every pew was filled with relatives and friends who had journeyed long distances to celebrate Easter in the heart of Székelyföld. Many of them had either grown up in the village or spent their childhood summers and school holidays there. This time, I danced through serving communion with a happy heart and a sober expression—though my soul kept reminding me that it was smiling, and who would tell their soul to stop smiling?

After the service, which ended with the surprise tractor delivery, several people thanked me for "singing Easter through for us." One man said, "Connection to your California church gives us a reason to hold to the old ways. It's good, because the old ways are closer to God." That startled me. I had assumed our partnership was providing a means for the Transylvanians to move into new ways. In fact, I think our partnerships have provided *me* a path into those old ways that are closer to God.

———————— ⌘ ————————

At the end of the week, Mária drove me to the train station. Watching through the back window of the car for a last glimpse of the Unitarian church steeple rising above the fields, it came to me that they had not held the Saturday night music service for me. They held it to keep faith with the 800 Easters that have been celebrated spring after spring in the Homoródszentmárton church.

As the train hurtled through a different kind of long night toward Hungary and the West, I realized our partners might never know that by inviting me to share their dark, cold, faith-keeping service they freed me to leave behind what I had always feared and disdained about Easter and opened me to what I could treasure about it—the commitment and renewal of *keeping watch*. My partnership connections have in this and so many other ways strengthened my faith in the blessings that happen when people reach out to one another across what separates them— ethnicity, language, geography, religion, history, politics, economics. They reaffirm my faith that when we walk in each other's shoes we know we are the same, at least in the things that matter, and especially in matters of the spirit, of human worth, and the heart.

———————— ⌘ ————————

Closing Story:
Our Faith Can Give Us Wings

As members of the San Jose congregation became partnership enthusiasts, we began to reach out not only to our partners but to other North American congregations with partners. Each had wonderful stories to tell us.[108] Jim Nelson, then minister of the Unitarian Universalist Congregation in Fairfax, Virginia told us the following story which I included in all my early talks about the "how tos," challenges, and blessings of being in partnership.

Attila Csongvay and his wife, Zsuzsánna, spoke during their first worship service at their US partner church.[109] Attila described how they felt as they boarded a plane for the first time. When the plane took off, they watched the patchwork of fields and roads recede below them, and Attila made an amazing discovery—that above the clouds the sun is always shining.

When he looked around to share his discovery with the other passengers (who were already sleeping, reading, or computing) he found no one else was paying attention to this miracle.

"I suddenly realized," he said, "that the other passengers could not have lived all their lives as we have, in a place where it often felt impossible to find the sun. For forty years, many of us in Transylvania forgot that in other parts of the world there were people who were 'living in the light.'

"That was the moment I began to make serious plans to build a strong bridge between the Unitarians in Fairfax and Szentgerice (Gălățen). We would build a bridge," Attila said, "over which sunlight could make its way into our valley, a church-to-church bridge to light up our lives and our homeland where the dark times have been very deep." The message of Attila's sermon on his last day in Fairfax was: "Our faith can give us wings to fly above the clouds."

Sadly, Attila Csongvay died not long after their visit, but the Fairfax and Szentgerice congregations are faithfully working together on his dream. I am sure Attila would have agreed with me that it is deeply satisfying to see our partner church hopes fulfilled by others who have taken up the work we all began twenty years ago.

Afterword:
József Kászoni

~~~~~

ircea Dinescu, the Romanian poet and perceptive critic of Romanian society, called the events of 1989–90 the period of "the great disorder." But in addition to disorder, that period brought wonderful changes into our life, the life of the Transylvanian Unitarians. New ways and new possibilities opened for us after a long period of feeling we were prisoners in our own country, in our own homeland.

This book tells stories about establishing the first partnerships between Transylvanian and North American congregations. This is what might be called the plot of the book. But more important than the facts described in the book are the feelings, personalities, and spiritual lives of those people who, for the first time in their lives, encountered a completely different culture and completely different way of living as a religious person. This is true for both sides of every partnership, though this book shows the point of view of the North Americans.

In the spring of 1990, traveling to Transylvania was far from as popular or as easy as it is today. Still, Gretchen Thomas, then one of two ministers at the Unitarian congregation in San Jose, risked that journey. Actually, she was a pioneer. It was the Pentecost when she first arrived in Transylvania at our parsonage in Homoródszentmárton. After evaluating her visit as successful and important, she repeated it several times, to our great delight. And day by day, without telling anyone, she took notes. The result of these carefully kept notes is what you have just read.

This book is outstanding and unusual. It describes how our partnership connections were organized at the very beginning, before there were North American, Transylvanian, and Hungarian partner church councils to help us. But most important, it is a story told with deep honesty and great empathy. On the basis of Gretchen's own experience, from her own point of view, she offers us a spiritual adventure which, while it is her own, is also that of other North Americans, as well as ours, the Unitarians of Transylvania, and mine. I feel deeply moved by Gretchen's desire to see through the obvious, past the surface, to the really important understandings and feelings that are sometimes impossible to express. In spite of this, with her great heart and perception Gretchen does her very best to express the inexpressible.

Those of you who have read this book and have already visited Transylvania will undoubtedly recognize here many events and spiritual adventures similar to your own. For those others who have never been to Central Europe, this exciting book may raise questions and draw you to see with your own eyes this part of the world, once locked away for so long.

I owe thanks to Gretchen Thomas, but not only for writing this book, which is a wonderful glimpse for the English-speaking world and our North American partners into our life here in Central Europe. I also owe her thanks personally for her true and devoted friendship with me and my family, which gave her the patience to be my sensitive guide in her own world, and for her wise and useful advice, always at hand when needed. May our friendship flourish across the borders and oceans, even though she and Robin have now moved to another, even more distant part of our world, a world we are binding together through global partnerships.

Budapest, Hungary, 2010

Afterword:
Gretchen Thomas

———— ∞∞∞ ————

When I moved from Canada to Scandinavia in 1998 and then to Australia in 2006, I became a removed observer of the North American partner church movement. As an outsider, I developed new, sometimes unusual, insights into what was happening with our partnerships. I am inspired by those all across the world who are carrying on the work we began in the early 1990s.

The creation of the North American Unitarian Universalist Partner Church Council in 1993, the Transylvanian Partner Church Council in 1999, as well as the Hungarian Partner Church Council soon after, were important turning points, and the decision to expand the North American connections beyond the early ones with Transylvanian Unitarians was a sea change for our movement. At first, partnerships focused on emergency relief and minority rights protection, but we have become both more realistic and more optimistic about what partnered congregations can accomplish together.

Today, partnered congregations engage in the personal connections and spiritual and cultural exchanges described in these stories, but also in projects that assess and improve a church or community's economy. And there have been deep changes in the socio-political environment. As Hungary and then Romania moved into the European Union, EU resources and human rights guarantees have come into play, so emergency relief and minority protection are less needed from North America. Like the Homoródszentmárton–San Jose partnership, some of these connections are almost twenty years old and have moved through several stages of development, while others are just beginning. The experiences of the North Americans doing partnership work have moved on from the excitement and frequent misunderstandings of the opening-up phase described in this book into more mutually beneficial projects. We exchange needlework, aprons, music, and recipes right alongside assisting villages in restructuring their economic base and enabling an entire generation of young rural Unitarians to complete high school and university education. At the same time, North Americans are stretching to become global thinkers and raising children who care about and want to be involved in what happens in distant parts of the world. In the course of rebuilding our churches, souls are also being rebuilt because we have crossed the bridge of our partnership's spiritual bonds to find ourselves transformed.

Our twenty year old movement is now made up of nearly 400 partnered congregations in nearly a dozen countries. Stretching across histories and economies is teaching us to truly connect, not despite our differences but because of them, not intermittently, but in a committed, long-lasting way. Even the Romanian government has come to believe that international partnerships like ours are an effective way to care about and help one another across national boundaries, ethnic differences, and religious entrenchments. As our connections confront us with the reality that our national, ethnic, and religious identities can either separate or unite us, ongoing partnerships are proving to be a powerful answer to the demands and opportunities of our ever more global world.

Where do you hold your faith? How important is it to you? Does it guide how you live your life? To answer these essential questions and then live by those answers have been the challenge and the gift of being part of the partner church movement.

I hope reading these opposite sides of the world stories from József Kászoni's and my own early partnership experiences will inspire others to write down their own. I will be one of their most avid readers.

Melbourne, Victoria, Australia, 2010

Acknowledgments

❧

This book has been made possible by the committed people in many countries who have worked creatively for the last twenty years with tireless enthusiasm to make the partner church movement a reality and a success.

I am grateful to my fellow Unitarians and Universalists in the United States, Canada, the Czech Republic, Great Britain, Poland, Transylvania, and Hungary. Their stories about how their partnership experiences affected their lives have enlivened and reshaped my thinking. The stories about Transylvania, North America, and Hungary formed the bones of this book.

I treasure the wisdom and faith of József Kászoni in Budapest, of Zoltán Veress in Stockholm, and of Judit Gellérd in Hawaii and Transylvania who thoughtfully questioned and carefully corrected my mistakes of perspective, memory, and fact. Receiving the help and respect of these accomplished authors was an education and a privilege.

Leon Hopper, Kim Kane, Jessica Vega, Cathy Cordes, Pat Rodgers, Nancy Crumbine, Elisabeth Leb, and Robin Room also generously read and carefully critiqued the manuscript, improving it substantially. We are all grateful to Cindy Spring for the careful notes she took during József's talk and her follow-up interview with him that made his story, "'Revolution' in Homoródszentmárton," possible.

I contacted everyone mentioned by name in the book, and they replied with permissions, corrections, and suggestions from their present locations, scattered across the globe.

Mary Benard at Skinner House Books was instrumental in making this collection of stories more focused and chronological. She convinced me to divide the original manuscript into two books—which has set me my next task: Volume II.

Many colleagues and loved ones, including Roz Reynolds, Harry Scholefield, and Helen and Jules Seitz, assured me these stories were not only worth telling, but worth writing down. Still, it was not until I joined the Stockholm Writers' Group, and later the Melbourne Life Writers, that my intentions became reality. These colleagues' sustaining belief in this book kept me working through to the end, despite my efforts to learn Swedish interrupting the book's beginning, and our relocation to Australia substantially delaying its end.

I am grateful to the Iranian/Swedish family who owns Kharazmi in Stockholm and to the staff of St. Jude's Cellars and The Journal Café in Melbourne. They welcomed me warmly, played wonderful music to write to, and fed my writers' groups as we noisily tore each other's writing apart and rebuilt it into something more significant and more satisfying.

The Fitzroy neighborhood (where St. Jude's is "my local," as the Aussies say) has rather miraculously provided me with many things that made this book possible: Sans Serif Editing and Publishing, particularly Alison Caddick, book designer Mal Oram, and Arena Printing and Publishing. It is a wonder to have all these resources, as well as new friends and colleagues, within an easy walk of home. Their dedicated, skillful efforts brought *Walking in Others' Shoes* into being.

I celebrate my parents' choice in 1949 to trust their children's religious education to the Tennessee Valley Unitarians. At first we went to Sunday school while they remained in the parking lot reading the Sunday *New York Times*. But eventually they crossed the threshold with us. Growing up Unitarian forged a path which led me forty years later into international partnership. Being a Unitarian Universalist engaged in the partnership movement has given me a faith I hold, and that holds me, at the very center of my life.

And I am grateful every hour for all Robin brings—rocks and light, roots and wings.

Gretchen Thomas

Placenames

Romanian is the only official language in Romania, but placenames in areas with large numbers of Hungarian and German residents are acknowledged officially in two or all three languages. The first time a place in Romania is mentioned in this book, it is identified by its Hungarian name, followed by its Romanian name in parentheses. The first time places outside of Romania are mentioned, their full location is given—state or province and, where appropriate, country. After their first mention, and for all other placenames and locations that need explaining, readers can consult the alphabetical list below.

Romania

Alabástromfalu (Cheia)
    aka Mészkő
Alsórákos (Racoş)
Arad (Arad)
Brassó (Braşov)
Bucharest (Bucureşti)
Csikszereda (Miercurea-Ciuc)
Déva (Deva)
Harghita (Harghita) County
Homoródalmás (Mereşti)
Homoródszentmárton (Mărtiniş)
Homoródszentpál (Sinpaul)
Homoródszentpéter (Petreni)
Homoródujfalu (Satu Nou)
Jánosfalva (Ioneşti)
Karácsonyfalva (Crăciuneşti)
Kiskapus (Copsa Mică)
Kolozsvár (Cluj Napoca)
Korond (Corund)
Kovászna (Covasna) County
Maros (Mureş) County
Menyő (Mineu)

Mészkő (Cheia)
    aka Alabástromfalu
Nagyajta (Alta Mare)
Okländ (Ocland)
Segesvár (Sighişoara)
Sepsiszentgyörgy (Sfântu
    Gheorghe)
Szentgerice (Gălăţen)
Székelyföld—the heart of
    Transylvania (especially
    Harghita, Kovásna, Maros)
Székelyudvarhely (Oderheiu-
    Secuiesc)
Temesvár (Timişoara)
Torda (Turda)
Torockószentgyörgy (Colteşti)
Volkán (Vulcan)

Hungary

Budapest
Debrecen
Füzesgyarmat
Kocsord

191

Australia
Melbourne, Victoria
Sydney, New South Wales

Canada
Montreal, Quebec
Toronto, Ontario

Republic of Ireland
Dublin

United Kingdom
Croydon, England
Edinburgh, Scotland
Hampstead, England
Hingham, England
Liverpool, England
London, England
Manchester, England
Norfolk, England
Northiam, England
Oxford, England
Tenterden, England

Continental Europe
Annemasse, France
Berlin, Germany
Dachau, Germany
Geneva, Switzerland
Helsinki, Finland
(Leningrad, Soviet Union)
Paris, France
Prague (Czechoslovakia)
Stockholm, Sweden
Vienna, Austria

United States of America
Anchorage, Alaska
Atlanta, Georgia
Bedford, Massachusetts
Berkeley, California
Boston, Massachusetts
Chicago, Illinois
Cleveland, Ohio
Concord, Massachusetts
Fairfax County (Oakton),
   Virginia
Florence, Massachusetts
Hingham, Massachusetts
Houston, Texas
Knoxville, Tennessee
Los Angeles, California
Lynn, Massachusetts
Madison, Wisconsin
Milwaukee, Wisconsin
Minneapolis, Minnesota
Montclair, New Jersey
New York (City), New York
Northampton, Massachusetts
Oakland, California
Portland, Oregon
San Francisco, California
San Jose, California
Seattle, Washington
St. Paul, Minnesota
Star Island, Isles of Shoals,
   New Hampshire
Weston, Massachusetts
Yellow Springs, Ohio

Endnotes

Preface

1   The early history of our 1990s partnership connections is thoughtfully discussed by Leon Hopper in "A Brief History of the Partner Church Council," in the UUPCC *Partnership Handbook*, 2006.

2   Leon Hopper's foreword to David Keyes, *Most Like an Arch: Building Global Church Partnerships*, Chico, California: Center for Free Religion, 1999, pp. 11–15, describes the 1920s and '30s sister church connections.

Introduction

3   Elizabeth Gilbert, *Eat, Pray, Love: One Woman's Search for Everything*, London: Bloomsbury, 2006, p. 79.

Part 1: Leading Us into Partnership, 1988–1989

4   Richard Henry's biography of Čapek is *Norbert Fabián Čapek: A Spiritual Journey*, Boston: Skinner House Books, 1999.

"Revolution" in Homoródszentmárton

5   Cindy Spring took careful notes during József's talk, conducted a follow-up interview with him, and shared her notes with me.

6   During the communist years, ten Unitarian parish ministers, three of their seminary professors, the Unitarian College librarian and archivist, and one of the ministers' spouses (as well as four Unitarian seminary students not included in the numbers below) were incarcerated for lengthy terms:

    1–4 years (1 professor, 2 ministers)
    5–6 years (2 ministers)
    7 years (2 professors, 1 minister)
    10 years (2 ministers)
    15 years (2 ministers)
    20–25 years (2 ministers, 1 minister's spouse).

To learn more about the experiences of imprisoned Unitarian clergy and their family members, read Judit Gellérd, *Prisoner of Liberté: Story of a Transylvanian Martyr*, Chico, California: Uniquest, 2003. This data is taken from pp. 79–80.

7   James Jeffrey, *Paprika Paradise: Travels in the Land of My Almost Birth*, Sydney: Hachette Australia, 2007, p. 134.

8   Two books that discuss the lives of Transylvanian Unitarian ministers during the Ceauşescu years are Judit Gellérd, *Prisoner of Liberté*, op. cit. and *Confession about Ourselves*, ed. Mózes Kedei, Odorheiu Secuiesc/Székelyudvarhely: Transylvanian Ministerial Fellowship, IN-FOPRESS, n.d.

9   For accounts of events in Temesvár, read László Tőkés, *With God, for the People: The Autobiography of László Tőkés*, London: Hodder and Stoughton, 1990, and Charles Colson, "The Story of the Church: Timişoara," in Charles Colson (ed.), *Being the Body*, Dallas, Texas: Word Publishing, 1992.

10   A detailed account of the Ceauşescus' 16–25 December 1989 flight, capture, and execution appeared in Celestine Bohlen, "Revolt in Rumania," *The New York Times*, 7 January 1990.

11   György Csanády wrote the words for the *Székely Anthem* in 1918 when Romania first occupied Transylvania and 200,000 Hungarians, including 50,000 Székelys, left Transylvania for Hungary and other countries. This depiction of their cares, despairs, and hope for a miracle starts with a question "Who knows where destiny will lead us?" It recounts the suffering the Székelys had already endured under the Tartars, Turks, and Habsburgs and is a prayer to God to save their homeland, Transylvania. Kálmán Mihalik composed the slow, lamenting melody, which is similar to that of the Hungarian National Anthem. Some Transylvanian partner churches have added copies of the *Székely Anthem* to their hymnals, including the English words to sing with their North American visitors.

Who knows where destiny will lead us
On this rough road and dark night.
Lead your people once again to victory,
Csaba, Prince Royal, on a heavenly path.

Our ancestors crumble to dust
Through these wars of nations, as cliffs on rough seas.
The flood is upon us, oh, overwhelming us a hundred fold,
Lord, don't let us lose Transylvania!

As long as we live, Hungarian Nation,
Our spirit shall not be broken;

Wherever we are born, whatever corner of the earth,
Whether our fate be good, or cruel.

Such sorrowful a past—our millennia of misfortune,
The ravages of Tartars and Turks, and Austrian yoke.
Let us inherit our nation, the land of the Székely,
In a free fatherland, to live in happiness.

(Translated by László Szelecki)

Unitarians? In Romania?

12   In *Out of the Flames: The Remarkable Story of a Fearless Scholar, a Fatal Heresy, and One of the Rarest Books in the World*, New York: Broadway Books, 2002, Lawrence and Nancy Goldstone describe in detail how Servetus was judged a heretic and burned at the stake. It also traces the histories of the three surviving copies of *Christianismi Restitutio (The Restoration of Christianity)*—Servetus' work that so infuriated Calvin. In the Goldstones' book there are pictures of Servetus (the frontispiece) and of the Champel memorial stone (p. 314).

The three surviving original books—all now priceless—are located at the Bibliothéque Nationale in Paris, France; the library of the University of Edinburgh, Scotland; and the Österreichische Nationalbibliothek in Vienna, Austria. The Vienna copy was owned from the 1660s to 1787 by the Transylvanian Unitarian Church. In the 1940s Earl Morse Wilbur hired a scribe to make a handwritten copy from the original in Paris. Wilbur's document was recently used in producing the first English translation, published by Mellen Press in 2007. Alicia McNary Forsey, formerly professor of church history at Starr King School for the Ministry, was the managing editor and director of this project, which has finally made Servetus' *Christianismi Restitutio* available in English.

13   John Calvin (1509–1564), Michael Servetus (1511–1553), John Knox (1513–1572), William Farel (1489–1565), Theodore Beza (1513–1572), István Bocskai (1557–1606), Martin Luther (1483–1546), Huldrych Zwingli (1484–1531), Ferenc Dávid (1510–1579).

14   My understanding of the tensions between Hungarian-Romanians and Romanian-Romanians during the 1980s and early 1990s has been formed primarily by my reading—for example the books by Judit Gellérd, Dervla Murphy, Anna Funder, and Helena Drysdale, listed

in the Bibliography. My reading sometimes differs from conversations I have had with Transylvanians about these tensions. None of the Hungarian-Romanians I have talked with believe that the Romanian majority suffered more than the Hungarian minority during the Gheorghiu-Dej and Ceauşescu years; while most Romanian-Romanians are convinced they suffered more than minority persons did.

15   Quoted in the American Hungarian Federation's issues statement, "Overdue Autonomy for Minority Hungarians! Time to Bury Trianon and Resurrect Democracy," 4 June 2008.

16   On this period, see Christine Morgan, *Alabaster Village: Our Years in Transylvania*, Boston: Skinner House Books, 1997, p. 17:

> At first the rabid nationalism seemed incredible. But just as incredible was the irresponsibility of the Allied governments in putting entire populations under alien rule, without sufficient respect for history and cultural autonomy. Contrary to agreements under the League of Nations, the Romanians had in effect confiscated Hungarian high schools, universities, libraries, museums, and hospitals, replacing Hungarian personnel with Romanians without compensation. Because the Romanian University entrance examination was made intentionally difficult for non-Romanians, 80 percent of the Hungarian students failed it. Unable to enter the university built by their ancestors, they were becoming manual workers.

Part 2: In Homoródzsentmárton, 1990

17   William Schulz, "Romania Resurrectus!" *The World*, March/April 1990, and Chester Atkins "Rumania: January 1990," *The World*, May/June 1990.

Wheresoever You Go, Go with All Your Heart

18   Despite the limitations of growing up in Transylvania during the difficult Gheorghiu-Dej and Nicolae Ceauşescu-led years, Judit Gellérd—known affectionately to her friends as Zizi—became a physician, a psychiatrist, and a concert violinist. Since moving to the United States she has written and published many books, studied social transformation with Professor Elie Wiesel at Boston University, and been ordained as a Transylvanian Unitarian minister. In his 1998

talk, "History of the UU Partner Church Council," Leon Hopper expressed his appreciation for Judit's central role in the 1993 creation of the Unitarian Universalist Partner Church Council and its formative years. For this work and her many other efforts on behalf of Transylvanians and the Transylvanian Unitarian Church, Judit has been awarded the UUPCC's first Louis Cornish Living the Mission Award, an honorary doctorate from Starr King School for the Ministry, and the highly prestigious Transylvanian Julianus Award, which honors people who have given extraordinary support to the Hungarian minorities in Transylvania.

19 Each of our tickets cost a bit less than 600 lei, then about 15 US dollars. In 1990 around 5 US dollars was one day's wages for a skilled carpenter, and the exchange rate was 21 Romanian lei = $1.

20 Pico Iyer, "Why We Travel: A Love Affair with the World," *Los Angeles Times*, 19 April 1998, Special Travel Issue, p. 32.

21 For more information about Ferenc Dávid, see János Erdö, *Transylvanian Unitarian Church: Chronological History and Theological Essays*, trans. Judit Gellérd, Chico, California: Center for Free Religion, 1990; Imre Gellérd, *"Truth Liberates You": The Message of Transylvania's first Unitarian Bishop, Francis Dávid*, trans. Judit Gellérd, Chico, California: Center for Free Religion, 1990; and Béla Varga, *Francis Dávid: What Has Endured of his Life and Work?* trans. Vilma Szantó Harrington, Budapest: Magyar Unitárius Egyház, 1981.

22 There are distinctly conflicting theories about the original source of the Székely who, along with the Magyar, belong to the language group that includes only Hungarian, Finnish, Estonian, Sami, and a few Siberian dialects. Claims are made for Székely origins in the Ural Mountains in Russia or for being decendants of either Attila's Huns or the Magyars. Sorting it out makes a good afternoon's reading on Google. It is certain that in 1003 about 1000 Székelys were sent by Stephen I of Hungary to the Harghita Mountains to invade and occupy the edges of Transylvania in order to defend its borders. According to Turkish accounts, in 1526, when Turkish invaders pushed the Magyars out of Transylvania into present-day Hungary, the Székely remained because they had settled within the more inaccessible areas inside the protective circle of the Carpathian Mountains and the Transylvanian Alps.

23 One hundred years before Ferenc Dávid founded Unitarianism, Prince Vlad III (1431–1476/77) known as Draculea (son of Dracu, the Dragon) and Tepes (the Impaler) was a crusader against the Turkish Empire. Becoming Catholic was a marriage condition of the family of his Hungarian wife. He married her to cement ties with powerful families from Hungary he expected would help him fight to keep the Muslim Turks out of Wallachia—the part of present-day Romania south of Transylvania—where Vlad was governor. Vlad despised the Turks after spending much of his childhood as a hostage to them and later spending fourteen of his adult years imprisoned in Turkey. After his wife's death, Vlad joined with the Orthodox Church to resist the Turks.

Vlad III is seen as a martyr and national hero by many ethnic Romanians, who revere his possible birthplace in Segesvár. Vlad is regarded with disgust and embarrassment by most ethnic Hungarians, who see him as a blood-thirsty, evil despot who ruled by fear, tortured and mutilated senselessly, and killed 100,000 of his subjects and enemies, often by impaling them on a forest of spikes around his castles.

The British author Bram Stoker used tales of Vlad the Impaler as the inspiration for his fictional Transylvanian vampire, whom he named Dracula.

24 In *Zen Mind, Beginner's Mind*, New York: John Weatherhill, 1972, Shunryu Suzuki discusses how complex situations are sometimes understood quite clearly by those who are seeing them for the first time, and how everyone can employ this "beginner's frame of mind" to reconnect with their fundamental desires and intentions.

25 A line from William Wordsworth's "The French Revolution as It Appeared to Enthusiasts at Its Commencement," lines 105–44 of *The Prelude*, XI, 1804.

Thinking American

26 Experts have estimated that in the worst of the Ceauşescu years one-third of the people in Romania were informers to the Securitate—at least seven million people. (See note 41.)

27 József translated my words by reading aloud the Hungarian version of my talk that had been prepared just before the service by Gabriela

Popa, his English teacher. The church bells were ringing the start of the service as she raced to finish her translation, and she declared it was the hardest English-to-Hungarian exam she had ever been given, teaching me early the importance of speaking and writing in straight-forward, simple sentences and verbs for those who are learning a new language.

28 Isabel Allende, *The Sum of Our Days*, London: HarperCollins, 2008, p. 173.

29 Quoted by György Andrási during an International Association for Religious Freedom panel presentation at the June 1990 UUA General Assembly when he was a visiting scholar at Meadville-Lombard seminary.

30 Dervla Murphy, *Transylvania and Beyond: A Travel Memoir*, Woodstock, New York: Overlook Press, 1993, p. 40.

Standing on Holy Ground

31 Imre Gellérd, "The Meaning of the Communion for Transylvanian Unitarians of Today," in Judit Gellérd, *Guidebook for Unitarian Universalist Partner Churches*, Chico, California: Uniquest and Center for Free Religion, 1997, pp. 164–73. Imre Gellérd spent the last fifteen years of his life (1965–1980) serving the Unitarians in Homoródszentmárton, as described by Judit Gellérd in *Prisoner of Liberté*, op. cit.

32 József Kászoni, "The Unitarian Meaning of the Lord's Supper in Hungary," in David Steers (ed.), *European Perspectives on Communion: Liberal Christian Approaches to Communion and the Lord's Supper*, Ulster: European Liberal Protestant Network, 2001, p. 38.

33 Elek Rezi, "The Lord's Supper in the Transylvanian Unitarian Church," in David Steers (ed.), *European Perspectives on Communion*, ibid., p. 41.

34 Ruth Gibson, E-message: "Why does our U*U* faith appeal to people who..." Posted 6 February 2010 on <pcc-chat@lists.uua.org>.

35 For more on the history of communion in North American Unitarian and Universalist Churches, read "The Communion Experience," in *The Communion Book*, Boston: the Unitarian Universalist Ministers Association, 1993, ed. Carl Seaburg, pp. 9–25.

Learning to Pray: Join Me as You Will

36 Translated by Judit Gellérd.

37 Kate Braestrup, *Here If You Need Me: A True Story*, New York: Back Bay Books/Little Brown, 2007, p. 109.

Learning Freedom behind Closed Doors

38 For a description of life under communism in East Germany, read Anna Funder, *Stasiland: Stories From Behind the Berlin Wall*, London: Granta Books, 2001.

39 Tobias Wolff, Foreword, Helena Drysdale, *Looking for George: Love and Death in Romania*, London: Picador, 1996, pp. xi and xii.

40 Dervla Murphy, *Transylvania and Beyond*, op. cit., p. 141.

41 The College for the Study of Securitate Archives has reported that the Securitate kept files on two million Romanians and that 700,000 citizens were informers. Critics say both these figures are so ridiculously low that they cast doubt on the validity of all of the Archives' studies. (See note 26.)

42 See Judit Gellérd's, *Prisoner of Liberté*, op. cit., or watch the 2007 prize-winning film, *The Lives of Others*, about life in 1984 under the East German Stasi. The film is an inside look at how a diabolically efficient and oppressive surveillance society, set up to discover and prey upon human weakness, has the ability to make everyone a potential subject/victim. The characters encounter impossible predicaments that force them to wager their talent, their souls, and their lives as they struggle to preserve their humanity.

43 Christian Mungiu's prize-winning 2007 film, *4 Months, 3 Weeks and 2 Days*, is about obtaining an abortion in Romania.

44 József Szombatfalvi, Sr. was speaking as an ambassador from the Transylvanian Ministers' Association to the 1997 annual meeting of the Unitarian Universalist Ministers' Association. His talk, "The Promised Land: New Heavens and New Earth," was published in *UUMA News*, Autumn 1997, p. 12.

Loaves and Fishes

45 This clever way of crossing the border does not work today because crossing on foot was soon forbidden in an effort to stem the large

number of black market goods and drugs that quickly began flowing across the Romanian–Hungarian border in the early 1990s.

The Walls Come Down

46   At the end of World War II, the city of Berlin—an isolated enclave entirely surrounded by East Germany—was divided by the liberating occupiers into four sections. The American, British, and French sectors were later united by the occupying powers and considered part of West Germany, while the fourth, Soviet, sector became part of communist East Germany.

There were eight East–West border crossings for different kinds of transportation and citizens of different nationalities, named Alpha, Bravo, Charlie, and so on. Checkpoint Charlie was used only by Allied forces personnel and foreigners to enter and exit East Berlin. Checkpoint Charlie was originally policed by the US military on the western side, and by East German border guards on the east. Nearby there was a separate checkpoint for international train passengers at the Friedrichstrasse station. In many parts of Berlin, the Wall was actually two walls with a cleared, paved "death strip"' between— giving a clear field of fire to guards. Despite there being more than 100 watchtowers, it is estimated that there were about 5000 successful escapes. Between 136 and 200 people were killed attempting to cross from East to West Berlin. (The numbers are strongly disputed.) The Wall was rebuilt—each time to make it higher and more permanent—in 1962, 1965, and 1975. The final Wall was 3.6 m (12 feet) high and 140 km (96 miles) long.

A replica of the Checkpoint Charlie guardhouse was reconstructed in 2000 as a memorial museum on its former site at Friedrichstrasse. In 2004, a 140 m (460 foot) replica of the Wall was built by the Allied Museum next to a field of 1065 burial crosses representing each of the victims who died attempting to cross from East Germany into West Germany.

Part 3: Practicing Partnership at Home, 1990–1992

The First Unitarians: Ferenc Dávid and János Zsigmond

47   'Stories for all Ages' are often included in Unitarian Universalist weekly worship services. This one is a dramatic reading by an

amateur actor who is speaking particularly to the children (ages five to twelve), though people of all ages are present.

48   Aladár Körösföi-Kriesch's famous painting *The Proclamation of Religious Freedom [at] The Diet of Torda, 1568*, can be viewed at <www.uniuniques.com/UniFineArt/Printwork/Prints.htm>. Copies of this photogravure hang in most Unitarian churches and in many Unitarian homes in Transylvania.

A print of the painting with a page telling the history of the Edict of Torda and identifying all the people can be purchased from UniUniques or from John Gibbons at <minister @uubedford>.

49   Having rejected the authority of the Roman Catholic Church, Ferenc Dávid and other Protestant (protest-ing) ministers chose to wear academic gowns instead of priests' robes, symbolizing the Protestants' choosing reason and scholarship as the source of their theological authority.

50   According to legend, Dávid carved into the wall of his prison cell in Déva Castle these words: "Neither the sword of the Pope, nor the image of torture and death—nay, no earthly power shall stop truth in its course. I write what I feel and what I have felt and I have truly preached with a trusting soul—and I am firmly convinced that after my death the doctrine of false teachers will perish. Amen."

They Hold the Future in Their Hands

51   A message posted on <pcc-chat@uua.org> in 2007 by the Unitarian Society of Northampton and Florence (Massachusetts), which is partnered with Karácsonyfalva (Crăciuneşti), tells about the annual summer youth pilgrimage to Transylvania:

> This year, four members of Northampton's youth group participated in the annual Partner Church Council Youth Pilgrimage to Transylvania. It was the first time our congregation was represented. Several partner church committee members—all previous travelers to Transylvania—met with the group a few days before they left and again after their return. What a difference! They were subdued before the trip, mostly trying to think of more things that might go wrong and trying to digest our advice. They came back tired, but full of wonder and enthusiasm—praising the Transylvanian church for its youth programs, feeling a strong connection to historical Unitarianism, and eager to share their

experience in a worship service. The Youth Pilgrimage is a wonderful way to make your partnership intergenerational and to make a contribution to the lives of teens as they make important decisions concerning their future direction.

Part 4: In Northern California, 1992

52 "Sándor Kovács Speaks at General Assembly," in *Partner Church News*, vol. 3, no. 2, September 1996.

A Transylvanian Look at Our Faith

53 One of the reasons the spouses of Transylvanian ministers traditionally have been expected to be Unitarians at birth or to become Unitarians is to prevent a minister's children being raised in another faith—which would happen for the opposite-sex children if the spouse was not a Unitarian. (Even though this policy denies free religious choice, as the step-parent of three non-UUs, I feel some sympathy for this unwritten, though usually followed policy of the Transylvanian Unitarians.)

54 John Buehrens and Forrester Church, *A Chosen Faith*, Boston: Beacon Press, 1998.

Keeping Moving in the Right Direction

55 Martin Luther King, Jr., speaking in 1960 at Marion Wright Edelman's alma mater, Spelman College, Atlanta, Georgia.

Which of Us Is Poor?

56 The term "panhandle" originated in San Francisco. Unsuccessful 1850s gold prospectors stood on the street holding out the empty pans they had previously used to sift gold from gravel, hoping to collect enough coins from passers-by to pay for a train ticket home.

57 There was also a small—but needed and welcome—monthly stipend provided by the government for ministers of all faiths. (I was told the stipends to the "other" denominations were to justify the much larger support the state gave to the Romanian Orthodox Church. Since Romania is a secular state, there is no official national religion or state church, and all religious communities are supposedly equal before the law.)

58 There is a sharp divide between US and Canadian Unitarians on this

community versus individual continuum, with the Canadians being more like the Transylvanian Unitarians. In 1990 a Canadian religious educator told me, "If Canadians were asked to reorder the UUA's list of principles, we'd put the interdependent web first and the worth and dignity of the individual last." At the time I was surprised by that, but walking in Transylvanian Unitarians' shoes has moved me much closer to the middle of the individual vs. community continuum.

Part 5: Finding Our Roots in the 1920s, 1930s, and 1940s

59 A good listing of important historical events can be found in Dervla Murphy's chronology, in *Transylvania and Beyond*, op. cit., pp. 236–40.

60 Conrad Rudolph, *Pilgrimage to the End of the World: The Road to Santiago de Compostela*, Chicago and London: University of Chicago Press, 2004, p. 38.

61 In David Parke (ed.), *The Epic of Unitarianism: Original Writings from the History of Liberal Religion*, Berkeley: Starr King Press, 1957, Harry C. Meserve is quoted on the page following the dedication page.

Warming up to History: Earl Morse Wilbur

62 Voltaire is quoted in an article by Jill Lepore, "A Critic at Large: Prior Convictions: Did the Founders want us to be faithful to their faith?" *The New Yorker*, 14 April 2008, p. 72.

63 Conrad Edick Wright, "A Son's Appreciation," in "Conrad Wright: Historian of American Unitarianism," reproduced at <http://www. harvardswquarelibrary.org/unitarians/wright-conrad.html>.

64 David Parke (ed.), *The Epic of Unitarianism*, op. cit., dedication page.

65 Henry Wilder Foote, "Earl Morse Wilbur: Historian of Unitarianism 1886–1956," *The Unitarian Yearbook 1957–58*, reproduced at <www.harvard squarelibrary.org/unitarians/wilbur.html>.

66 Alan Seaburg, "Earl Morse Wilbur," *Dictionary of Unitarian and Universalist Historical Society*, reproduced at <www25.uua.org/ uuhs/duub/articles/earl morsewilbur.html>.

67 Alicia McNary Forsey is writing a book on the interactions between János Zsigmond's mother (Queen Isabella Sforza Zápolya) and the Ottoman Empire during the rule of the Turkish Sultan Süleyman.

68 Henry Wilder Foote, "Earl Morse Wilbur: Historian of Unitarianism," op. cit.

69 Ibid.

Lighting the Dark: Louis C. Cornish

70 Several colleagues are helping me construct a list of the people who preceded or followed Louis Cornish as the American Unitarian Association's and then the Unitarian Universalist Association's staff responsible for international relations. Some were paid part-time staff and a few were titled "the AUA field Secretary," though more were volunteers or paid through release time from their full-time work as congregational ministers. The names we have confirmed so far are John G. Palfrey (who began his international responsibilities in 1828); Henry Ware (from 1829); Charles Wendt (1908); Sydney B. Snow (1927); Herbert Hitchen; Ed Cahill; Donald Harrington; Homer Jack (1965); Max Gabler; Max Kapp; Mel Hoover (1987); Polly and Ted Guild (1990); Ken MacLean (1993); Olivia Holmes (2000); Cathy Cordes (interim, 2005); and Eric Cherry (2007).

71 Frances E. F. Cornish, *Louis Craig Cornish: Interpreter of Life*, Boston: Beacon Press, 1953, p. 60.

72 See note 2.

73 Minutes of an informal meeting of the Commission on Hungarian Relief, 1 June 1921, p. 3:

…the following recommendations were made to the Continuing Commission for the Relief of the Transylvanian Churches: FIRST: That the American Unitarian Churches assume responsibility for the further and stated support of 112 Unitarian parishes in Transylvania in accordance with the lists submitted by Mr. Csiki and that it be recommended to the Unitarian Churches in Great Britain, through the British and Foreign Unitarian Association which has expressed to the Secretary of the American Unitarian Association its desire to do its share, that they give assistance to the headquarters, the college in Kolozsvar, and to the three high schools maintained in other places.

74 Quoted in Edgar A. Collard, Elizabeth C. Speyer, and Charles Eddis, *Montreal's Unitarians, 1832–2000*, Montreal, Quebec: Church of the Messiah, 2001, p. 257.

75 Helena Drysdale, *Looking for George: Love and Death in Romania,* op. cit., p. 54.

76 Louis C. Cornish, *Transylvania in 1922: Report of the Commission Sent by the American and British Unitarian Churches to Transylvania in 1922,* Boston: Beacon Press, 1923, p. vi.

77 Louis C. Cornish, *The Religious Minorities in Transylvania,* London: Grant Richards, 1926 (also published by Beacon Press, Boston, 1925) pp. 22–23. Cornish compiled this report in collaboration with the American Committee on the Rights of Religious Minorities.

78 Louis Cornish, *Work and Dreams and the Wide Horizon,* Boston: Beacon Press, 1937, p. vi.

79 Frances E. F. Cornish, *Louis Craig Cornish,* op. cit., p. 19.

80 Ibid.

81 Louis Cornish, "Celebrating Twenty Years of Unitarian Summer Meetings on Star Island, June 15, 1916," Pamphlet, Boston: Star Island Corporation, 1916, p. 10.

82 Recipients of the Louis C. Cornish Living the Mission Award:
2009 – Rev. John Eric Gibbons
2008 – Rev. Dr. Spencer Levan
2007 – Rev. Dr. Arpad Szabo
2006 – Natalie Gulbrandsen
2005 – Rev. Richard Boeke
2004 – Rev. Peter Raible
2003 – Patricia Rodgers
2002 – Rev. Richard F. Beal
2001 – Rev. C. Leon Hopper
2000 – Rev. Dénes Farkas
1999 – Rev. Dr. Judit Gellérd

An Early East–West Partnership: Christine Frederiksen and Ferenc Balázs

83 The program is named for Ferenc Bálazs, a visiting scholar in 1926–28. The Transylvanian ministers who have been Balázs Scholars at Starr King School for the Ministry are:
Róbert Bálint (2009–2010)
Endre Nagy (2008–2009)
Béla Botond (Bélu) Jakabházi (2007–2008)

Erika Orbán (2006–2007)
Zsolt Solymosi (2005–2006)
Csaba Tódor (2004–2005)
Mária Pap (2003–2004)
Lajos Lőrinczi (2002–2003)
Zsuzsánna (Gyerkes) Bartha (2001–2002)
Botond (Boti) Koppandi (2000–2001)
Kinga-Réka (Zsigmond) Székely (1999–2000)
László Kiss (1998–99)
Csaba Mezei (1997–98)
Sándor Kovács (1995–96)
Sándor Léta (1994–95)

84 Christine Frederiksen's (later Morgan) life in Transylvania is described in her book *Alabaster Village*, op. cit., which József Kászoni has translated into Hungarian: *Mészkő (Alabástromfalu): Balázs Ferenc felesége az Erdélyben töltött évekről 1930–1937*. In 2007 the Unitarian Universalist Partner Church Council published a bilingual (English and Hungarian) version.

85 From a biographical sketch of Christine Morgan by Ernest Morgan in *Poems by Christine*, self-published, p. 5.

86 Christine Morgan, *Alabaster Village*, op. cit., p. 130.

87 Ibid., p. 10.

88 Ibid., p. 65.

89 Ibid., p. 95.

90 Ibid., p. 130.

91 Translated by József Kászoni in Christine Morgan, *Alabaster Village: Our Years in Transylvania*, Bedford, Massachusetts: Unitarian Universalist Partner Church Council, 2007, p. 237.

My Life Has Been a Field of Stars: Gábor Kereki

92 G. Peter Fleck, *Come as You Are: Reflections on the Revelations of Everyday Life*, Boston: Beacon Press, 1993, p. 15.

93 Gábor Kereki, *'Egy az Isten' Unitarianism: Some words of Gábor Kereki*, London: Lindsey Press, 1996.

94 Gábor Kereki, "I have seen the longest of winters," a framed statement hanging in the office of the First Unitarian Church of Budapest, Hungary.

95 Christine Morgan, *Alabaster Village*, op. cit., p. 74.

96 In June 1948 the Social Democratic Party was forced to merge with the Communist Party, creating the Hungarian Working People's Party, which was dominated by the communists. Anti-communist leaders were forced into exile or excluded from the party. Soon after, President Zoltán Tildy was also removed from his position, and replaced by a fully co-operative Social Democrat, Árpád Szakasits. In 1949 all non-communist parties were organized into a so-called People's Front, with a Soviet communist leader, while opposition parties were declared illegal and their leaders arrested or forced into exile.

97 George Grieve was a lifelong internationalist. He was the visiting preacher at King's Chapel in Boston on 3 September 1939, the day Britain declared war on Germany. The congregation, which has its own British roots, greeted Grieve's entry into the church by rising to sing the British National Anthem.

98 Compiled from the obituary of Gábor Kereki in *The Inquirer*, no. 7368, 24 June 1995, p. 6.

99 Csilla (Lakatos) Dale, the co-coordinator of UUPCC travel services with her husband John Dale, is working on a PhD in counseling that focuses on Transylvanians who have settled in Hungary.

Part 6: In Homoródszentmárton, 1993

100 Today, thanks to EU-required bank reforms, aid monies are no longer carried by hand. It is now possible to wire funds from bank account to bank account.

101 For a lovely package delivery story, see "Nine Days in September," by Gary Smith in Judit Gellérd (ed.), *In Storm, Even Trees Lean on Each Other: Unitarian Universalist Sermons on Transylvania*, Chico, California: Center for Free Religion, 1993.

A Transylvanian Village Wedding

102 Reinhold Niebuhr, quoted in Nancy Jay Crumbine, *Humility, Anger, and Grace: Meditations Towards a Life that Matters*, Norwich, Vermont: NorthBoundBooks, 2004, pp. 24–5.

Sounding Our Faith

103 Judit Gellérd, *Prisoner of Liberté*, op. cit., pp. 90–1.

Keeping Watch

104 On the day the church tractor was delivered, two different people
told me this joke:
> Upon handing over his deposit for a tractor, a Romanian farmer
> was told:
> "Your tractor will be delivered to you seven years from today."
> "Will that be in the morning or the afternoon?" asked the farmer.
> "Why do you need to know that now?"
> "Because the telephone installer is coming that afternoon."

During the years when telephone installation in Hungary was taking
an extraordinarily long time, a member of the Hungarian parliament
sarcastically proposed it should enact a law allowing children to
inherit their parents' telephone applications.

105 Knowing and performing Gyula Péterffy's *Unitárius Passió* was the
final exam in József's seminary music course. The comprehensive
course was taught by Péterffy himself, an accomplished, highly
respected Unitarian composer. The Unitarians in Transylvania
practice the ancient tradition of singing a Good Friday Passion. József
told me that every Unitarian congregation with an organ and a
cantor will try to sing Péterffy's *Unitárius Passió* during the long
weekend.

106 The youth of the Unitarian Church of Füzesgyarmat, Hungary can
be viewed on an internet clip celebrating Easter customs, including
carol singing, dying eggs, reciting poems, and spraying perfume at
<http://www.youtube.com/watch?v=iaELn7ydlQw>.

107 James Agee, *The Morning Watch*, London: Peter Owen, 1964.

Closing Story: Our Faith Can Give Us Wings

108 Judit Gellérd published some of these stories in: *In Storm, Even Trees
Lean on Each Other*, op. cit., and in *Ending the Storm: Unitarian
Universalist Sermons on Transylvania*, Chico, California: Uniquest
and Center for Free Religion, 1996.

109 Attila Csongvay was the minister of the Transylvanian Unitarians in
Szentgerice (Galateni), and Zsuzsánna is the sister of Dénes Farkas,
who was then part of the Transylvanian Church's headquarters staff
and also drove the Partner Church van for small groups of pilgrims
to Transylvania.

Bibliography

Agee, James. *The Morning Watch*. London: Peter Owen, 1964.

Allende, Isabel. *The Sum of Our Days*. London: Harper Collins, 2008.

American Hungarian Federation. Issues statement for the 88th anniversary of the Treaty of Trianon: "Overdue Autonomy for Minority Hungarians! Time to Bury Trianon and Resurrect Democracy," 4 June 2008. Reproduced at <http://www.american hungarian federation.org/ news_trianon_88Anniversary.htm>

Atkins, Chester. "Rumania: January 1990," *The World: Journal of the Unitarian Universalist Association*, May/June 1990.

Bohlen, Celestine. "Revolt in Rumania," *The New York Times*, 7 January 1990. Reproduced at <query.nytimes.com/gst/fullpage.html?res= 9C0CE1D61631F934A35752C0A966958260&sec=&spon=&page wanted=all>.

Braestrup, Kate. *Here If You Need Me: A True Story*. New York: Back Bay Books, Little Brown, 2007.

Buehrens, John and Forrester Church. *A Chosen Faith*. Boston: Beacon Press, 1998.

Collard, Edgar A., Elizabeth C. Speyer, and Charles Eddis. *Montreal's Unitarians, 1832–2000*. Montreal: Church of the Messiah, 2001.

Colson, Charles. "The Story of the Church: Timişoara," in Charles Colson (ed.), *Being the Body*. Dallas, Texas: Word Publishing, 1992.

Commission on Hungarian Relief. Minutes of an informal meeting, 1 June 1921, p. 3.

Cornish, Frances E. F. *Louis Craig Cornish: Interpreter of Life*. Boston: Beacon Press, 1953.

Cornish, Louis C. "Celebrating Twenty Years of Unitarian Summer Meetings on Star Island, June 15, 1916." Pamphlet, Boston: Isles of Shoals Corporation, 1916.

——— *Transylvania in 1922: Report of the Commission Sent by the American and British Unitarian Churches to Transylvania in 1922*. Boston: Beacon Press, 1923.

——— in collaboration with the American Committee on the Rights of Religious Minorities. *The Religious Minorities in Transylvania*. Boston: Beacon Press, 1925; London: Grant Richards, 1926.

—— *Work and Dreams and the Wide Horizon.* Boston: Beacon Press, 1937.

—— *Philippines Calling.* Philadelphia: Dorrance, 1942.

—— *Transylvania: The Land beyond the Forest.* Philadelphia: Dorrance, 1947.

Crumbine, Nancy Jay. *Humility, Anger, and Grace: Meditations Towards a Life that Matters.* Norwich, Vermont: NorthBoundBooks, 2004.

Drysdale, Helena. *Looking for George: Love and Death in Romania.* London: Picador, 1996.

Erdö, János. *Transylvanian Unitarian Church: Chronological History and Theological Essays,* trans. Judit Gellérd. Chico, California: Center for Free Religion, 1990.

Farkas, Sándor Bölöni. *Journey in North America, 1831,* trans. and ed. Árpád Kadarkay. Santa Barbara, California: American Bibliographical Center-Clio Press, 1978.

Fleck, G. Peter. *Come as You Are: Reflections on the Revelations of Everyday Life.* Boston: Skinner House Books, 1993.

Foote, Henry Wilder. "Earl Morse Wilbur: Historian of Unitarianism 1886–1956," *Unitarian Yearbook* 1957–58. Reproduced at <www.harvardsquarelibrary.org/unitarians/wilbur.html>.

Funder, Anna. *Stasiland: Stories From Behind the Berlin Wall.* London: Granta Books, 2001.

Gellérd, Imre. *"Truth Liberates You": The Message of Transylvania's First Unitarian Bishop, Francis Dávid,* trans. Judit Gellérd. Chico, California: Center for Free Religion, 1991.

—— "The Meaning of the Communion for Transylvanian Unitarians of Today," trans. Judit Gellérd, in Judit Gellérd (ed.), *Guidebook for Unitarian Universalist Partner Churches.* Chico, California: Uniquest and Center for Free Religion, 1995. Reproduced at <www.uupcc.org>.

Gellérd, Judit (ed.) *In Storm, Even Trees Lean on Each Other: Unitarian Universalist Sermons on Transylvania.* Chico, California: Center for Free Religion, 1993

—— (ed.) *Ending the Storm: Unitarian Universalist Sermons on Transylvania.* Chico, California: Uniquest and Center for Free Religion, 1996.

—— *Prisoner of Liberté: Story of a Transylvanian Martyr.* Chico, California: Uniquest, 2003.

Gilbert, Elizabeth. *Eat, Pray, Love: One Woman's Search for Everything.* London: Bloomsbury, 2006.

Goldstone, Lawrence and Nancy Goldstone. *Out of the Flames: The Remarkable Story of a Fearless Scholar, a Fatal Heresy, and One of the Rarest Books in the World.* New York: Broadway Books, 2002.

Henry, Richard. *Norbert Fabián Čapek: A Spiritual Journey.* Boston: Skinner House Books, 1999.

Hopper, Leon. Foreword, in David Keyes, *Most Like an Arch: Building Global Church Partnerships.* Chico, California: Center for Free Religion, 1999.

—— "A Brief History of the Partner Church Council," 2006. Reproduced at <www.uupcc.org/docs/handbook.pdf>.

Iyer, Pico. "Why We Travel: A Love Affair with the World," *Los Angeles Times*, Special Travel Issue, April 1998.

Jeffrey, James. *Paprika Paradise: Travels in the Land of My Almost Birth.* Sydney: Hachette Australia, 2007.

Kászoni, József. *Csak Neki Szolgálj!* Budapest: Unitárius Egyházközség. n.d. (A collection of sermons, in Hungarian.)

—— "The Unitarian Meaning of the Lord's Supper in Hungary," in David Steers (ed.) *European Perspectives on Communion: Liberal Christian Approaches to Communion and the Lord's Supper.* Ulster: European Liberal Protestant Network, 2001.

Kedei, Mózes (ed.) *Confession about Ourselves.* Odorheiu Secuiesc/Székelyudvarhely: Transylvanian Ministerial Fellowship, INFOPRESS, n.d.

Kereki, Gábor. *'Egy az Isten' Unitarianism: Some words of Gábor Kereki.* London: Lindsey Press/General Assembly of Unitarian and Free Christian Churches, 1996.

Keyes, David. *Most Like an Arch: Building Global Church Partnerships.* Chico, California: Center for Free Religion, 1999.

Kovács, Sándor. "Sándor Kovács speaks at General Assembly," *Partner Church News*, vol. 3, no. 2, September 1996.

Lázár, István. *Transylvania: A Short History.* Budapest: Corvina, 1997.

Lepore, Jill. "A Critic at Large: Prior Convictions: Did the Founders Want us to be Faithful to their Faith?" *The New Yorker*, 14 April 2008.

MacCulloch, Diarmaid, *Reformation: Europe's House Divided 1490–1700*. London: Penguin Books, 2003.

McNulty, Karsten D. *Romanian Folk Art: A Guide to Living Traditions*. Farmington, Connecticut: Aid to Artisans, 1999.

Miller, Russell E. *The Larger Hope: The Second Century of the Universalist Church in America*, Vols 1 and 2. Boston: Unitarian Universalist Association, 1979.

Morgan, Christine. *Poems by Christine: Spring 1994*. Pamphlet, 1994.

——*Alabaster Village: Our Years in Transylvania*. Boston: Skinner House Books, 1997.

——*Mészkő (Alabástromfalu): Balázs Ferenc felesége az Erdélyben töltött évekről 1930–1937*, trans. József Kászoni. Budapest: Készült a Cerberus Nyomdában, 2002.

——*Alabaster Village: Our Years in Transylvania* in English and Hungarian, trans. József Kászoni. Bedford, Massachusetts: Unitarian Universalist Partner Church Council, 2007.

Murphy, Dervla. *Transylvania and Beyond: A Travel Memoir*. Woodstock, New York: Overlook Press, 1993.

Parke, David B. (ed.) *The Epic of Unitarianism: Original Writings from the History of Liberal Religion*. Berkeley: Starr King Press, 1957.

Ranck, Shirley Ann. "Cakes for the Queen of Heaven: A Ten-Session Adult Seminar in Feminist Theology." Boston: Unitarian Universalist Women and Religion, 2009. Reproduced at <www.uuwr.org/index.php?option=com_content&view=article&id=88&Itemid=74>.

Reed, Christine and Patricia Hoertdoerfer. "Neighboring Faiths: Exploring Religion with Junior High Youth." Boston: Unitarian Universalist Association, 1997. Reproduced at <http://archive.uua.org/re/currmap/curriculum.php?CurrID=107>.

Rezi, Elek. "The Lord's Supper in the Transylvanian Unitarian Church," in David Steers (ed.) *European Perspectives on Communion: Liberal Christian Approaches to Communion and the Lord's Supper*. Ulster: European Liberal Protestant Network, 2001.

Rudolph, Conrad. *Pilgrimage to the End of the World: The Road to Santiago de Compostela*. Chicago and London: University of Chicago Press, 2004.

Schulz, William. "Romania Resurrectus!" *The World: Journal of the Unitarian Universalist Association*, March/April1990.

Seaburg, Alan. "Earl Morse Wilbur," *Dictionary of the Unitarian Universalist Historical Society*. Reproduced at <www25.uua.org/ uuhs/ duub/articles/earlmorsewilbur.html>.

Seaburg, Carl (ed.) "The Communion Experience," *The Communion Book*. Boston: The Unitarian Universalist Ministers Association, 1993.

Servetus, Michael. *De Trinitatis Erroribus*. 1531. (The Earl Morse Wilbur Rare Book Collection at Starr King School for the Ministry, Berkeley, California contains a second edition copy of *On the Errors of the Trinity*.)

—— *Christianismi Restitutio*. 1553.

—— *The Restoration of Christianity: An English Translation of Christianismi Restitutio*, trans. Christopher A. Hoffman and Marian Hillar, project director Alicia Forsey. Lewiston, New York: Mellen Press, 2007.

Stoker, Bram. *Dracula*. London: Penguin Classics, 2003.

Suzuki, Shunryu. *Zen Mind, Beginner's Mind*. New York: John Weatherhill, 1972.

Szacsvay, Imre and Sándor Kicsi. *Erdélyi Utakon*. Budapest: A Kossuth Nyomda Kiadása, 1989. (A three-volume photo essay of Transylvania.)

Szombatfalvi, József. "The Promised Land: New Heavens and New Earth," *UUMA News*, Autumn 1997.

Tőkés, László, as told to David Porter. *With God, for the People: The Autobiography of László Tőkés*. London: Hodder and Stoughton, 1990.

—— *In the Spirit of Timişoara: Ecumenia and Reconciliation*, ed. Zoltán Barabás. Királyhágómellék: The Hungarian Reformed Church, 1996.

Unitarian Universalist Partner Church Council. UUPCC *Partnership Handbook*, 2006. Reproduced at<www.uupcc.org/docs/handbook. pdf>.

Unitárius Egyház. *Négyszáz Év 1568–1968: Emlékkönyv*. Kolozsvár: Unitárius Egyház, 1968. (A Transylvanian Unitarian Church yearbook containing pictures of many churches, published on the 400th anniversary of the Edict of Torda.)

Varga, Béla. *Francis Dávid: What Has Endured of His Life and Work?* trans. Vilma Szantó Harrington. Budapest: Magyar Unitárius Egyház, 1981.

Wilbur, Earl Morse. *A History of Unitarianism: Socinianism and Its Antecedents.* Cambridge: Harvard University Press, 1945; and Boston: Beacon Press, 1977.

——*A History of Unitarianism in Transylvania, England, and America to 1900.* Cambridge: Harvard University Press, 1952; and Boston: Beacon Press, 1977.

Williams, Betsy Hill. "Who Are Our Partners Around the World?" Unitarian Universalist Partner Church Council Religious Education Materials Group, 2004. (Religious education curriculum for eight to fourteen year olds.) Reproduced at <www.uupcc.org/re/introductions/introduction.htm>.

Wolff, Tobias. Foreword, in Helena Drysdale, *Looking for George: Love and Death in Romania.* London: Picador, 1996.

Wordsworth, William. "The French Revolution as It Appeared to Enthusiasts at Its Commencement," *The Prelude.* 1804. Reproduced at <http://www.cooper.edu/humanities/core/hss3/w_wordsworth.html>.

Wright, Conrad. *Beginnings of Unitarianism in America.* Hamden, Connecticut: Archon Books, 1976.

Wright, Conrad Edick. "A Son's Appreciation," in "Conrad Wright: Historian of American Unitarianism," Notable American Unitarians series. Reproduced at <http://www.harvardswquarelibrary.org/unitarians/wright-conrad.html>.

Films and other media

4 months, 3 weeks and 2 days 2007, motion picture, Romania. (Christian Mungiu, director)

The Lives of Others (Leben der Anderen, Das) 2006, motion picture, Germany. (Forian Henckel von Donnersmarck, director).

Youtube, video clip, <http://www.youtube.coüm/watch?v=iaELn7ydlQw>. (Easter rituals in Füzesgyarmat, Hungary.)

Péterffy, Gyula. *Passió az Unitárius* ("The Unitarian Passion" or "The Good Friday Passion"). Cantata. 1957.

Aladár Körösföi-Kriesch. *The Proclamation of Religious Freedom [at] The Diet of Torda, 1568.* Painting. (The 12 square meter painting, completed in 1896, currently hangs in The City Museum of Budapest.)

Unitarian Universalist Partner Church Council Resources

For Unitarian Universalist Partner Church Council resources go to <www.uupcc.org>, email <office@uupcc.org> or phone (+1)-781-2751710.

For religious education materials go to <http://www.uupcc.org/re.html>.

For UUPCC membership go to <www.uupcc.org>, email <office@uupcc.org>, or phone (+1)-781-275-1710. Or contact the Unitarian Universalist Partner Church Council (UUPCC) PO Box 88, Bedford MA USA 01730-0088.